Thinking About National Security

D1711195

Perhaps the most basic national security question that U.S. leaders and the body politic continuously face is where and under what circumstances to consider and in some cases resort to the use of armed force to ensure the country's safety and well-being. The question is perpetual—but the answer is not. This insightful text helps students make sense of the ever-changing environment and factors that influence disagreement over national security risks and policy in the United States.

The book takes shape through a focus on three considerations: strategy, policy, and issues. Snow explains the range of plans of action that are possible and resources available for achieving national security goals, as well as the courses of action for achieving those goals in the context of a broad range of security problems that must be dealt with. However, there is little agreement among policymakers on exactly what is the nature of the threats that the country faces. Snow helps readers frame the debate by suggesting some of the prior influences on risk-assessment, some of the current influences on national security debates, and suggestions for how future strategy and policy may be shaped.

Donald M. Snow is professor emeritus of political science at the University of Alabama, where he specialized in international relations, national security, and foreign policy. He has also served as visiting professor at the U.S. Air, Army, and Naval War Colleges and the U.S. Air Command and Staff College.

Thinking About National Security

Strategy, policy, and issues

Donald M. Snow

 Routledge
Taylor & Francis Group

NEW YORK AND LONDON

First published 2016
by Routledge
711 Third Avenue, New York, NY 10017

and by Routledge
2 Park Square, Milton Park, Abingdon, Oxon OX14 4RN

Routledge is an imprint of the Taylor & Francis Group, an informa business

© 2016 Taylor & Francis

The right of Donald M. Snow to be identified as author of this work has been asserted by him in accordance with sections 77 and 78 of the Copyright, Designs and Patents Act 1988.

Library of Congress Cataloging in Publication Data
A catalog record for this book has been requested

ISBN: 978-1-138-90291-6 (hbk)
ISBN: 978-1-138-90292-3 (pbk)
ISBN: 978-1-315-69722-2 (ebk)

Typeset in Times New Roman
by Taylor & Francis Books

Contents

Introduction

Where We Are Now

The major national security question that always faces the country is where and under what circumstances the United States must consider and in some cases resort to the use of armed force to ensure its safety and well-being. It is arguably the most basic question with which any national government deals: it is not clear what good a government is that cannot protect its people from harm, ultimately death. It is also a perpetual question: the problem of national security never goes away.

The answer to the question, however, changes with time and circumstance. Sometimes the answer seems obvious and clear enough to virtually everyone that there is essential agreement both on what the problems (usually expressed as threats) are and what must be done about them. Such situations, however, occur relatively rarely and are generally limited to times of great and obvious peril. The declaration of war on the United States by Germany and Japan in 1941 and the recognition of the existential threat that Soviet nuclear-tipped rockets highlighted during the Cuban missile crisis of 1962 and afterward are examples of extraordinary circumstances that produced a virtual unanimity of purpose around the dictates of national security.

Most of the time, such consensus does not exist, and the result is some level of disagreement within the body politic and among political leaders about the answer to the national security question. Normally, those periods are associated with less compelling, more unambiguous threats to the national existence and appropriate responses to them. In simplest terms, that is the condition in which the United States finds itself today. The most basic fact of the matter is that although the national security question may be perpetual, the answer is not: it is a variable that changes as the environment becomes different.

Introducing some of the factors that influence the current disagreement over national security policy and the possible range of solutions in the current environment are the purposes of this volume. It approaches this task through several lenses suggested in the title. Part of its framework derives from the question of U.S. national security *strategy*. This broadly used term has its genesis in military affairs (the basis of the word strategy comes from the Greek word for "generalship"), but it has been appropriated by numerous other disciplines, notably business. As used here, the term refers to the broadest level of application, sometimes called "grand national strategy" (see Dennis M. Drew and Donald M. Snow, *Making 21st Century Strategy*) and refers to *a plan of action for achieving goals and resources for particular goals*, in this case national security.

A closely related concept is *policy*, defined here as *a course of action adopted or proposed by a government* to achieve strategically determined goals. Policies implement strategy by providing direction and substance to responses to strategic plans and especially challenges to them. These challenges normally come in the form of threats to interests the state has that are expressed in grand strategy. The results are policy *issues, problems with multiple policy alternatives*, among which national security concerns must be reconciled.

This process of translating strategy to policy applied to issues is relatively straightforward when there is broad agreement about the nature of the threat the country faces. World War II strategy and policies were directed at defeating fascism. The only major issue was in what order the major fascist states should be dispatched. Similarly, the Cold War focused on containing communism. There was consensus on these needs, and the result was widespread agreement on the general orientation (or *paradigm*) for dealing with it. With the partial exception of terrorism, there is no current overarching threat to provide such unity and thus direction for strategy, policy, and issue responses. The search for a new, options-clarifying paradigm is also part of the task of this volume.

One useful way to think about national security problems in need of solution is captured in the concept of *risk*. A common dictionary definition of risk is the "chance of harm or loss." Synonyms include hazard, peril, and jeopardy. So stated, the concept seems comparatively benign, because it does not include any assessment of the extent or gravity of risks one might encounter. In some cases, risks are minor and tolerable. There is some risk of getting a paper cut from turning the pages in this book, for instance, but neither the chance of this happening nor the consequences are particularly severe.

National security risks, on the other hand, can both be grave and have enormous potential consequences, and are thus of a different order of magnitude and concern. The possibility of national extinction as a result of an all-out Soviet nuclear attack against the United States was a grave and alarming risk to the American public brought home in 1962 during the Cuban missile crisis, and the brief confrontation between Russia and the United States in May 2014 over Russian actions in Ukraine was a reminder that this potential peril was still at least a distant possibility. A major difference between national security and other forms of risk is in the potential consequences.

These two instances provide a useful benchmark about the pervasive nature and impact of risk in national security. In 1962, the Soviet "missiles of October" (to borrow the title of Robert Smith Thompson's 1992 book) seemed an imminent and very deadly source of national and personal jeopardy, and the reaction to it helped congeal a national security paradigm and strategy for the Cold War (discussed in Chapter 4). In 2014, the danger of nuclear war seemed sufficiently far-fetched that hardly anyone took the physical risk seriously, and the outcome did nothing to relieve the general national disagreement about national security policy. A paradigm congealed around one threat, but not in today's environment. President Obama captured this salient difference in his address to the graduating cadets at West Point on May 28, 2014: "The odds of a direct threat against us by any nation are low," he said, "and do not come close to the dangers we faced during the Cold War." Situations change, and policy must change with them.

Risk can be thought of as consisting of two basic components: threats and capabilities. I have reduced the relationship between the two concepts to an intuitive, if not precisely mathematical formula (in *National Security for a New Era*, fifth edition) where Risk = Threat − Capability. Generally speaking, threats are promises to do something harmful in the absence of compliance with them, and they are made by or toward adversaries. There are a wide variety of threats and consequences of their realization, and they are the basic "stuff" with which national security deals. The purpose of national security policy is to negate or neutralize the most important threats so that the harm they promise does not occur or is mitigated.

The problem with threats is that they are both variable and subjective. Variability means they tend to change across time and circumstance, so that solving today's threats may solve current problems, but does not mean there will not be new (or even returned) issues with which one will have to deal in the future. The problem is perpetual. Subjectivity means that everyone is not equally affected physically or psychologically by particular threats: what is frightening to some (and fear is one emotion threats are intended to engender) does not necessarily frighten someone else as much or even at all. Thus, threats are matters of disagreement.

The second element in the risk "formula" is capability. For this purpose, capability is defined as the ability to negate or control threats—to make them less threatening or non-threatening. Operationally, what to do about threats is the problem of national security policy, which includes the consideration or actual use of military force as the means to reduce national risk.

This is all conceptually fairly neat and simple, but in actual application, it is not. If the answer to the national security question is risk reduction, the question is what threatens security (creates risk) and must be contained if the national security is to be maintained. The risk formula can be rephrased, where risk equals "what needs to be done to secure the country?" (threats) minus "what is the country able and willing to do to reduce risk?" (capability). The variability of threats—few Americans had given much thought to international terrorism before September 11, 2001—and their subjectivity—how big and what kind of threat does terrorism represent?—demonstrate the major source of policy disagreement.

Particularly in the post-Iraq and -Afghanistan era, the exact nature of threat and what is necessary to deal with it are major questions with which policymakers must struggle. Americans are all concerned about terrorism, but they differ in the degree and intensity of their fear of this ongoing threat. Partly as a result, they also disagree both on what the country can do to negate or lessen the threat (reduce risk) and about what the country ought to do in different circumstances. These disagreements provide the yeast for a lively ongoing debate over national security policy.

It is the purpose of this volume to explore some of the factors that have been, are, and presumably will be parts of the ongoing debate. The purpose of these discussions is not to "solve" the problems by offering bold or innovative solutions, because doing so would be both presumptuous and probably extraordinarily ethereal. Rather, the intent is to help put something of a frame around the general debate by suggesting some of the prior influences on the situation, some of the current influences on the debate which may affect both its present and future status, and to offer a few suggestions about how that future may be shaped.

The text is divided into two parts. Part I: Context examines how the United States got to the policy position in which it now finds itself. It consists of four chapters, each of which looks at a different aspect of the environmental mix as it has evolved. Chapter 1, "U.S. Policy in Transition," argues that two major categories of factors largely shaping the situation come from the international environment: threats and opportunities that have arisen and to which the United States has responded; and the domestic environment in terms of changing capabilities and perceptions about when those capabilities should be employed. It examines in particular how uniquely American influences have a distinctive impact on how this country sees the world and its place in it. Chapter 2, "War... What Is It Good For?" examines how attitudes and circumstances about the utility of force have evolved. Chapter 3, "Humanitarian Intervention?" analyzes how contemporary rationales for using force are influenced by humanitarian concerns and how those changes affect support for the use of force. Chapter 4, "The Cold War Paradigm," focuses on the content and impact of the Cold War consensus on national security and it still influences American strategic attitudes and structures.

Part II: Influences consists of three chapters that look at aspects of the current environment that affect what the United States will do in the national security environment in the upcoming years. Chapter 5, "Factors in the New Environment," examines some dynamics that will help form parameters in the near future that are not always included in standard discussions. These include limits deriving from perceptions about recent past American military activities, the ambivalent impact of the fruits of military technology (drones in particular), and military manpower in light of recent experiences. Chapter 6, "The Syrian Microcosm," focuses on the American decision not to involve itself with active armed forces in the Syrian civil war and what kind of precedent that may set for the future. Chapter 7, "Paradigm for a New Era," raises the question of whether American national security policy is adequately served by the conceptual framework it inherited from the Cold War period and whether a new paradigm is needed. It also raises some elements that might be included in such a reconstruction.

Bibliography

Drew, Dennis M., and Donald M. Snow. *Making 21st Century Strategy: An Introduction to Policy and Problems*. Montgomery, AL: Air University Press, 2006.

Obama, Barack. "Transcript of President Obama's Commencement Address at West Point." *New York Times* (online), May 28, 2014.

Snow, Donald M. *National Security for a New Era*. (5th edn). New York: Pearson, 2014 (especially Chapter 2).

Thompson, Robert Smith. *The Missiles of October: The Declassified Story of John F. Kennedy and the Cuban Missile Crisis*. New York: Simon and Schuster, 1992.

Part I
Context

1   U.S. Policy in Transition

At the most basic conceptual level, national security is not all that complicated. Most national security problems can basically be understood and
analyzed with principal reference to three core concepts suggested in the
Introduction. National security issues can sometimes seem perplexing and
unfathomable, but centering discussions on these basic notions allows a
manageable conceptual economy and approach to the national security
predicament.

This simplicity can be both beguiling and misleading. A good bit of the
contextual setting of real life national security analysis tends to be either very
technical (the detailed lethal characteristics of one's own and adversaries'
weapons capabilities, for instance) or clandestine (such as intelligence analyses
of adversary intent in particular situations) or both. While there are
always important complicating influences that cannot be known or easily
fathomed by the lay person, this should not obscure the fact that the basic
dynamics of the national security equation can almost always be reduced to
the core ideas. Because the devil is usually in the details, the average citizen may
be at a disadvantage reaching detailed judgments in particular situations; it
does *not* mean that citizens cannot reach sound judgments on core concerns.
Those who suggest (and there are many of them) that national security judgments are beyond the grasp of the interested citizen are simply wrong or have
some personal agenda that is served by shielding matters from public scrutiny.

The contemporary environment in which national security operates is highly
contentious, largely on two grounds. The first and overarching source of
disagreement stems from the general malaise of American politics. Among
the consequences of that pathology is a tendency to polarize and make
partisan all issues regardless of content. The area of national security is not
exempt from the adversarial personalization and polarity of the public on all
issues. Matters such as the ongoing controversy over the killing of American diplomats and intelligence officers in Benghazi and ongoing dissent
about U.S. policy toward the Syrian Civil War are examples.

The impact of the hyperpartisan debate on discussions of national
security may be largely artificial, born not so much out of concern over
the topic *du jour* as it is with gaining political points in the partisan

bloodletting that marks so much political dialogue in this country. There is, however, a more fundamental and legitimate basis of disagreement that is always part of the national security dialogue. This disagreement is more deeply philosophical and reflects basic differences in judgment arising from the subjective nature of so much of the fundamental subject matter. While it is necessary to mention the partisan poison that hangs like an obscuring fog over political discussions, it is necessary to "burn away" that fog and to examine the more fundamental issues that divide Americans and that form the enduring basis for the national security debate.

In order to pursue that understanding, this introductory chapter will proceed sequentially through a series of conceptual building blocks that cumulatively form the basis for evaluating current and future issues. It will begin by defining and placing in context the basic concepts around which national security questions gravitate, including some discussion of the implications of the concepts, the relationships between them, and how the seemingly endless debate of American policy toward Iraq illustrates these dynamics. It then moves to an assessment of the current state of the debate, in the process trying to cull the wheat from the chaff of ongoing questions and disagreements. Because part of the perspective that the citizens of any country have toward national security is influenced by idiosyncratic experiences and interpretations of those experiences, the discussion moves to a section on uniquely American influences and how Americans frame national questions and answers. It concludes with a brief assessment of the national security "equation" for the United States.

The National Security Equation: Variables and Constants

The national security enterprise does not exist in a vacuum. Rather, its context lies within a competitive framework in which the United States interacts with other countries and groups within countries and where the major objective of all participants is to maximize their security. The common elements in dictionary definitions of security are safety and a *sense* of safety. This suggests that there are two basic elements to security: physical safety (the objective inability of hostile others to cause one harm) and the feeling (or sense) of security. The former element of security is physical and, generally speaking, fairly objective and agreed upon. Americans, for instance, did not worry much about being physically attacked and conquered or killed by their enemies after the British quit trying during the War of 1812 until the Soviets perfected nuclear-tipped ballistic missiles capable of attacking and destroying the country (if with awful consequences to themselves) after 1957. Americans were physically safe for 140 years of American history and thus had little reason to concern themselves with this most elemental form of security.

The conditions that make people *feel* safe are an entirely different matter and the cornerstone of most national disagreement over security policy. The simple fact is that different conditions and situations affect different people in different ways. These differences form the basis of much honest (and occasionally not so honest) debate about what imperils the national condition and what must be done to rectify it. The disagreements at this level can often be very visceral and deeply felt and can inflame discussions among those who have them to the point of arousing the hyperpartisan passions that so trouble political discourse generally. As an example, the question of how important the physical security of Israel is to the *American* sense of safety is guaranteed to ignite very passionate advocacies on both sides of the issue of how important particular world conditions are to Americans.

There is another concern that is virtually unique to national security analysis and adds to the controversies that often surround it. That concern is the potential *physical consequences* of national security decisions. A bad judgment in most areas of politics may inconvenience or harm specific Americans and groups, but mistaken national security decisions could literally imperil the existences of Americans by placing them at irretrievable physical peril. Had John Kennedy guessed wrong during the Cuban Missile Crisis of 1962, the United States might have been largely destroyed and a significant part of the population killed. Such consequences hardly ever arise in any other policy area. The gravity of possible consequences very much colors the national security debate.

Within these parameters, the conceptual basis of national security can be laid out. Its basis is in the meaning and relationship between three basic concepts, *interests*, *threats*, and *risk*. Their relationship is sequential and cumulative. Understanding how they apply will not answer all the nuances of particular problems and situations, but they go a long way toward defining their meaning.

Interests

The idea of interests, or more specifically national interests, stands at the core of unraveling the rationale for national security concerns. The term "interest" is a difficult, slippery idea, because it is used to mean a variety of things, from a desire to know about something (have an interest in a topic) to a fee paid for the use of funds. In the parlance of international relations (and especially so-called realist interpretations of international dynamics), the qualifier "national" is normally attached to the core concept, helping to give it a specific meaning and establishing the idea at the base of national security concern. Within the hierarchy of things states seek to do in their relations with other states and groups are to maximize those conditions and situations in which they have interests. The most important interest a state has is its physical safety, and a variety of surrounding conditions and situations contributes to how safe a state's citizens feel about their situation. Thus, a link between interests and security is established.

As the term is used in international relations, an interest refers to a matter of national concern and importance, a condition or situation the state deems important to its health and well-being. The French term *raison d'etat* (purpose of state) is often used as a synonym and suggests that the major purpose of a country's government is to ensure that national interests are realized. National security strategy and policy is a basic avenue through which the national interest is pursued.

The problem with interests is that they are competitive. What this means is that not all interests of individuals and groups coincide: what one state or other entity views as a desirable, even necessary, condition may not be viewed in the same way by others. In some cases, this competition may take the form that the interests of the groups are mutually exclusive and conflicting: both cannot simultaneously enjoy their desirable conditions, and at worst, the realization of one group's interests may only be achievable at the expense of another group's interests. This condition is *conflict of interest*, and when the incompatibility between desired situations affects countries and has important, fundamental proportions and consequences, the results are very consequential and important to national governments. These kinds of situations are common within the relations between states and form the grist of national security concerns and efforts to ensure the national security. Without interests that come into conflict with the interests of others, national security would be a far less central concern than it is in a world where interests clash.

The idea of interest must, however, be refined with two additional, related qualifications. The first of these is the comparative importance of various interests in the national hierarchy of values: all interests are not of equal importance. The second, and related, qualification is the means that will be employed to realize particular interests: not all means are appropriate or proportional to the interests in whose defense they are proposed. Both qualifications are debatable and, to some extent, subjective, adding spice to the general cauldron of disagreement on national security topics.

Clearly, states have interests of varying importance, and this variation can be related to the basic distinctions regarding security more generally. Within the realm of national security, the most important interests relate to the physical security or safety of the country, and more debatable interests are attached to the conditions that make people *feel* safe. The importance of core, physical interests is generally well established and agreed upon; disagreement begins to occur when one moves to discussing the psychological conditions that make people feel safe and the degree of interest the state has in realizing those conditions, including what it may be willing to do in that realization. Much of the debate over national security can be isolated to this area of interests.

One of the most common ways to distinguish the importance of interests is through a simple dichotomy (that I have developed more extensively in the various editions of *National Security for a New Era* (Snow 2014)) between *vital interests* (VIs) and *less-than-vital interests* (LTVs). The distinction is intuitive. VIs, as the name implies, are situations where the failure to realize a value would be nationally intolerable (its realization is vital to national survival or well-being). There is a finite list of such interests (e.g. the sanctity of national borders), but they are generally well agreed upon and unchanging. LTVs, on the other hand, are conditions that might be unfortunate, inconveniencing, or even compromising of national values, but whose realization is not intolerable. The list of LTVs is long, changing, expandable depending on circumstances, and the area where there is the most disagreement, either based on whether an interest exists or on its importance. Almost all the divisiveness over national security policies surrounds LTVs.

The other distinction is about what means the state will use to realize its interests. In national security matters, this distinction centers on the question of whether the state should be willing to use force—and if so what kinds and extent of force—to realize its interests. Because the employment of armed forces is an extreme act, determining when the state should or will use force, generally or in particular situations, is a matter of ongoing contention. This is particularly true because of the expense of raising, maintaining, and employing different kinds and levels of forces.

The two distinctions come together. Generally speaking, the more important an interest is, the more likely force will be viewed as an appropriate tool to realize it. The general "line in the sand" is whether VIs exist in particular situations. The realist position is that armed force should be limited to situations where VIs are threatened, and while some find this too restrictive, it is a generally agreed upon standard (at least partly because most military professionals support it). As a result, debates about invoking American forces for use in particular situations will almost rhetorically be framed in VI terms, with proponents arguing they are and opponents denying that assertion. Indeed, it is not unfair to typify most of the national disagreement on national security matters as a lack of consensus about where the line between vital and LTV interests lies.

Threats

The second link in the chain is threats, a concept introduced and defined in the Introduction. Threats are the problem that arises from conflicts of interests between the United States, other states, and groups within or between states whose interests differ significantly from American interests. Incompatibility of interest, however, is not the sufficient trigger of national security concern. Rather, what makes a situation rise to a national security problem is when an adversary (someone whose interests are incompatible with one's own) asserts the intention to realize his or her preference at the expense of one's own. The threat is the mechanism by which another party asserts his intention to realize his interest at your expense (or vice versa).

Threats are related to but not identical to interests. Interests, particularly physical interests that translate into VIs, are generally reasonably stable and unchanging over time. Non-hostile regimes on American borders and the freedom and independence of most of Europe and northeast Asia are examples. Some interests are more transitory than others, of course, which is the source of disagreement about them. What, for instance, are American interests in East Africa, and how important are they? The answer is such interests are debatable and changeable. Threats, on the other hand, change, depending on a variety of factors. Western European freedom from harm was fundamentally threatened by potential Soviet aggression during the Cold War, but no equivalent threat exists today. A half-century ago, few Americans were very concerned about threats to stability in the Levant, but such threats clearly exist in the contemporary environment.

As noted in the Introduction, threats are also subjective. What conditions or changes are threatening to some people are less threatening (or not threatening at all) to others, and these conditions and the emotions they produce change as well. Most of this disagreement arises because different parties emerge at different times in different places who assert contradictory interests and who threaten to act upon those differences at American expense. The threat posed by international religious terrorism is clearly of this nature. At the same time, people can and do disagree about some more enduring obstacles to the realization of American interests that are enduring but at least somewhat ambiguous. Does China pose a threat to the United States, for instance? If it does, what kind of threat is it? And what can be and should be done to deal with the peril it presents?

Threats are the problems that arise from the existence and clash of interests between parties. There is a core both of interests and threats on which almost everyone agrees and thus on which there is concord about what to do about them. Posing a counter-threat to the Soviet ability to obliterate the United States with nuclear weapons was so compelling and obvious to most Americans that there was little dissent about policy to deal with it. The problems arise, of course, because disagreement exists about how important interests are, what means should be used to protect them, and about the nature and changing constellation of threats to national interests. The policy debate revolves around first defining what the problems are (interests and threats to them) and about how to respond to the perils the environment provides. Risk and risk management is the art and science that deals with this part of the equation.

Risk

The nature of threats means that risks vary as well. How many risks one takes, the dangerousness of those risks to national security, and the relative importance of individual risky situations depends on an assessment of the threat posed by each situation and by their accumulation. Since risk reduction requires the commitment of resources (capabilities) to deflect or remove threat, the degree of the capability a country must devote to making itself safe and feel safe also varies. There is an old political saw that "policy is what gets funded." In that sense, the assessments of interests, threats, risks, and the capabilities necessarily devoted to those threats are at the heart of the political process, particularly since national security resources also tend to be very costly.

All areas of public policy, of course, can be assessed using the risk formula of Risk = Threat − Capability introduced earlier. There are potential negative consequences for not dealing with any political problem. What sets national security threats apart is that they emanate from sources that do not wish the country well and that may, given the opportunity and felt need, do grievous injury to the country.

The potentially damaging, even apocalyptical in some extreme cases, consequences of national security policy color discussions about the subject in ways generally not true in other policy areas. Because some of the disagreements about threats and the risks they pose are deep and honestly felt, many of these disagreements are fundamental and difficult to reconcile. The upshot is that national security policy will always have at least a partially adversarial quality. The exception is situations where there is broad agreement about the severity of the threat and the necessary means that must be applied to negate it. World War II provided such an aura, and it was largely present during the darkest days of the Cold War, which is discussed in detail in Chapter 4, and these periods create nostalgia for a return to these "simpler" periods of national accord. Such periods of agreement are, however, the exception rather than the rule, and those conditions clearly do not apply today. One of the reasons dissension is so jarring and upsetting for many Americans is because it stands in sharp, unfavorable contrast to a remembered past the attractiveness of which inevitably increases as detailed memories of its reality fade from the public recollection. It is far easier to wax nostalgic about the general agreement on policy than it is to remember living in the shadow of Soviet nuclear annihilation.

The Iraqi Conundrum

The seemingly never-ending drama of American relations with Iraq is highly amenable to understanding within the framework of interests, threats, and risks. While such an analysis may not plumb all the vagaries and innuendos of the Iraqi–U.S. national security relationship, it does both illustrate the dynamics and provide a useful bridge to looking at the current state of national security thinking more generally.

Begin with American interests in Iraq. Historically, the United States had very little common history and thus essentially no mutual interests with Iraq. The United States, like all petroleum-dependent developed countries, had some peripheral concern with access to Iraqi oil reserves, among the largest in the world in terms of traditionally exploitable reserves (i.e. non-shale reserves). American companies were basically denied access to that oil by the regime of Saddam Hussein that came to power in 1979, and Iraq remained off the American policy radar until 1980. Before that, American interests in Iraq were minimal.

The Iran–Iraq War, which began in 1980, raised the public profile of Iraq in American policy eyes. The war occurred at the same time as relations between the United States and Iran, heretofore the center of American interests in the region, soured. The Iran hostage situation from 1979 until early 1981 highlighted that change from ally and client to implacable adversary. In that context, the willingness of the Arab Sunni regime in Iraq to confront the new Persian Shiite fundamentalist regime raised American interest in both the country and its regime, and the United States became a supporter and supplier of the Iraqis in their anti-Iranian efforts. That relationship also soured in 1990, when Saddam Hussein invaded and conquered neighboring Kuwait, causing the United States to assume the leadership of a coalition that militarily threw Saddam's forces out of the country in early 1991. In the process of a little over a decade, Iraq moved from a minor area of concern to ally to adversary, and American interests shifted and apparently intensified in the process.

The attacks of September 11, 2001, and the subsequent "war on terrorism" made Iraq a national security concern of the U.S. government. The vehicles were accusations (that later proved false) that Iraq was both developing and deploying weapons of mass destruction (WMDs) that it might use against neighbors and that it had ties with anti-American terrorists, with whom it was feared they might share their WMDs. This prospect elevated perceptions of American interests in the Saddam Hussein regime and created the perception of a threat argued at the time as vital to the United States. The result was the decision to invade Iraq and to overthrow the government of Saddam Hussein. Rather than risk the possibility that Iraqi-bred terrorists or WMD might be used against the United States, the United States used its military capabilities to negate the Iraqi "threat." The result was an American occupation of Iraq that was not terminated until 2011. When the situation visibly deteriorated in that country in 2014, an American debate over what it should do resurfaced.

In 2014, as in 2003, the question boiled down to American interests in Iraq and who governed it. In 2003, accusations of hostile actions and intentions appeared to dictate a threat-reducing action, and the war ensued. Many Americans at the time wondered about the veracity of the accusations against the Iraqis, which were unproven at best and simply false at worst. Without those conditions being met, most Americans came to believe that American interests in Iraq were not sufficient to warrant military action, meaning U.S. interests in Iraq did not rise above LTV status. When Sunni radicals associated with the terrorist-related Islamic State or Iraq and Syria or more broadly the Levant (ISIS, or ISIL) began to grab large parts of Iraq as the largely Shiite army of Iraq disintegrated in 2014, questions about American reactions arose again.

The 2014 debate was influenced by the earlier experience. Neither the level of American interest nor the threat posed by ISIS/ISIL was accepted at face value by a war-weary American public. Advocates of a "resolute" U.S. response including an American military assistance program (but not ground forces) argued that the total disintegration of the country or its rule by the rebels was intolerable for the United States, thus invoking implicitly American vital interests. Most of the arguments concentrated on regional destabilization, which opponents argued would inconvenience the U.S. but not be intolerable (involve LTVs, in other words) to U.S. friends in the region. Skeptical because of the Bush administration arguments that vital interests were at risk in 2003 when most had concluded they were not, the debate was joined.

The Iraqi situation is a likely harbinger for many future national security debates. In the contemporary environment, there is what I have elsewhere called an "interest-threat mismatch," a situation where America's most vital interests are not particularly threatened and where threats are to lesser interests. Most world problems with potential national security implications currently occur in the developing world. Iraq is a microcosm of these situations, because it is not clearly and unambiguously within America's vital interests, but neither is it inconsequential. Events and their consequences thus fall in the psychological realm of what makes Americans *feel* safe, always a source of disagreement. These kinds of situations form the context of most current debates.

The State of the Debate: Fundamental (and Not So Fundamental) Disagreements

The following scenario has become a virtually ritual characteristic of the contemporary American political "game" as it applies to national security matters. A crisis breaks out, usually in some part of the developing world that involves gruesome violence toward the civilian population. The carnage is captured by international media like the 24-hour cable TV networks and publicized worldwide. American note is taken, and immediately calls ring out from one end of the political spectrum or the other for an American response.

The administration issues some sort of response to the crisis. That response is immediately criticized and condemned by some political elements and supported by others, and the rhetoric escalates to make the crisis seem vastly more important, especially to the United States, than it might appear under closer examination. It does not matter where or what the crisis is, and it probably does not matter who makes the decision regarding an American response: it will be controversial and reflect the general political divide in the country.

Why does this happen with such startling regularity? The quick answer is that it is because there is no basic, underlying agreement on the nature of international threats and how the country should respond to them, but that answer begs the more important underlying question, which is why such a situation exists. The answer to that question is more complex, but it contains at least two important considerations. One of these is the nature of the international environment. Unlike the Cold War confrontation with communism, there is no central, compelling threat around which to organize policy that helps pre-program responses (no paradigm that directs strategy). The other factor is domestic: American politics is overwhelmingly dominated by often vituperative disagreement about virtually everything, and this dissention inevitably spills over into the area of national security. These two factors combine to create a particularly poisonous policy environment mix.

The International Environment

Disagreements about national security tend to get magnified in the current political atmosphere. The major source is the general chasm that exists among political actors in the country and which radiates to all areas of public policy, including national security. Discussions about national security issues and problems arise in a setting of some ambiguity in the international arena, where conditions are in general flux and where the threats to American interests are of debatable magnitude and importance. The result is to make differences appear more frequent and thus more important than they might seem otherwise.

What is most noticeable about the contemporary world environment is the ambiguity of the external threats to the United States. Were the threats clearly peripheral and unimportant, there would be neither the need nor the interest in fashioning clear and strong responses to them. Once the breakup of the Soviet empire was physically complete and it was becoming apparent that there would not be cataclysmic consequences of that disintegration, the remainder of the 1990s was basically tranquil, and such national security actions as the United States experienced were in places where the risks and consequences were relatively low: in effect, the United States had the luxury of "sweating the small stuff" in places like the disintegrating Yugoslavia (Bosnia-Herzegovina and Kosovo) and Haiti. These were arguably situations where questions could have been raised about what the United States was doing inserting itself into situations that hardly merited the effort, but criticism was muted by the fact that the enterprises were, in national security terms, cheap and relatively safe. There was no real emerging consensus around a successor framework to the Cold War posture for dealing with threats, but one did not appear to be needed.

This ambiguity was largely the result of the collapse of the old communist threat that had provided a unifying force during the roughly forty years of the Cold War. It was increasingly apparent that the conditions justifying the very high financial and physical commitments of the Cold War no longer existed, and early in the 1990s, there were even vague promises that this could result in a "peace dividend" of reduced spending that never quite materialized. The cost of the end of the Cold War was the unifying consensus of opposition to Soviet communism and its worst manifestation, nuclear war. This loss caused some analysts like John Mearsheimer to lament, in an article with that title in 1990, "Why We Shall Soon Miss the Cold War." It was a frequent regret of many of the Cold Warriors, who had taken a cold comfort of sorts from the need to rally around policy to blunt a very real and compelling threat. The 1990s were a period of confusion regarding the nature and severity of the external threat. Fortunately, the environment was also confused and tranquil enough that this condition was not especially dangerous for U.S. security, and it thus did not require coming to serious grips with how to cope with a changed threat environment.

This tranquility was, of course, shattered by the terrorist attacks against New York and Washington, DC on September 11, 2001. Suddenly, Al Qaeda introduced the United States to a new form of threat: international terrorism. Terrorism was not, of course, a new phenomenon; historians of the subject date it back at least to Jewish resistance to Roman rule during biblical times, and the modern phenomenon is normally associated with the Reign of Terror during the latter stages of the French Revolution.

There were, however, two things about the phenomenon that were unique and added up to a need for American national security efforts to focus on the problem. It was the first time that the United States had been the apparent systematic objective of a foreign terrorist campaign, and especially one with a religious base. Previous American experiences with terrorism had been mostly with home-grown practitioners, such as the nineteenth-century anarchists who assassinated President James Garfield in 1881 or contemporary "lone wolf" terrorists like Timothy McVeigh, who engineered the bombing of the Murrah Federal Building in Oklahoma City in 1995. Outside a small and dedicated community of analysts and scholars who studied the subject in the United States, the idea of terrorism as part of the *international* threat environment was novel. Most Americans did not understand it, but they were frightened by it and wanted something done about it.

The other thing was that the United States had neither a comprehensive, coherent strategy for dealing with terrorism nor the forces and methods effectively to negate the threat. Terrorism is not a clearly and unambiguously military activity, and it is not clear that military responses play more than a supporting role in its suppression. Thus, the United States flailed at developing an internal governmental structure and set of policies and strategies to deal with the threat amid a loud and insistent public outcry that the country "do something" about it.

Terrorism replaced international communism as the focus for security policy. One can argue that the overlay was imperfect. The terrorist threat was never as severe as the potential destruction of a nuclear holocaust, but the prospects of some kind of personal jeopardy galvanized certain Americans to insist on dealing with this new national security peril. In the wake of 9/11, some policies were probably misguided overreaches: the willingness to accept the notion that Iraq was in league with the terrorists when all evidence and logic suggested they were not is one example. The expansion of an effort in Afghanistan originally conceived as a discreet mission to capture or kill Osama bin Laden and his colleagues to a general defense of the Afghan government is another. These misapplications in turn have weakened support for the "war on terrorism" declared by President George W. Bush atop the rubble of the Trade Towers in lower Manhattan in September 2001.

As the middle of the 2010s arrives, terrorism remains a nagging problem. It is sometimes said by the terrorism experts that individual terrorists and terrorist groups come and go, but the phenomenon of terrorism is ubiquitous: it never goes away entirely. With that realization in mind, the question of the central nature of the international terrorist threat and what should be done has become a lively one. At the same time, there is a lack of consensus and apparent precedent for dealing with the nagging world instabilities that are currently concentrated in the Middle East, Africa, and Asia.

Most of these conflicts are internal in nature and are artifacts of map imperfections created at the time independence was granted. Such developing world internal conflicts (DWICs) are perplexing. They are often very bloody and furtive contests between rival ethnic or religious groups walled within common political states to which they do not have primary loyalty. Thanks to modern communications capabilities the worst bloodshed and atrocities of these conflicts are often beamed to worldwide audiences, creating reactions of horror on humanitarian grounds and of calls for intervention on geopolitical grounds. For American policy, the problem is that U.S. interests in these countries are normally neither entirely clear-cut nor overwhelmingly important: they are almost uniformly LTV situations. In that atmosphere, there is fertile ground for disagreement with any action the U.S. government proposes to take or not to take.

The Domestic Dimension

The other source of dissonance in the national security policy process is domestic in the form of the extreme, highly vocal, and often vitriolic debate among political factions in the United States, generally along party lines. The level and venom of the political atmosphere in Washington has been steadily growing worse since the turn of the century, and while it has been partially moderated in the national security area by the unifying impact of transnational terrorism, it has come to dominate all facets of the political system. The result has been to paralyze the policy process to the point where it has become impossible either to debate civilly or objectively basic policy areas or to contemplate changes in policy direction beyond the peripheries of concern.

The detailed nature and sources of dissention are extensive, complex, and beyond the scope of this study. What is important is that the political system is effectively trapped in a situation of decisional gridlock wherein the ideas of proposing or especially implementing changes of direction in any policy area are next to impossible. National security policy, which is arguably in need of a re-examination because of changes in the international environment, is one of the areas where basic change is both needed and probably impossible unless things change.

The dimensions of governmental gridlock are staggering and daunting. The United States has not, for instance, passed a federal budget since 2009, and there is little prospect that such an act will occur during the remainder of the Obama presidency. The reason is that the political parties, manifested in different party control of the executive and legislative branches of government, cannot reach agreement on the shape of such a document. Disagreements include how much the government should spend (expressed in tax increases versus cutting government spending) and what it should spend its resources on. Because the divisions are ideological and both serve and are stoked by philosophical differences in the electorate (often encouraged by partisan political appeals), elected politicians are unwilling to compromise on budgetary matters for fear of arousing constituent wrath, the basis of which they may have created or intensified. Because the differences are so great on these issues, neither side seriously pursues accommodating positions the other might find acceptable but which might displease their particular constituencies. The result is gridlock in the decision process.

In this situation, the government functions by simply doing the same things it has before. The vehicle for this perpetuation of the status quo is "continuing resolutions" passed periodically that authorize a continuation of government budgets at the same levels and with basically the same priorities that were passed the last time a budget was adopted by Congress and signed by the President. Effectively, the federal government today is largely carrying out the wishes of the 2009 Congress and Executive, with some minor tweaks to the numbers. If policy is indeed what gets funded, policy reflects yesterday's priorities.

Changes in public policy almost always require the reallocation of public resources away from abandoned and toward reformulated public ends. The implication of this realization is sobering from a strategic perspective. A re-examination of American military policies, especially those aimed at fresh determinations about who the United States will be willing to fight and where and how Americans will fight, will almost certainly result in some change of emphasis. That change will, in turn, require change that almost certainly cannot be accommodated within the continuing resolution dynamic. Any attempt to try to devise and implement a change in American posture is thus effectively the hostage of partisan gridlock that extends to the national security area, a part of governmental activity that most Americans undoubtedly think is supposed to be above the petty wrangling of politics as usual.

One of the obvious consequences of this situation is that national security questions become part of the general cacophony of American politics. Something happens in the world, the political sides adopt positions that are designed to assuage their political supporters, and this effectively means attacking other partisans' positions. By constitutional intent, the functions of national security decisions tend to focus on the executive branch, and whoever occupies the White House is the central "target" in the political exercise about how the United States should reply. In many cases, the reactions are so predictable and ideological that they can effectively be ignored. When the President is contemplating a response, however, he cannot avoid realizing that whatever decision is reached, it will be criticized by some political elements, and the effect may well be to make implementing any decision more difficult. Particularly if the decision may require the allocation of new resources, the inertial drag of a political process that cannot decide anything may well effectively preclude even considering some options.

The Intermestic Intersection

There is an old saw in the area of foreign relations that used to form the cornerstone regulating the intersection between the international environment and partisan domestic politics. That first principle was that "politics ends at the water's edge," and it meant that while normal political discourse might be highly contentious, when the United States faced outward toward the world, and especially hostile elements in the global environment, such differences were put aside and the country operated as one united force. This principle dominated the period from American entrance into World War II and through the Cold War. It is now an apparent dead letter. Its demise arguably compromises American stature and effectiveness in the world, but it is also a matter of simple reality in the contemporary scene.

The "intermestic intersection" (elaborated in Donald M. Snow and Patrick J. Haney, *American Foreign Policy in a New Era)* is the confluence of international and domestic impacts. Indeed, the term "intermestic" is a hybrid of *inter*national and do*mestic* and suggests that the two factors interact with and affect one another. The question in any specific situation is whether their interactive influences support or weaken one another.

The current situation combines a low or ambiguous threat environment with a high level of domestic dissention. One can think of this as a "happy" coincidence in the sense that while the domestic political scene is so adversarial that it cannot act decisively on essentially anything, there is nothing momentous in the international environment that truly requires or dictates resoluteness on the part of the domestic system. The relationship is less than ideal if one believes, as this volume argues, that the current paradigm for organizing national security policy does not apply especially well to the current situation and would benefit from rethinking and reformulation.

The international situation might well benefit from a reformulation and reorientation of the American stance, but at the same time, the status quo is tolerable, if occasionally disagreeable. Re-examining and reforming security policy would require considerable agreement among political actors and the ability to pass significant legislation, most prominently in the budgetary area. Since the domestic political scene is frozen into inaction, such decisiveness is difficult to imagine. It is thus probably a good thing that the international environment is not so hostile as to require decisive American response, since it is not clear that the system can act decisively.

This situation would be far less tolerable were there a clear and pressing national security challenge. If a basic and overriding threat to the integrity of the United States were to appear, the contemporary deadlock of the American political system would arguably be intolerable and might actually jeopardize physical security. From an intermestic viewpoint, the current tolerability of the international environment permits continued political paralysis, because although gridlock may produce unfortunate domestic consequences, it does not endanger fundamental national security concerns.

It should be noted that disagreement over national security matters is not a key contributing factor in domestic political gridlock, but rather derives from domestic turmoil. Occasionally national security matters get entwined in the domestically venomous rhetoric of the political competition, but they are not the cause of that venom. The Benghazi sideshow is illustrative. In more agreeable times politically, that incident probably would not have created a cause célèbre but would have been viewed as a simple national tragedy not unlike the bombing of the U.S. Marine barracks in Beirut in which 243 American service members were killed. Objectively, Beirut was a much larger tragedy than Benghazi, but the Reagan administration was subject to virtually none of the venom that has been directed at the Obama administration over Benghazi. There will always be a question about whether the Marines should have been on guard duty at the Beirut Airport, a job for which the Army was much better prepared: was that somehow a lesser form of negligence than allegedly having inadequate security in Benghazi, a known hotbed of CIA activity? What is the difference? One answer is the 1980s were a much more tranquil time domestically than are the 2010s.

How might the two environments be brought into a dynamic and productive relationship? The answer, of course, means that one or both would have to change. The most obvious solution would be a shift in the domestic political scene away from ideology-driven confrontation and disharmony back to the spirit of compromise and accommodation that has historically marked politically productive periods in the past. Such a change, however, would require some basic changes both in people's attitudes and in the ways that politicians seek to shape, reflect and exploit the differences that exist. At heart, after, all the basis of difference is nothing new, pitting those who seek an activist, interventionist role for government in the national existence versus those who seek a more limited role for government. Arguments on specific issues tend to flow from these basic differences on the role of government in society. These disagreements have been present since the founding days of the republic and have formed a lively part of political dialogue. Occasionally, those debates have been rancorous and have compromised the ability of government to carry out its functions, but it is hard to remember a time when that corrosiveness was as bad as it is today.

The basic disagreements are not likely to be solved or resolved entirely. What makes the current period distinctive is the depth that belief in one set of values has assumed and an overriding sense that one's position is so correct that it must prevail for the good of the country. This depth of conviction has produced an atmosphere where straying from the ideological line is seen as virtually an act of apostasy, and the result has been to undermine the sense that pragmatism is a necessary and noble way to solving national problems. To change the effects of the current dynamic of division will require a fundamental reformulation of the orientations of everyday citizens whose votes those in power covet and on which they rely. Until the public says decisively they have had enough political division and vitriol and demand a return to a period when pragmatism and compromise were the norm, it is hard to see much change occurring.

Ironically, the emergence of a truly menacing threat to national security might cause this effect. A truly looming threat would provide something about which virtually the entire political spectrum could agree, forming a sliver of consensus in a vast sea of dissention. If the country truly needed to unite around such a threat, it could also break the sense of deadlock that currently keeps government gridlocked. Such a transformation might well take a while: before World War II, for instance, it took a long time for almost all Americans to agree that Nazi Germany was a menace to the United States and to abandon their opposition to siding with the Allies. A strong dollop of suggestion that such opposition might be less than patriotic helped still the voices of the opposition, like Charles Lindbergh's "America First" movement. A cooperative enemy can aid in this creation of consensus: Pearl Harbor and the German declaration of war on the United States made it impossible to oppose American engagement in World War II.

The prospects of either of these things happening in the short term can hardly be viewed as good. There seems to be no easing of the level or intensity of animosity on the domestic scene, and it is hard to see how a uniting figure or movement could arise and prosper in the current atmosphere. There is also not a great likelihood that a truly compelling external threat will arise in the short run that could act as a stimulus to moderation of the political climate and a resurgence of a spirit of cooperation. For most purposes, the miniscule prospect of a compelling threat is a good thing, as a real outside danger is more appalling and threatening than a merely dysfunctional political system that bumbles along in both the domestic and international environments. A real and overwhelming threat might bring some desirable benefits with it, but the costs are potentially higher than anyone would propose.

The net effect of influences on the current political climate militates against major change and in favor of a torpid status quo. The intermestic intersection neither encourages nor necessitates the kind of political debate that might produce a new and more realistic American national security strategy, but that same situation also means there are not dire consequences of doing what is being done, which is essentially nothing.

The *American* Equation

The attitudes that any country's citizens have regarding how to view and deal with national security problems are to some extent idiosyncratic, and part of any country's national security "equation" includes calculating those unique attributes, conditions, and experiences that shape how it thinks not only about the past but also the future. The United States is no exception to this observation.

For present purposes, it is possible to identify at least three areas that have been important in shaping the American national security culture. The first of these is the physical situation of the United States and how that has influenced the way that American attitudes toward force have evolved. The second is the American tradition of "exceptionalism," the belief that the United States has unique characteristics to which others should aspire. This belief contributes to contradictory evangelical and isolationist strains in American attitudes. The third is a distinct American military culture nurtured by the general success of the country at arms and manifested most clearly in the "can do" tradition. These three factors do not individually or collectively explain all the influences that compose what is idiosyncratic about the American view of the national security problem, but they do help put some useful parameters on the discussion.

Geography and History

The United States enjoys one of the most benign geographic inheritances of any country in the world, and the accident of that geography has helped shape the way the United States sees the world, its place in it, and its perceptions of national security threats. There are two broad geographic categories of factors that compose that heritage, location and natural resource abundance. Their combined impact has helped to shape American military history and thus the context of how Americans view threats in the world.

The first geographic factor is location. Along with Australia (and basically uninhabited Antarctica), North America is arguably the most physically isolated continent in the world, protected by wide oceans both to its east (the Atlantic) and its west (the Pacific) that form a natural barrier to outside intrusion from the two most intrusive continents historically, Europe and Asia. The protection is not perfect, of course: European colonialists were able to subjugate the continent when it was only sparsely populated by indigenous "Indian" tribes whose ancestors themselves mostly came across the Aleutian land bridge from Asia. Once the outsiders were expelled in the eighteenth and nineteenth centuries, however, the result was to provide a formidable barrier to outside threat.

This protection was particularly prominent for the most populous and powerful of North American countries, the United States. When combined with fairly weak, non-hostile regimes to its north and south, the United States was from the latter 1700s until the middle of the twentieth century effectively an island state, and one to which the term "fortress America" was often not inappropriately applied. During most of the early, formative period of American history, physical national security and the instruments for its execution were simply not a large problem for the United States. This pristine, virginal situation stands in strong contrast to the conditions of most European and Asian states, which had long histories of predators on their boundaries against which vigilance was necessary. This condition of virtually absolute physical invulnerability lasted from the end of the War of 1812, when the British quit trying to subjugate American soil, until 1957, when Soviet nuclear weapons aboard intercontinental range ballistic missiles began to threaten American soil.

The other geographical influence was resource abundance, and it has taken two basic forms that historically helped insulate the United States from the vagaries of the outside world. The first form is abundant and fertile farmland that has been basically capable of feeding the American population. While this is a given for most Americans, it is not for many of the world's peoples. The fertile Nile Valley, for instance, has been a coveted piece of real estate throughout history mostly because it has been a granary capable of sustaining both populations and armies in an area of the world where that is not always the case. The United States is self-sufficient agriculturally except for exotic goods that are not or cannot be grown in the United States (certain spices like cinnamon, for instance) or for fresh foods during winter in the northern hemisphere (e.g. Chilean grapes). It is a happy luxury and source of national security that the United States is able to be a food exporter rather than an importer.

In addition to abundant agricultural regions, the United States is also blessed with great enough supplies of the mineral and energy sources that have been necessary to propel the United States into a position as a global industrial power. These have included large and generally handily collocated supplies of natural endowments like iron ore and coal for a steel industry and large supplies of energy such as coal, petroleum and natural gas to power and sustain the American economic machine. This abundance has also meant that for most of American history the United States has not been forced to rely on foreign sources of the necessities for prosperity, a luxury not available to many other states. When states are deficient in natural resources (Japan may be the best global example), their national security may require looking outward and securing both supplies of resources and secure means to get those resources to home markets. Historically, the United States has simply not had this burden.

The resource availability equation has changed for the United States in ways that illustrate how geography affects national security. While the United States has abundant supplies of most mineral resources, some industry now requires minerals that are simply not available in the United States and must be imported, creating a dependency with national security implications. Titanium is an example. There is virtually no titanium ore in the United States, and only a small and inadequate supply in Canada. Most of the world's supply comes from two countries: Zimbabwe (former Rhodesia) and Russia. Titanium in alloy hardens steel and allows it to tolerate much greater heat than steel can tolerate without it. This heat resistance is necessary for the nose cones of projectiles re-entering the earth's atmosphere (nuclear warheads or space vehicles) and for jet airplane engines. Because both of these products are vital to aspects of the national security effort, securing access to reliable quantities of titanium at reasonable cost is a national security imperative that simply did not exist before the second half of the twentieth century.

An even clearer example is that of petroleum. The United States has large amounts of traditionally exploited petroleum in a number of areas (Texas, Oklahoma, and Alaska, for instance), but those sources have been extensively exploited (except for Alaska). Remaining reserves are more difficult to reach and bring to market, and the cost of doing so is much greater than in the "glory days" when petroleum was both abundant and cheap. Depletion coincided with a growing world (including American) dependency on petroleum for things like transportation and electricity production.

In this circumstance, the United States joined other countries that had long been dependent on foreign sources of abundant, reliable, and affordable petroleum. The result, of course, was to create a strong national security interest in the Middle East where one had not previously existed. Without the need for oil, would the United States have any reason to invest much of its national security efforts in this most unstable, volatile part of the world? Would, for instance, Islamic terrorism be directed at the

United States in the absence of a large and intrusive American presence dictated by the geopolitics of petroleum dependency?

These kinds of questions make the emergence of the shale oil and gas revolution in the United States particularly geopolitically intriguing. In the past few years, it has become technologically and economically feasible to extract natural gas and oil deposits locked in shale formations through the use of a technology known as "fracking," a technique developed for getting hard-to-exploit conventional oil from oil fields that have been largely depleted. The technique involved pumping a mixture of water, sand, and chemicals into the formation freeing the deposits from the formations and allowing them to be "mined." Although the technique has been available for years, it has become controversial because of environmental concerns over its large-scale use.

The effect of exploiting shale gas and oil has been geopolitically dramatic and could become even more so. The United States is now the world's largest natural gas producer and will soon become a net energy exporter with very small needs for imported petroleum, and specifically for petroleum from the Middle East. As this occurs, American dependency on Middle East imports has declined substantially to the point that securing and guaranteeing the uninterrupted flow of petroleum from the region is much less an American problem than it is a problem for other countries. This raises the prospect that the United States, with reduced interests in the area, could begin to reduce the extent of its commitment and presence in this volatile area. Some of the possible effects of such a decrease on American national security policy and more specifically on American military and anti-terrorist efforts are explored later in the text.

American Exceptionalism

Americans have generally believed that this country has a special place in the world based on a uniquely desirable culture that offers a model and ideal for other peoples. This sense that the country is a special—an exceptional—place is based on the appeal of American democracy and freedom, an American egalitarianism that allows for anyone and everyone to succeed and live "the American dream," and a sense of welcome that is represented by the quotation from an Emma Lazarus poem inscribed on the Statue of Liberty to "give me your tired, your poor, your huddled masses yearning to breathe free."

This sense reflects the American experience and hence the belief among many Americans that the United States is a special place. All Americans are, after all, immigrants at some remove, and many of those who migrated to the United States did so to flee the political and economic tyranny of their native lands. President Ronald W. Reagan captured the self-image that most Americans have of themselves and their relationship with the world when he said, "America is a shining city upon a hill whose beacon light guides freedom-loving people everywhere."

Whether this self-image is accurate or not is almost beside the point, since it is what many Americans believe and how they view the world and the American place in it. Certainly one can quibble about some of the details of American nobility that the image implies, and many people worldwide undoubtedly do. The self-image suggests a kind of selflessness and benevolence toward others that differs with the experience some peoples and countries have had with Americans, and it has always been somewhat difficult for many Americans to understand why others are not as grateful to the United States as these Americans feel they should be. Adverse indigenous reactions to prolonged American occupations of places like Vietnam and Iraq are cases in point. Moreover, the sense that the United States is indeed an exceptional place has undoubtedly suffered because the United States appears to many to have become "just" another great power in the power politics of the world.

What is important about this influence for present purposes is that it motivates both the historical strands of American sentiment about its world role and thus its definition of its national security. Those strands are *evangelism/activism* and *isolationism*. Both have strong constituencies in the United States, both have been dominant sources of influence over American foreign and national security policy, and each has very different implications for the American role in the world.

Of the two strands, isolationism is the older and has been the dominant sentiment of Americans for a longer part of its history. The heart of this belief is based on the moral judgment, very strong at the time of the formation of the country, that the outside world is corrupt and tainted. Flight from conditions of political and religious tyranny and lack of economic opportunity, after all, were the motivating force behind much of the original surge of migration to the New World. As a result, there has always been a strong sense that the United States should shield itself from the taint and corruption the outside world brought with it. The United States welcomed those seeking asylum from the Old World, but it expected the immigrants to leave the outside baggage of their prior existences behind when they arrived on American soil.

The isolationist strain dominated the first century and a half of American existence. Both George Washington in his Farewell Address and Thomas Jefferson in his First Inaugural famously warned Americans to avoid entanglement with foreign politics and influences, and being left alone suited an American desire for aloofness so it could concentrate on the important "manifest destiny" it had to settle and civilize the American continent (a process liberally fertilized by foreign capital from European banks, it might be added). This period was temporarily interrupted when the United States felt compelled to enter World War I and pluck European "chestnuts" from the burning coals of potential chaos and tyranny. Disgust at the settlement of the war triggered a return in the form of "splendid isolationism" between the world wars. As a pure position and advocacy, the Japanese attack on Pearl Harbor on December 7, 1941 revealed the impracticality of a policy of isolationism in the modern world, and the idea of literal isolationism has been in eclipse ever since.

The basis of specialness and wanting to be left alone has never died altogether, however. Its clearest expression has been in the policy positions of the libertarians, whose general disdain for government activism extends to foreign policy, and especially military, activism. Political figures like Senator Rand Paul (R-Ky.) offer the clearest expression of this position, but its strands remain a lingering shadow in debates about foreign and national security policy.

The other strain is activism, which suggests that the United States must be an active participant in the affairs of the world, and that is irresponsible for the United States not to act in that way. The rationale is both empirical and moral. Empirically, the United States has been the most powerful country since the end of World War II, and thus it arguably cannot shrink from playing a role in world affairs. This obligation is particularly great in a world where others do not share American visions and who would in the absence of prominent American leadership in world affairs attempt to reorder the world in ways inimical to American values and their pursuit. The Cold War confrontation with Soviet communism provided exactly such an environment. Without American leadership, the perception was that communism would spread globally and threaten the United States and that only a long-term, active American role in the world could stem that advance. In that atmosphere, activism became the dominant operational base for American policy, a position it continues to occupy. Morally, the belief in the superiority of the American vision contained an evangelical strain suggesting the United States had a moral obligation to "uplift" the world. The only problem has been that not all parts of the world have embraced the uplifting experience the United States offers.

Whether the American sense that it is exceptional is accurate or not, it has been a dominant ongoing strand that underlies much of the American view of national security. It contains both a belief in the inherent superiority of the American "way" and a conviction it should be universalized. It is a letter of faith for most Americans that almost everywhere in the world would be better if it adopted American values and institutions, for instance. This creates a sense of disillusion among some Americans when others resist or even reject that appeal (e.g. the leaderships in Iraq and Afghanistan). At the same time, a major element in the evangelical base of spreading the American way has been the result of American self-perception of its success in the past, a belief with a significant military component.

The American Military Culture: Can Do

All countries develop distinct attitudes about their own military and their generalized experience with using it. Combined with beliefs about the efficacy of force in different kinds of circumstance and in general, the collection of those attitudes forms something that is sometimes referred to as a military culture.

The American military culture is premised on the belief that the U.S. armed forces have been a positive force that has served the country well. Moreover, basic attitudes include a strong conviction that the American military has been almost universally successful in serving the interests for which it has been used to protect and promote. This attitude is by no means unique to the United States and is shared as part of the national pride of most countries. The basic repository of this belief and its promotion has been held within the United States military itself.

Much of this belief arises from historical perceptions about the use of armed force through the American experience. Generally speaking, the United States has prevailed when it has employed armed force, and this has bred a belief in the prowess and tradition of success of that force. While this historical interpretation is partly romantic, containing elements that look much better in broad brush than they do at close inspection, the basic contour of U.S. military success is accurate. It has bred a sense of superiority and invincibility about the American armed forces that is captured in the "can do" tradition of the American services, an attitude that asserts whenever the military is called upon to perform a task, it will achieve the desired results.

This tradition is complex and has been the subject of many excellent studies, possibly the most famous of which are Russell Weigley's *The American Way of War* and T. Harry Williams' *A History of American Wars.* What is critical to note is that most of this tradition is the result of looking at how the United States has performed in traditional, European-style, or what is now sometimes called *symmetrical* warfare. The ultimate symmetrical conflict was World War II, and it is not coincidental, as Carl Builder noted in *The Masks of War* in 1989, that this is America's most romanticized conflict within the armed services, the war that produced what each service views as its shining hour.

The American record has not been so exemplary or noteworthy in what is now referred to as *asymmetrical* warfare, where opponents' armed forces are neither organized nor fight in accepted European ways. The United States has a long and uneven history in this form of fighting. When it has been an asymmetrical warrior, as it was in many of its more successful experiences during the American Revolution, it has been relatively successful (see Snow and Drew, *From Lexington to Baghdad and Beyond* for a discussion). When it has had to fight against asymmetrical warriors, it has not fared as well. During the nineteenth century, for instance, it faltered during the Seminole War in Florida, in some of the campaigns against the plains and western Indians, and in its attempts to subdue an insurgency in the Philippines at the end of the century and into the twentieth century.

The vulnerability of the American armed forces in this kind of warfare was first widely exposed in the Vietnam War. Over an eight-year period, the United States was unable to subdue a North Vietnamese force that was by all conventional measures far inferior. The American military was not defeated in any traditional manner, but the fact that it did not prevail in subduing the opponent won the Vietnam experience the debatable epithet as the first war the United States "lost." Why this occurred and what it means has been hotly debated ever since but not resolved. Neither has the "solution" to defeating asymmetrical warriors been discovered in any demonstrable way. Ominously, asymmetrical wars are almost the only kinds of opportunities to use military force on the international horizon, and the traditional, conventional wars at which the United States excelled have essentially disappeared from the military map. No one is predicting that these conflicts will return in the foreseeable future.

The American "can do" tradition must be assessed in this light. It was a tradition born and nurtured in a military environment and applicable to conflicts that no longer occur. When crises break out in the world, one predictable response from part of the American political spectrum is recourse to American arms. The implicit assumption underlying these calls arises from the military's "can do" tradition that, regardless of the mission and how difficult it may be, the military will somehow solve the problem. The problem is that it may be a false expectation in the contemporary world.

One of the major questions confronting American national security policy in the future is what the United States can and cannot do to arrange the world in ways compatible with its national interests. More particularly, can American military might, by far still the most prodigious in conventional terms, be brought to bear to correct world problems (at least as they are perceived by the United States)? If these kinds of situations are not isomorphic to the kinds of situations that bred and support the "can do" tradition, does that tradition apply? If it does not, should there be an addendum to "can do" that specifies where and in what circumstances the United States "can't do"? These issues are pursued in some detail in the next chapter.

Bibliography

Bacevich, Andrew C. *Washington Rules: America's Path to Permanent War.* New York: Metropolitan Books, 2010.

Brodie, Bernard. *War and Politics.* New York: Macmillan, 1973.

Builder, Carl. *The Masks of War: American Military Styles in Strategy and Analysis.* A RAND Corporation Research Study. Santa Monica, CA: RAND Corporation, 1989.

Clausewitz, Carl von. *On War.* Revised edn. Translated and edited by Michael Howard and Peter Paret. Princeton, NJ: Princeton University Press, 1984.

Dupuy, Ernest, and Trevor N. Dupuy. *The Encyclopedia of Military History.* New York: Harper and Row, 1972.

Gaddis, John Lewis. *Strategies of Containment: A Critical Appraisal of Postwar American National Security Policy*. Oxford: Oxford University Press, 1982.

Gwynne, S. C. *Empire of the Summer Moon: Quanah Parker and the Fall of the Comanches, the Most Powerful Indian Tribe in American History*. New York: Scribner, 2010.

Hassler, Warren W. Jr. *With Shield and Sword: American Military Affairs, From Colonial Times to the Present*. Ames, IA: Iowa State University Press, 1984.

Keegan, John. *A History of Warfare*. London: Hutchison, 1993.

Leckie, Robert. *The Wars of America*. Revised and updated edn. New York: Harper and Row, 1981.

Mearsheimer, John T. "Why We Shall Soon Miss the Cold War." *Atlantic Monthly* 262, 2 (August 1990), 35–50.

Millett, Allan R., and Peter Maslowski. *For the Common Defense: A Military History of the United States of America*. New York: Free Press, 1984.

Pfaff, William R. *The Irony of Manifest Destiny: The Tragedy of America's Foreign Policy*. New York: Walker Publishing, 2010.

Polk, William R. *Violent Politics: A History of Insurgency, Terrorism, and Guerrilla War*. New York: Harper Perennials, 2008.

Snow, Donald M. *Distant Thunder: Patterns of Conflict in the Developing World*. 2nd edn. Armonk, NY: M. E. Sharpe, 1997.

Snow, Donald M. *National Security for a New Era*. 5th edn. New York: Pearson, 2014.

Snow, Donald M., and Dennis M. Drew. *From Lexington to Baghdad and Beyond: War and Politics in the American Experience*. 3rd edn. Armonk, NY: M. E. Sharpe, 2009.

Snow, Donald M., and Patrick J. Haney. *American Foreign Policy in a New Era*. New York: Pearson, 2013.

Waltz, Kenneth. *Man, the State, and War: A Theoretical Analysis*. New York: Columbia University Press, 1959.

Waltz, Kenneth. *Realism and International Politics*. New York: Routledge, 2006.

Weigley, Russell F. *The American Way of War*. New York: Macmillan, 1973.

Williams, T. Harry. *A History of American Wars: From Colonial Times to World War II*. New York: Alfred A. Knopf, 1981.

2 War...What Is It Good For?

"War—Good Gawd Y'all, what is it good for?" is the opening line of an anti-Vietnam song recorded by Edwin Starr in 1970. After posing the question, the artist provides an answer: "Absolutely nothing!" That response represented a lament of the imbroglio in which the United States found itself by the end of the 1960s, and which, at that point in time, seemed to have no concrete prospects of conclusion, successful or not. In that setting, both the question and response were understandable and shared by many—especially many young Americans facing conscription into the armed forces and possible involuntary combat service in the Vietnam War. Regardless of the context, Starr's question is a good one.

War is one of humankind's most venerable, recurring institutions. The fact that humans have come into conflict with and fought and killed other humans who differed from them in one regard or another is simply a fact of human history. Through time, the recourse to war has been both glorified and vilified as bringing out both the best and the worst in the human species. Those who go forward to fight others have been depicted as social heroes exercising mankind's most noble instincts through their bravery and willingness to engage in self-sacrifice, and the warriors have been more darkly portrayed as blood-thirsty savages acting out and glorifying the basest blood lust of the species. It has always been and remains a contentious question: What about humankind impels us to fight and slaughter our own? It is an interesting metaphysical question, but it is not one that can be satisfactorily answered empirically.

War persists, and this chapter looks at the traditional pattern of warfare and how that pattern affects the ways we now view war and its conduct. Since our focus is on American policies, the chapter examines the American concept of war and how that view has been conditioned by the experience this country has had at war through its history. The content of the "American way of war" contains elements of the reasons for which the country has taken up arms (why it has fought), the ways it has done battle (how it has fought), and the successes and failures we have endured as a people (what outcomes have occurred). All three dimensions are relevant to questions about how the U.S. force should be used in the future.

The result of this examination is a distinctive American military culture which is, in turn, a part of the larger western tradition of warfare. That western tradition produced both a distinct way for conducting war and distinct ways to decide why and how to apportion success and failure. This tradition reached an epitome in World War II. Because so much of American history has occurred in the European-centered international system often known as the Westphalian peace, our military history has historically experienced little influence from other traditions, notably the eastern, Asian tradition the United States has increasingly encountered in developing world conflicts in the past few decades and will likely continue to confront in the foreseeable future. Contrasts in eastern and western views about war include differing and sometimes incompatible beliefs about the functions of war, and these are increasingly salient in the post-Cold War and post-9/11 environments that the United States has faced and in which it will make future decisions about whether and where it will make war. World War II, the last "good" war, stands as a watershed in this intellectual development.

Basic Definition of War: What Is It?

Any discussion of a phenomenon as complex and consequential as war must begin with at least some distinctions about what war is. Much of the definition is commonsensical, but the term is used so widely to cover so many phenomena that do not meet normal specifications as to require some comment. Making "war" on poverty, illiteracy, or drugs, for instance, is hardly the same thing as making war against Iraq or Afghanistan. The expansion (arguably bastardization) of the term is not uncommon among militarily based terminology: the only pure meaning of the word "strategy," for instance, is its military use, but hardly any organization or movement fails to have a "strategy" in modern parlance, as noted in the Introduction. The same is true of war.

There is a generally accepted core meaning of the term "war." Its core is that war is organized, armed and often prolonged conflict between political communities. The distinctions here are a hybrid of definitions from a variety of sources, but the core of the concept is that war is, in terms used by this author in a 2000 text, "armed violence directed by one politically defined group against another." Some students of war have sought to make finer distinctions based on things like the duration and level of casualties to distinguish war from lesser forms of conflict, but the core of the concept remains: organized armed violence between political communities.

At the risk of splitting hairs, a distinction should be made between conditions and legal states of war. It is necessary to note that the armed conflicts in which the United States has been involved since World War II have technically not been wars. Why? Not all armed clashes that otherwise meet the definition of war are considered war in a strict legal sense; indeed, the United States has only technically been at war five times in its history (the War of 1812, the Mexican War, the Spanish–American War, and the two world wars), although it has engaged in actions that technically meet all other standards of war hundreds of times. Rather, formal wars require that one side makes a legal declaration of war against another, and this hardly occurs at all in the modern era. The basic reason is that formal states of war create a large and burdensome array of legal obligations, stipulations, and conditions both for the combatants and those who interact with the combatants in areas that states seek to avoid (neutral rights is an example). This may be a technicality and a diversion from the major thrust, but it does clarify the status of contemporary military actions for the purist. It is not, of course, an effective inhibition that keeps states and others from making war against one another. What the distinction does, however, is to create the legal technicality that armed conflicts that are war by any other criterion can legally not be war. Thus, the United States has fought a number of conflicts since it was last in a legal state of war in 1945, but those engagements are not technically war, even if that is what they are called (e.g. the Vietnam War).

This legal distinction has particular importance in the United States, and it has been the source of considerable political and constitutional concern across time. Under Article 1, Section 8 of the U.S. Constitution, only Congress has the power to declare war; at the time the founding fathers fashioned the framing document, it was generally agreed that this gave exclusive, overriding power to the Congress over the commitment of American forces into harm's way (with the possible exception of minor employments in the event of emergencies). Thus, the war-declaring power was a fundamental part of the original checks-and-balances principle that underlies the American political system.

The fact that wars are no longer declared (by virtually anyone in the world) undermines that exclusive power and check on executive authority. The question about the extent to which the president as commander-in-chief can commit the armed forces of the United States into conditions resembling states of war has become a sharply debated and contentious issue in American politics. The precipitant for this debate was the Vietnam War, where the only Congressional authorization of what is now the country's third longest war was a single joint resolution (the Gulf of Tonkin Resolution of 1964) that was subsequently rescinded. The response of the Congress was to pass the War Powers Resolution of 1973, designed to create a presidential obligation to consult the Congress before sending forces into warlike situations and to regulate the conduct of hostilities (including their duration), but it has been an imperfect solution which all presidents since have more or less actively opposed. Major actions like Iraq and Afghanistan were not preceded by any formal sort of declaration of hostilities.

What is common to all senses of what constitutes war is its physical nature: organized armed violence between political communities. As we will explore in a later section of this chapter, what war seeks to accomplish is a matter of some greater disagreement: is war a conscious political act designed to achieve concrete political objectives, or is it something else? Some of the answers, including nuances, are found in how war has developed and changed across time.

A Brief and Highly Selective Historical Tour of War

The history of war is a mammoth subject, and one that goes very far beyond the purpose of this book to address in any detail. It has been the subject of countless political and historical analyses that are notable for their length and detail: in the American scholarly tradition, possibly the landmark study is Quincy Wright's *A Study of War* originally published in 1942, a tome published as World War II raged across the globe and was dedicated to both the understanding and, ultimately, the abolition, of war. Any attempt to replicate, summarize, or add to the enormous literature and impressive body of thought that has been devoted to the subject here would be pretentious. It would also go beyond the more modest purpose of this chapter, which is to try to set some kind of context for helping to understand why the United States appears to be having such difficulty adapting to the contemporary conduct of wars in places and by means apparently alien to the American tradition.

These rejoinders noted, a few observations can be fairly safely put forward that will help move the discussion forward. The first is that, as already noted, war is an enduring phenomenon. For whatever reason based in human psychology, chemistry, genetics, or group dynamics, the institution of war has been virtually universal in the human experience. Anthropologists have found a handful of societies, generally so isolated that they have no, or hardly any, contact with anybody but one another, where war, and even individual violence, is not a normal form of behavior. The vast majority of human social contrivances, however, have included some notion of intergroup violence. The Old Testament of the *Bible*, for instance, is largely the chronicle of the usually violent interactions of early human groups in the Middle East, and no corner of the inhabited globe has been exempt from the reality of war.

Regardless of its underlying bases in metaphysics or elsewhere, this reality suggests something important about how we look at the problem of war. War has been too immutable a part of the human condition to suggest that it will wither and disappear anytime soon, and efforts to move toward its abolition have proven sufficiently unsuccessful that one probably can conserve and redirect the energy one might otherwise devote to the elimination of the "beast."

On a more positive note, the pattern of war, both within and between groups and locales, has changed over time, ebbing and flowing both in its pervasiveness, frequency, and bloodiness. The recently concluded twentieth century was arguably the bloodiest in human history (some military historians may challenge that assertion), but whether it deserves that distinction or not, it was certainly more violent than most and should not be viewed as the golden mean—some kind of "normal" level of mayhem. Indeed, there is a distinction between the two temporal halves of the century: the first half was dominated by two world conflicts and numerous internal uprisings, whereas the second half lacked major, systemic warfare between the most powerful states in the world militarily.

What this may suggest is that the problem of war is not so much its elimination or even reduction as it is in the management of the recourse to war. In a nuclear-armed world, for instance, global dominion may simply have disappeared as an attainable military goal and thus as a reason for which groups go to war. There has not, for instance, been a major interstate war where the clashes could realistically lead to systemic war in over a half century. Instead, warfare has moved to the geopolitical peripheries, where nuclear possibilities are remote.

A second observation about war is that it continues to be fought for a dizzying array of reasons. Power and control over other humans is a kind of catch-all overall purpose, because that power and control is usually desired for some other stated purposes. Among the more popular reasons, the imposition of some sort of political order (the expansion of empires is a recurrent historical theme), the promotion of a particular religious belief system ("conversion by the sword"), access to or control over mineral or other natural endowments, control over important (e.g. "strategic") locations, or a belief that a particular group has some form of divine or other mandate to control places or people (American "manifest destiny" over the West). Any overview of the history of war reveals the ingenuity of reasons that man has employed to justify war.

That recognition has at least two further implications useful in thinking about future wars. One is that people have gone to considerable lengths to justify the call to arms. This suggests that there is something about human nature that is certainly not inimical to engaging in war, or possibly that impels people to find violent ways to resolve their differences. Without moving toward either end of the metaphysical debate about whether humans are inherently violent or non-violent, the historical record supports the assertion that engagement in war is certainly not incompatible with whatever human nature may be. If war were such a disagreeable state for humankind, one would think that human groups would have avoided it much more than they have.

This leads to the second implication, which addresses efforts to reduce or eliminate the recourse to war. The basic argument that war somehow violates human nature and makes people act in ways that violate that nature inevitably must explain why so much of the time, people have found themselves placed in this unnatural situation. The standard response is that there are societal defects in the way society is organized that creates these conditions, and if those conditions were removed, the reasons for war would disappear as well. The problem here has been human ingenuity. The sheer variety of reasons for which people have gone to war in the past suggests at least the possibility that if all the reasons people have said they were going to war in the past were ameliorated, people would simply find other things to fight about. They might not, of course, but they also might.

Disagreements about the virtues of war and warriors form another recurrent historical theme. Is the warrior a heroic creature because of the virtues of placing himself in mortal danger to achieve some end, someone to be revered for the protection he provides to his group? Is the willingness to bear arms in pursuit of "a heavenly cause," in the words of Don Quixote, the Man from La Mancha, a sign of purity and virtue? Should the warrior be idolized because of his prowess at overcoming warlike others in the protection or promotion of what we hold dear? At the other extreme, is the warrior a barbarian, someone so primitive and unreasoning that he engages in blood lust because of some inherent psychological or intellectual shortcomings that make him feel that beating opponents into submission (or the grave) is somehow an heroic activity, whereas opposition to war smacks of weakness, even an effeminate tendency? Is the warrior a "man's man," whereas those who decry and eschew war are "lesser men" than those who pursue it?

Fourth, while warfare seems to have been something of a constant in the human experience, it has changed over time. At a minimum, the evolution of warfare can be seen through the answers to three interconnected questions: Who fights? How do they fight? And why do they fight? Looking at each of these questions helps color our picture of war and its role in contemporary society.

Who Fights?

The degree to which different kinds of individuals and groups within warring societies have been part of war is one changing variable. Two major traditions regarding who fights have competed historically, and each is present in the pattern of modern warfare.

One tradition is that every member of the group (state, tribe, or whatever) is a part of war, either directly as combatants or indirectly as potential victims of whatever fighting occurs. This tradition suggests war is an encompassing struggle—societies fighting societies—in which there are no exemptions from the rigors and horrors of war. Such warfare tends to be particularly desperate in its conduct, and few rules are observed or enforced about how groups make war on one another. This is the historical norm recorded in places like Carthage and much Old Testament fighting among tribes. The epitome of this tradition is the Golden Hordes of Mongols sweeping across the Asian steppes, in which no members of groups who found themselves in the path of the hordes escaped the violence. This concept is war at its most elemental, savage, and uncivilized in the sense of lacking social restraints. While the actions of the Mongols represent the extreme in this form of warfare, this "model" is not unusual historically or in the contemporary world. In fact, it may be making a comeback in places like the Middle East.

The notion that there should be a distinction between those who fight and those who do not has gradually evolved in the western military tradition. From the chaotic, savage conduct of the Thirty Years War of the seventeenth century, rules of western warfare gradually came to make a sharp distinction between combatants and non-combatants and to make the purposive assault on non-combatants a war crime punishable under the laws of war. In the process, warfare conducted against non-combatants came to be thought of as cowardly and unacceptable, stigmatizing those who carried out such forms of war. This does not mean, of course, that instances of atrocity by organized armed forces against non-combatant portions of adversary populations have disappeared from the conduct of war, but it probably did contribute to lesser instances of such behavior.

The key question is whether a distinction is clearly made between those who do the fighting (the combatants) and other members of the particular group who are present but who do not directly engage in violence (non-combatants). This distinction itself is easier to make in the abstract than it is in concrete situations: where to distinguish between combatants and non-combatants as legitimate targets of war is not always so clear. This is particularly true in internal wars like the DWICs.

Particularly in the twentieth century, the trend has been gradually to expand those considered legitimate targets (effectively, combatants) to include not only the physical warriors but also those who support the traditional combatants and allow them to continue fighting. In World War II, for instance, aerial bombardment included targeting factories that produced the war materiel on which modern armies depend. When these targets were attacked, plant workers with no direct combat role or status were inevitably victims of the bombers' ordinance. One way to justify these casualties is to consider them "collateral damage" (unintended consequences of the attack on the factory itself). Another is to expand the definition of what constitutes combatant status to include those who provide necessary aid to the soldiers.

The trend in modern warfare has been progressively to blur the distinction between combatants and non-combatants, effectively increasing the number and percentage of population members considered, if not direct combatants, at least not a category immune from attack. Partly, this expansion reflects acknowledging and attempting to justify the fact that collateral damage has increased; partly that some approaches to war do not make a strong distinction between the two categories, if they make any distinction at all. This latter factor is reflected throughout the book. A large part of this adaptation is the result of the nature of air warfare, and specifically aerial bombardment: it is difficult if not impossible for aerial bombers to be so precise that they only kill "eligible" victims, and one response has been simply to broaden the definition of legitimate targets.

This distinction is relevant to modern violent environments in at least two ways. One is that the participants in modern, asymmetrical warfare typically have different ideas about whether there is any distinction between combatants and non-combatants. Insurgents, for instance, are likely to deny that there is any distinction at all (this is particularly true of terrorists, who can only justify targeting "innocent" civilians because, by their definition, there is no such thing as an "innocent"). Western inter-veners like the United States tend to adhere to western distinctions between combatants and non-combatants and are thus reluctant to target those who, under traditional laws of war, are supposed to be exempt from such attacks. The problem with this reluctance has been that air-delivered collateral damage has become an increasing part of modern warfare as practiced by western-style armed forces, resulting in sizable casualties against civilians. The clearest contemporary case in point is the use of drone (e.g. Predator) air attacks against suspected concentrations of the enemy in Afghanistan and Pakistan. These attacks often include casualties among people who would otherwise be considered non-combatants. Call-ing these unintended results collateral damage does not leave the victims any less dead and raises the suspicion among survivors that such distinc-tions are mostly hypocritical. Those survivors can become the core of bitter oppositions as a result.

The notion of who is a legitimate target in war extends to the rules of combat—how people fight, with similar implications. Traditional rules of war limit both where and how armed forces fight. Those rules and the mores associated with them preclude (or certainly discourage) combat where the danger of physically engaging non-combatants is greatest. For this kind of prohibition to work, both sides have to agree, at least impli-citly, where they will meet in combat and in the rules of engagement (ROEs). In the historic western tradition, this meant armies clashing in areas outside cities rather than in urban confines, for instance, and eschewing prohibited violence against civilians who are in the way. This tradition basically died in the air and on the ground in World War II. In addition to aerial bombardment, many urban areas were the site of concerted combat as well.

How Do They Fight?

Prohibitions have extended to how combat is conducted. Certain forms of warfare have always been prohibited. The use of poison gas was outlawed after it was introduced into the trench lines in World War I, and before the "Great War," the developers of laws of war decided that the submarine could only attack surface vessels if it first surfaced (thereby giving warning of its intent) and had adequate provision to take on all survivors of its attack.

For such inhibitions to be enforceable, all parties must agree to abide by them. This is true because the newer methods presumably give some advantage to those who employ them that both sides have to agree not to exploit. Thus, the purpose of using gas in the World War I trenches was to poison the defenders in the opposing trenches, thereby incapacitating or killing them and allowing a successful assault breaching the otherwise impenetrable line. Both sides agreed to prohibit the use of gas at least partly because its application could not be controlled (if the wind changed directions, it might end up effectively attacking those who dispensed it) and because of countermeasures that could be taken (gas masks, for instance). Thus, beyond removing the inhumanity of gas attack effects on combatants, the prohibition made military sense as well. With limited exceptions such as Iraq in the 1980s and Syria in 2013, these bans have been effective deterrents.

Prohibitions on how and where to fight thus require the tacit agreement of both sides to honor whatever conventions are being enforced. When that agreement either does not exist or is not practiced by both sides, the orderliness the rules are supposed to promote may disintegrate. This is particularly a problem for the combatant who adheres to the rules and who faces an opponent who does not honor those rules. One consequence is to remove what minimal predictability there is in combat; even if one does not know exactly what the enemy is trying to do, the rules of war provide some idea how he will try to do it. For another, the rules are included in the normal ROEs for the rule-abiding combatant, who is generally prepared to fight others using the same ROEs. When an opponent does not, the rule-follower must adjust, and the soldiers who have been trained in these ROEs are likely to view a "rule breaker" as somehow less professional (if no less dangerous) than the side that "plays by the rules."

There is absolutely nothing new about the situation. In a general sense, the rules of war are constructed to regulate acts of war carried out by particular forces acting out of particular politico-military traditions. Those rules are clearly most applicable and "fair" for those who are prepared to fight by them, but they may be quite unfair to the side that has neither the same force traditions nor configurations.

Those with lesser forces may not be able to play by the same rules. The situation of a weaker foe facing a superior armed force that it cannot possibly contest on the stronger side's terms is as old as warfare itself. What is the weaker foe to do? The options are few and stark. One is to accept the situation and fight on the terms of the stronger foe. The consequences are predictable: defeat and probable death. The second is to avoid fighting altogether, either getting out of the way of the superior force or submitting to its domain. Flight may not be possible and submission comes with unpredictable and quite possibly unacceptable results (extinction, enslavement, etc.). That leaves a third option, which is to fight, but to adopt rules of fighting (including no rules at all) that minimize the advantage of the stronger force and may make it possible for the weaker to compete and prevail.

Of the three options, the third may be the most acceptable. Resistance by changing the rules and hopefully "leveling the playing field" is as old as warfare. Its current manifestation goes under the name *asymmetrical warfare* and is a concept the United States is currently seeking to understand and adapt to in its military planning and execution. This approach does not always succeed, but it does so often enough in the contemporary world that it has come to dominate the contemporary pattern of warfare and especially those instances where the United States (the consummate rule player) is faced by opponents (e.g. the Vietnamese and Afghans) who recognize they cannot (or could not) compete with the Americans playing by the Americans' rules and thus ignored or changed those rules.

This kind of calculation also has relevance in the case of intrusion on foreign soil by outside invaders. Whether the intent of the invaders is malicious (the extension of empire) or benign (humanitarian intervention) is, in these terms, virtually beside the point. Such intrusions will be resented by the hosts, who will want the intruders to leave. If they do not do so willingly (which they rarely do), resentment turns to rejection and resistance. At this point, the resisters have the disadvantage of inferior force and the certainty that standing up to the invaders on their own terms will fail. Thus, they are likely to choose the third option. This may, in turn, frustrate the occupiers and eventually cause them to leave, which is the asymmetrical warrior's goal.

Why Do They Fight?

How people fight is related to why they fight. To understand this dimension of the equation, a distinction must be made between total and limited objectives in war, and it is reflected in who fights and how they fight. The distinction, which I have made in collaboration with Dennis M. Drew (see Snow and Drew, *From Lexington to Baghdad and Beyond*) is imbedded in the dual political and military senses of the objectives of war.

At the military level, a total objective is aimed at destroying the ability of an opponent's armed forces to continue either through its physical destruction or the disruption of its military cohesion to the point that it cannot function effectively. The most obvious manifestation of achieving a total military objective is the surrender of the enemy armed forces. In total war, the purpose is the complete subjugation of the opponent, and it follows that the combatants will make a total military effort to achieve their ends. Historically, this has meant that all military means will be committed to the effort. Nuclear weapons have, however, altered this part of the equation for nuclear weapons possessors.

The nuclear qualification particularly affects countries like the United States. Totality of military means refers to the use of all military capabilities one possesses, not to some abstract notion of what level of various kinds of weaponry constitutes totality. Frequently in contemporary warfare, warring parties with much more modest military capabilities will fight total wars (i.e. fighting with everything they have) against larger and more robustly equipped opponents who do not employ all that they possess. In such cases, the more powerful opponent may use far less than its total capability against a more modestly equipped foe who is fighting all-out. Most obviously, a nuclear weapons state will not use its nuclear weapons and may not use other weapons for fear of escalation. In these circumstances, the more modestly equipped contestant may be committing its total, but comparatively more restrained, capabilities, while the stronger party may be fighting a limited engagement.

This situation can be anomalous and even frustrating, particularly for the more powerful combatant. Fighting a war of less than total means may seem less whole-hearted than the natural desperation of war seems to dictate, and those who are constrained may complain about having to fight "with one hand tied behind their backs" (an accusation frequently made about the American efforts in Korea and Vietnam). Restraint may, however, create other problems as well. It may affect military morale and may undercut political support for the war effort.

Politically, a total objective is one that requires the overthrow of the opponent's regime and its replacement with a government that will be more amenable to the political conditions demanded by the triumphant state(s). The overthrow and replacement of the fascist governments of the Axis powers is a classic total political objective achieved. Total military and political objectives are usually conjoined because defeating an opponent's armed forces is often necessary to force regime change on the loser.

Limited objectives cover the range of purposes short of the total defeat of an opponent's armed forces or overthrowing the enemy's government. Militarily, a limited goal seeks to bring enough military pressure on an opponent to make that adversary conclude that further resistance is futile and should be abandoned (exceeding "cost-tolerance"). This goal can, however, sometimes (even often) be realized without the formal surrender of the opponent's armed forces. The difficulty is that an outcome wherein the opponent's forces are not vanquished is not as "clean" and definitive as a solution where the adversary waves "the white flag." Politically, a limited objective, by definition, does not require a forced change of government but, more modestly, changing the objectionable policies or practices that precipitated war in the first place. The range of these situations varies considerably.

Three points should be made about the contrast between total and limited political purposes. The first is the relative frequency of occurrence of wars fought for one or another purpose. Historically, most armed conflicts have been limited in scope, conduct, and the reasons for which they are conducted. Many of the biggest, more spectacular, and most consequential wars have been total and have been the most chronicled because they were more likely to result in momentous political changes. History tends to distort the relative occurrence of total wars, downplaying the importance of less-than-total conflicts.

The second point is the satisfaction that surrounds total as opposed to limited wars. Put very simply, the attraction of total war is its intellectual and moral simplicity. An obvious reason to overthrow and replace an opponent's government is because either its personnel or policies (or likely both) are so odious that they require removing. At an intellectual level, this means that conditions are intolerable in terms used here. Morally, such diametrical opposition is generally easy to depict in terms of good and evil, making the removal of the opposing leadership a matter of era- dicating evil. So justified, it is relatively easy to rally support around the war effort, including the maximum, total commitment of resources to accomplish the task.

Contemporary wars are hardly ever total for all participants. Most are limited, at least for major powers like the United States. Limited wars involve influencing and changing behavior rather than overthrowing opposing governments, it is more difficult to depict them as moral cru- sades to fell evil leaders (although that objective was sometimes alleged, as in the case of Saddam Hussein in 2003), diminishing the moral force of the effort. Limitation extends to military conduct, with a country like the United States normally using only some fraction of its military might. Rallying public support behind an effort that may appear half-hearted is entirely more difficult than ridding the globe of some monstrous evil.

Since contemporary wars are generally internal contests, those opposing the United States are likely to view them as total—the overthrow or replacement of a government—and desperate, since the fate of those who lose civil wars is typically not pretty. For outsiders like the United States, their objectives are likely to be limited: relieving human suffering, for instance. The difference favors internal elements, since achieving their goal is more important to them than the outsider's goals are to the intruder. This imbalance in objectives and the consequent contrast in the importance of outcomes is a major factor in why these kinds of wars tend to be unwinnable for an outside power like the United States: ultimately, the out- comes are more important to our opponents than they are to the United States.

The third point follows in terms of the implications of totality versus limitation in the contemporary scene. The United States has not fought a total war since 1945, and it is extremely unlikely that it will fight one anytime in the foreseeable future. The United States has not had total wars fought *against* it but it has intruded into the violent internal affairs of other states. A major reason the United States has not fought total wars, of course, is that any war of total means for the United States would involve the use of nuclear weapons. The only countries against which the United States might ever have fought or fight such a war are against another state with the same capabilities. At the same time, in almost any case where the United States intervenes in a country's internal violent affairs, it will face an opponent who has a total purpose and is willing to engage all means at its disposal while the United States is self-limited in how it fights. This is a considerable disadvantage for the United States that has adversely affected its performance in the three major post-1945 wars in which it has failed to prevail, and it is a dynamic present in contemporary situations. No matter how evil they may be, the United States will not use nuclear weapons against ISIS(L), for instance.

The Functions of War: What Is It Good For?

Wars, of course, have been fought for multiple reasons throughout history. The functions of war, in other words, vary, and they do so in at least two important ways. One is about the purposefulness of war: why do people fight? It can be divided into two schools of thought. The other is the setting of war and the context of those engaged in it: who fights where? This can also be divided into two basic categories.

The first question is about the instrumentality of war, and it asks if war is principally a self-justifying act that people engage in because it a natural thing for them to do, or whether war is a device to achieve other objectives, notably political ends. In western thought, the idea that war is mainly an act to achieve political ends has been dominant for at least the last three centuries, but some military historians and thinkers maintain that this interpretation of war's function is an historical anomaly and that war is simply a natural human activity that requires no outside justification.

The idea that war is fought for mainly political purposes is most frequently associated with the philosophy and writing of Carl von Clausewitz, a Prussian staff officer of the nineteenth century whose master work, *On War*, was published in 1832. The book, which is both a statement of principles and a detailed history of the Napoleonic Wars, is most famous for its assertion, known as the Prussian dictum, that "war is the continuation of politics by other means." In this conception, the function of war is to serve the political ends of the political community waging it.

An important aspect of war defined as a political act is the impact it has on defining success and failure in war. Popular images often portray "victory" and "defeat" in mainly military terms measured by the success of armed forces in their combat with other armed forces. Certainly military victory is an important part of warfare and, since fighting is the primary physical activity in war, it is an obviously relevant measure. The Clausewitzian definition, however, changes the emphasis and meaning of success or failure to the achievement of the underlying political objectives for which war is undertaken. Ultimately in this construction—which is the dominant way in which westerners, including Americans, view the function of war—the party whose political objectives are achieved is the true victor and is not always the side whose forces prevail on the battlefield.

The possible difference between military, battlefield definitions of success and victory defined in political terms is one of the major points of contention in the contemporary world and a clear sign of how the utility of military force has changed. In traditional, Western-style warfare, the link between the military and political dimensions was intimate: military success was necessary to strip away the protection an adversary had to avoid being compelled to accept the policies that justify the war. There is a sequence and necessary relationship between the two aspects of war: military victory is prerequisite to achieving the ultimate, political objective. World War II is a clear example. In contemporary warfare, that link has largely been severed: prevailing in battle may or may not be the prerequisite for achieving the political objective, and experience has even shown that one side can actually fail by traditional military means of measurement and still prevail politically. The fact that modern warfare is more often internal rather than international is at the heart of this change.

The second distinction arises from the setting in which war occurs. Broadly speaking, one way to differentiate wars is as *interstate* conflicts (wars between fully sovereign states) and *intrastate* wars (conflicts fought primarily within the boundaries of a single state). Traditional, western-style warfare and preferences are largely built around the model of interstate war, whereas the vast majority of contemporary wars are either intrastate or have internal dynamics as their major characteristic. The two kinds of wars are sufficiently different in such a large variety of ways that a mindset and preparation for one kind does not necessarily prepare one well for the other.

Interstate wars—conflicts between countries—are the more comfortable forms of warfare from a western intellectual vantage point. They pit distinct peoples and governments against one another for what are normally easily understood reasons: control over disputed territory (the control of Texas in the Mexican War), the attempt of one state to spread its domain over others who oppose that extension (the Nazis in Europe, the Japanese in the Pacific), or the redress of grievances (the sinking of the *USS Maine*), for instance. In the western tradition, these wars are fought by similarly configured and equipped armed forces adopting the same ROEs, and each side has definable political and military definitions of success. They also generally have discrete beginnings and ends. Sometimes they are fought for profound, basic reasons (the World Wars) and sometimes the reasons may be fairly trivial (the War of 1812). They may be either total (once again, the World Wars) or limited (the Mexican War), but at least they are fairly clear and easy to comprehend. Limited wars are a bit harder to understand, because the question of whether the effort was worthwhile will always be raised and because limits will usually be imposed on the conduct of the war.

Interstate wars have virtually disappeared in the contemporary world. A few such wars pop up from time to time, and some have major implications, such as the various wars between India and Pakistan and between Israel and its Arab neighbors. The most important countries, such as the United States, no longer become involved in these kinds of wars. The reason is simple: interstate wars between the most powerful countries are potential nuclear wars, and the fear of escalation to nuclear holocaust has made such wars unthinkable. Interstate war between the major powers has further been diminished since all major powers share a common economic, and to some extent, political worldview: there is simply nothing dividing these countries worth fighting over that is not trumped by the reasons for them not to fight.

Since 1945, most of the world's conflicts have either been intrastate or have had strong intrastate overtones. This should not come as a great surprise. A major dynamic of this period has been the breakup of colonization in the developed world. Most of the new countries came into being without either political traditions or properly prepared personnel to lead them peacefully through the nation-building process. A large number of the new states created were historical fictions, wherein multiple peoples with histories of antagonism toward one another were grouped together in new, absolutely artificial states and told to get along. Most of the Middle East and much of Africa are this way. At the same time, the new borders split apart people of the same nationality from one another against their wills: the Kurds, Palestinians, and Pashtuns are notable examples.

During the Cold War, the superpowers stirred the pot. For most emerging countries, the ideological bases of the Cold War rivalry were largely irrelevant, but they were important to the evangelical leaderships in Washington and Moscow, who sought to win friends and allies and to turn the map "blue" or "red" by gaining predominant influence in these new countries, a theme explored in Chapter 4.

The predominance of intrastate warfare has continued. With the communism-anticommunism ideological base of conflict negated, such outside interests as now exist have gravitated to the banner of opposition to terrorism and the influence of terrorists (rather than communists) as an incitement to interfere. What has emerged, however, is that the politico-military form that western (i.e. American) involvement has taken is intervention in civil conflicts. This form of involvement did not work particularly well during the Cold War, and it does not work well today, for largely the same reasons. These include the application of a concept of traditional interstate warfare to a world where that analogy does not clearly apply. The major misapplication has been implicitly to equate modern warfare with World War II.

World War II: The Last "Good" War

World War II is the implicit model by which most Americans measure war. In surveys of Americans, it is consistently rated as their "favorite" war, and thanks to Tom Brokaw, those who fought it are the "greatest generation." If all wars were like World War II, there would not be much current quandary over when to use force in the future. Current reality, unfortunately, is not so simple.

The World War II Model

World War II was conflict on a grand scale. It was the largest war in human history, with combat occurring virtually everywhere there were human populations: of the globe's major land masses, the only one that avoided combat altogether was Antarctica. It was also the world's bloodiest conflict, with an estimated 70 million people killed during its conduct, almost half of whom were civilians. In some ways, it was a Russian war, since the Soviet Union endured the most casualties by a large measure. Although no one kept exact statistics, Soviet losses were at least 20 million, more or less equally divided between civilians and uniformed combatants.

Moreover, World War II was also the epitome of the evolved western, European military tradition in action. It was a war that, in large measure, started in Europe (Japan would probably not have been bold—or foolhardy—enough to start a war with the United States in the Pacific in the absence of a second front in Europe to divert some American energies), was fought by European-organized and equipped armed forces fighting under rules of conduct devised by Europeans for quintessentially Clausewitzian purposes. It was truly the logical extreme of the principles and rationales of the European tradition. It also was the last hurrah for that form of war.

It is the character of the conflict that makes World War II such a popular memory, at least among the victorious states who participated. This is especially true in the United States, which suffered comparatively light casualties (official figures are about 405,000 killed) and virtually no wartime damage to American property other than in colonies, e.g. the Philippines. What marks the unique character is that the second great conflagration of the twentieth century was quintessentially a crusade of "good" against an "evil" the destruction of which carried enormous moral as well as political and military weight.

Romantic recollections of the war are reflected in both military and political terms. As Carl Builder pointed out in *The Masks of War*, all of the major services remember actions from World War II as their finest hours: the Army the campaigns in Europe beginning with Normandy, the Navy the decisive naval battles in the South Pacific, the Marines the amphibious assaults on Japanese-held Pacific islands, the Air Force the strategic bombardment campaign that helped bring Nazi Germany to its knees. Prior to World War II, the place of the military services in American life was much more peripheral than it was in the war and as it has evolved since.

The impact of World War II on the military and the evolution of both thinking about and organizing American force can scarcely be overstated. During the war, over 12 million Americans were under arms. American forces had never even approximated this size before, and the growing complexity of warfare—the extension of war into the air and beneath the world's oceans, for instance—created the need for a much larger, more diverse, and complex structure than had ever been witnessed before.

The traditions honed and sharpened in World War II dominated the postwar military both physically and in terms of how the military thought about itself and how it should fight. The "Army's war" had been fought principally in Europe, and this experience helped shape the army's organization and preferences for the postwar world. The European theater was a "heavy" war fought between large armies emphasizing large ("heavy") equipment like artillery and armor leading the infantry. This experience shaped the postwar military in part because the new opponent, the Soviet Union, was organized and thought much the same way. As a result, the heavy warfighting specialties came to dominate the upper echelons of the Army and thus to perpetuate these preferences, even after the Soviet Union disappeared and no other opponent organized in a similar fashion emerged.

The Navy and Air Force were the same. The "Navy's war" was in the South Pacific, where the contest between Japan and the United States centered around the clash of large capital fleets in which the aircraft carrier became the centerpiece, supported by the submarine, and this experience continued after the war when the Soviets tried (with marginal success) to replicate the American Navy. The Air Force, separated from its World War II tethering as the Army Air Corps, established the ability to overfly enemy territory and to attack and cripple the enemy's war-making ability as its legacy. That experience remains the hub around which the advocacy of airpower is nurtured. Of the services, only the Marines, the poor cousin of the Navy and the only service that perpetually fears its own demise, saw the handwriting on the wall, realized that its future did not lie in storming island beaches in the future, and began to pivot toward DWICs (in which it had some experience) as a primary mission.

Both because it was such a success and was followed by a conceptually similar Cold War, it followed that the World War II military model would be carried over into the postwar environment. It had worked admirably to defeat fascism, and it had created a whole new class of military professionals born and honed in its traditions who felt most comfortable thinking about military problems and solutions in "traditional" ways. The military clung to the World War II model because it had worked in the past and because of the dire potential of a failure to keep the Cold War cold. Competing with the Soviets was much like competing with the Nazi Germans, and it helped perpetuate a way of thinking that has transcended the Cold War. Thus, airmen continue to promote the most sophisticated fighter, the Navy enhanced carrier-based battle groups, and the Army bigger, more lethal tanks in a world where the opponents have no air forces to shoot down, navies to sink, and few paved roads on which to drive tanks. Nonetheless World War II retains great popularity, and this is critical in political democracies, which cannot effectively conduct war without continuing support from the people.

The World War II Model in the Contemporary World

World War II reinforced the western model of war, and especially the centrality of the political purposes for which war is fought. War is a very strenuous, stressful, and dangerous enterprise, and the public must be convinced of the worth of a particular war effort. This is the role of the political objective, the articulation of the rationale for war. It serves two major purposes. One is to explain why war is necessary to create and sustain popular support: the objective as a rallying cry. The second purpose is to provide direction to the military aspects of the war: the objective as guidepost. In this sense, the relationship between the political objectives and military actions becomes clear: the political objective defines necessary conditions at the end of war and provides guidance to the military about what it must do to attain those conditions.

In the American historical experience, "good" political objectives for war—objectives that capture and sustain adequate public support to prosecute war to its successful conclusion—have tended to possess four characteristics, not necessarily in any order. Those four standards are clarity and simplicity, moral worth, attainability, and importance (or necessity). World War II met all four; most contemporary engagements do not.

The first is *clarity and simplicity*: the objective must be clear and it must be easy to articulate and understand by the average American. It is the application of the "KISS" principle: "keep it simple, stupid!" I have suggested what I call the bumper sticker rule to describe this criterion: it must fit on an automobile bumper sticker and be readable at three car lengths behind the vehicle displaying it. Succinctness and simplicity (even oversimplification if the objective is not distorted in the process) are virtues. "Destroy Hitler!" met this criterion; "create the conditions wherein a strong central government can arise that will not allow terrorists to return" in Afghanistan arguably does not.

The second standard is *moral loftiness*: the objective must embody some high moral imperative, preferably defined in terms of some good versus an evil that needs to be removed. The need to feel one is acting on behalf of some higher purpose may not be uniquely American, but it is certainly a characteristic that motivates Americans at arms. Put simply, Americans are much more highly motivated when they believe "we are doing good," and are uncomfortable with rationales for fighting that are clothed in gauzy, morally ambiguous or neutral geopolitical justifications. This assessment includes some positive belief in the moral worth of the enterprise. Ignoring the felt need to be engaged in a lofty enterprise is asking for trouble in terms of durable public support.

The third standard is *attainability*: whatever the objective may be, it must also be something that can be attained. It is part of the American military culture's self-image as winners, and this positive belief extends to the conviction that Americans are successful at war: the United States wins the fights into which it gets. It is at least partly mythological, since there are some instances where the United States "won" by only the most generous interpretations of victory (the War of 1812 is a prime example). Nonetheless, Americans believe that when they enter war, they leave as winners. One cannot always know in advance whether a particular conflict will be successful, meaning this standard affects not so much initial support for a war effort as it does sustaining that support as the war proceeds.

The fourth standard is *importance*: what are the consequences to the United States if it fails to attain its wartime goals? This particular criterion is a way of restating the realist limitation on the use of force in support of vital interest. If a favorable outcome is clearly necessary for the national condition, then resolve is likely to be stronger in the face of adversity; if the outcome does not appear so important, then that assessment may undermine that same support.

These four criteria are clearly interactive. Simplicity and moral worth are clearly linked in the sense that a short, easily understandable goal stated in moral terms represents a very appealing combination, and removing either of these criteria (and especially both) will clearly undermine the basis for support. The more easily attainable an objective is, the less any of the others will count (who, for instance, can remember why the United States invaded Grenada?). On the other hand, if attainment is difficult or problematical, as it has proven in so many contemporary situations, the result is a strain on all three of the others, and the strain on popular support increases with the length and indeterminacy of outcome. The necessity of prevailing can trump all other concerns if a war's successful prosecution is truly vital to the country.

World War II clearly met all four criteria. Defeating Nazi and Imperial Japanese imperialism was a succinct, easily understood goal, and the fascist regimes and their practices represented a clear evil that appealed to American crusading zeal. In other than the darkest days when the war began, the final goal was clearly attainable. Most importantly, the attainment of the goal was clearly necessary if the postwar world was to be acceptable to the United States and its allies. Americans believed they *had* to win, and that resolve effectively overrode any other concerns. In the context of the American experience to that point, World War II was a long war (never a positive factor in a democracy), but American resolve never wavered. World War II was a war fought for all the right reasons.

It was also a conceptually straightforward conflict. World War II was a classic, Clausewitzian war of both total means and ends. Wars of total purpose tend to arise and be justified in moral terms, and the veneer of good versus evil logically translates into a preference for the application of total means to eradicate the evil one opposes. In the situations since 1945, American goals have generally been limited (forcing the North Koreans to return to North Korea but not overthrowing them, or preserving the sovereign integrity of South Vietnam, for instance). Limitation of ends generally leads to limitation on how and toward what ends one fights: the goal is not to destroy the enemy's armed forces and compel their surrender, but to persuade that enemy to quit doing something deemed unacceptable. Translated backward from conduct to purposes, it means not destroying evil, but rather making it act a little less evilly. Given the rigors and sacrifices that war entails, that is not always an easy sell.

Wars of total ends and means are conceptually easier to direct and conduct. A war with the express intent of overthrowing the enemy's government presupposes an intensive physical effort in which the total means available will be invoked (wars between nuclear-armed opponents are an exception). Given the life-threatening nature of combat, military commanders naturally want to take whatever steps necessary to maximize the prospects of success and minimize personal losses. This natural proclivity translates into a preference for doing as much as one can: in the direction of a totality of effort.

The result is a likely synergism and general uniformity of military and political leaders in total warfare. This synergy will never be total or complete, but in total war, both groups are "on the same page," and this translates into a support for most, if not all, the military can do from political authorities, a situation that promotes unity of effort. By contrast, wars of limited purpose tend to produce inhibitions on the means appropriate to pursuing them, creating friction between civilian and military authorities, a theme and problem that will recur in these pages.

Distillation: The Preferred American Way of War

The World War II experience created an ideal set of expectations that is an effective albatross around America's understanding of and preparation for contemporary contingencies. World War II was, however, the end of an era, not the reflection of what future war would be like. The biggest total war in human history by every measure, it was not the way wars usually are. Historically, total wars have been the exception, not the rule in history. The simplicity, even simultaneity, of total purposes and means that helped make the war so supportable does not happen very often in human history. Employing the World War II experience as a kind of ideal model around which to tailor thinking thus distorts the lens through which one views current and likely future reality in unhelpful ways. The benchmarks and virtues of that experience really do not apply to the present very well at all.

One dimension of this misfit may be the application of the Prussian dictum. War may remain a political act, but not necessarily in as conscious a way as the dictum's description of war as a continuation of politics connotes. In all wars, the outcomes have political repercussions: some people or groups gain power at the expense of others. Whether this relationship is as overt and self-conscious as Clausewitz and those who have followed him described may not be as direct as the dictum suggests. In developing world internally based conflicts, the political influence may be very indirect and even unrecognized by those doing the fighting. The dictum effectively westernizes a phenomenon that is not entirely western.

The model distorts matters in other ways as well. Five stand out. The first is in the relationship between political and military objectives. Traditional, Clausewitzian war is fought for clearly defined reasons that help rationalize the reasons for going to war and its conduct. This process implies a kind of orderliness in the nature of and relationship between the warring parties that is true in traditional war but is not so clearly true in more contemporary conflict. More specifically, warfare in the World War II tradition is generally between independent, sovereign governments that have similar armed forces and have similar relationships between their political and military sectors. Both opponents view ends and means in similar ways. Within these confines, wars are fought for clearly defined and understood objectives at a state-to-state level.

This clarity and "model" do not apply to most contemporary conflicts. Most are not interstate. Rather, they are basically internal (intrastate) wars between factions within a country. These are asymmetrical conflicts, meaning the two sides neither fight the same way nor have the same clear relationship between political and military authorities. They only develop an interstate aspect when some outsider intervenes to tip the conflict toward one side or another. The reasons for intervention are normally complex, subtle, and contentious. For the internal contestants, they are usually about who rules and they are desperate: the losers are likely to suffer grievously. For the outsider, the reasons for supporting one faction or the other are likely to be opaque and difficult to articulate to the population at home. The objectives, in other words, are likely to violate both the bumper sticker rule and some or all of the criteria for a good objective. All of these factors make support for the war within the intervening population more fragile, problematical, and prone to erosion over time.

A second problem is that these wars do not conform to the American model which defines war as a discrete interruption of peace. Traditional wars can neatly be divided into a beginning, middle, and end, each of which are distinct and contain milestones to allow one to note passage from one phase to another. Wars begin and end.

Contemporary war is clearly not like that. Most contemporary wars do not have a clear beginning point. The invasion of Iraq by the United States is an exception, but the underlying issues within Iraq that the war brought to the surface precede the war by centuries. The war in Afghanistan, by contrast, can be traced back at least to the end of the Soviet occupation in 1989, but finding a clear starting point is a futile endeavor. The conduct of war is also protracted, not marked by decisive military clashes but instead by prolonged campaigns of attrition aimed more at wearing out the enemy than defeating him. This is especially true for wars in which countries like the United States intervene; the natives know they cannot "defeat" the Americans in battle (overcome hostile ability), so they instead wage protracted campaigns aimed at wearing out the American will to continue (cost-tolerance). It is a strategy that has been quite effective. Finally, these wars do not have dramatic endings where issues are settled and one can tote up victories and losses. When American forces leave Afghanistan the war itself will not be over, as has been the case in Iraq. Moreover, one side will not have decisively won or lost the war. Nobody surrenders; there is no peace treaty.

This disorder helps explain the third difference, which is the ambiguity of outcomes. World War II is the last American war that was ended by a definitive agreement between the sides that was enforceable and enforced (the Geneva negotiations posited the conditions for American withdrawal from Vietnam, but their provisions were not honored, and their violation had few consequences). The United States has left Iraq, but there is no peace agreement assuring that American objectives—a stable Iraq—will be met, and the final outcome is somewhere in the indefinite future. In the meantime, how are Americans to assess what happened? There is no defeat to mourn, no victory to celebrate.

This leads to the fourth and related difference, which surrounds notions of winning. The Prussian dictum defines the objective, and assessing the postwar political situation in terms of those goals allows one to determine accomplishment or failure, just as battlefield outcomes and the relative conditions of armed forces allow one to assess military victory or failure. These measures barely apply at all in contemporary wars. Whether the political objective is achieved is, if not totally unrelated to the war and its physical ending, generally something that does not emerge for some time after the smoke of war disappears. Internal armed forces that have not prevailed do not surrender and disband; instead they slink off to some sanctuary where they can repair and rejuvenate (the Taliban in Pakistan are a prime example). In these circumstances, who can say who has won or what they have won? Americans like outcomes figuratively displayed on a scoreboard so that one can see who scored the most points and thus who won. In contemporary wars, the numbers are more likely replaced by question marks or qualifying asterisks that leave the answers ambiguous.

The fifth difference reflects the importance of outcomes *to the United States*. World War II was clearly a war of necessity; it had to be fought and won. Virtually everyone agreed failure would have been intolerable. Contemporary wars, on the other hand, do not generally affect the most basic, vital American interests: even the worst possible outcomes are normally tolerable, if unpleasant. These wars of choice are much more difficult to rationalize to the American public than wars of necessity, which is why those supporting American involvement tend to describe the situation in terms of vital interests (see the discussion of ISIS(L) in Chapter 6 in this regard). Popular support is crucial to sustaining support for war, however, and inflation of importance can come to roost if the public changes its mind about the cause. As a partial result, new ways of rationalizing war have emerged, to which the discussion now moves.

Bibliography

Art, Robert J., and Kenneth N. Waltz. *The Uses of Force: Military Power and International Politics*. 4th edn. Lanham, MD: Rowman and Littlefield, 2004.

Brodie, Bernard. *War and Politics*. New York: Macmillan, 1973.

Builder, Carl. *The Masks of War: American Military Style in Strategy and Analysis*. A RAND Corporation Research Study. Santa Monica, CA: RAND Corporation, 1989.

Churchill, Winston S. *The Second World War*. (Six volumes). Boston, MA: Houghton Mifflin, 1948–1953.

Clausewitz, Carl von. *On War*. Revised edition translated and edited by Michael Howard and Peter Paret. Princeton, NJ: Princeton University Press, 1984.

DuPuy, R. Ernest, and Trevor N. Dupuy. *The Encyclopedia of Military History*. New York: Harper and Row, 1977.

Hassler, Warren W. *With Shield and Sword: American Military Affairs, Colonial Times to the Present*. Ames, IA: Iowa State University Press, 1984.

Keegan, John. *A History of Warfare*. London: Hutchison, 1993.

Leckie, Robert. *The Wars of America*. Revised and updated edn. New York: Harper and Row, 1981.

Peters, Ralph. *Fighting for the Future: Will America Triumph?* Mechanicsburg, PA: Stackpole Books, 2001.

Snow, Donald M. *UnCivil Wars: International Security and the New Internal Conflicts*. Boulder, CO: Lynne Rienner Publishers, 1996.

Snow, Donald M. *When America Fights: The Uses of U.S. Military Force*. Washington, DC: CQ Press, 2000.

Snow, Donald M., and Eugene Brown. *International Relations: The Changing Contours of Power*. New York: Longman, 2000.

Snow, Donald M., and Dennis M. Drew. *From Lexington to Baghdad and Beyond: War and Politics in the American Experience*. 3rd edn. Armonk, NY: M. E. Sharpe, 2010.

Stoessinger, John G. *Why Nations Go to War.* 11th edn. Belmont, CA: Wadsworth Publishing, 2010.

Sun Tzu. *The Art of War.* Translated by Samuel B. Griffith. Oxford: Oxford University Press, 1963.

Van Creveld, Martin. *The Transformation of War.* New York: Free Press, 1991.

Weigley, Russell. *The American Way of War.* New York: Macmillan, 1973.

Williams, T. Harry. *A History of American Wars: From Colonial Times to World War II.* New York: Alfred A. Knopf, 1981.

Wright, Quincy. *A Study of War: An Analysis of the Causes, Nature and Control of War* (abridged edn). Chicago, IL: University of Chicago Press, 1964.

3 Humanitarian Intervention?

Contemporary discussions of potential American military involvements tend to revolve around two pillars. Traditional arguments have been geopolitical, based on violations of vital interests if the United States does not become involved, and thus the necessity of American participation. These arguments are often difficult to make regarding DWICs, where levels of American interest are often opaque and arguable, making the potential involvement an act of choice.

Contemporary internal conflicts often have a tragic characteristic, which is great human suffering, often by innocent members of the society and graphically beamed worldwide by global electronic media. The ongoing sectarian slaughter in Syria and Iraq is a prime example. The situations become humanitarian disasters, and calls for intervention on humanitarian grounds have become an added element in attempting to gain support for the use of force in these situations. Such concerns are natural but unconventional. Because the horrors that activate these calls seem in no danger of disappearing, this rationale for military action merits consideration.

Calls for intervention on humanitarian grounds can be placed in the framework of interests, threats, and risks. Because these concepts have been the artifacts of traditional thinking about national security, however, the inclusion is not entirely comfortable.

Justifying military action on humanitarian grounds begins from the controversial premise the humankind has a universal, vital interest in protecting people from man-made atrocities, and that there is a universal duty to prevent humanitarian disasters from occurring, and when these tragedies happen anyway, to alleviate them and to punish their perpetrators. If this obligation is accepted (specifically the *vital importance* of the humanitarian interest), the idea of humanitarian intervention fits conceptually into conventional analysis. If one rejects the premise, it does not.

The importance of humanitarian threats is clearly related. If one is personally threatened, such threats are conventional in terms of risks and responses, but that is not the case for a country like the United States. Americans are more likely to view humanitarian violations to others and to assess whether such conditions are threatening to Americans. In a direct sense, they usually are not, so the cogency of threat must be assessed in universal, moral terms. Is everyone threatened when anyone is threatened by humanitarian disasters? The degree to which an impelling need for risk-reducing action exists (or does not exist) arises from this calculation.

Purely moral considerations are often uncomfortable concepts in traditional analysis of national security policy. The area is dominated by thinkers and practitioners who view national security primarily in military terms, and the mainstream of that thought is realist and geopolitical, not in the area of values and morality. To most traditionalists, arguments about the moral "right" and "wrong" of military action are "soft" and go beyond either their expertise or particular interest. Their basic values are implicit: the core is the protection of the state and its interests, and that value is so fundamental as to be beyond question or debate. Moral, humanitarian concerns have, however, snuck into the debate anyway.

There are several reasons for considering the moral dimension. One is certainly that the decision to use force in any manner is political, and political decisions are normally based on value considerations. In the case of decisions to invoke force, those reasons may largely be framed in terms of the threat to and pursuit of national self-interest (realism) or the strategic advantage or disadvantage of outcomes in situations where force is used or withheld (geopolitics), but there is also the question of whether such actions are somehow "right" in a value sense. At a minimum, in a political democracy, it is impossible to justify actions like intervention in the pursuit of amoral or immoral purposes. Doing "the right thing," President Clinton's justification for American action in Kosovo, is a powerful political appeal.

A second reason has been an international trend of justifying military action in moral terms. This theme's general thrusts are that there is some universal obligation to relieve human suffering wherever atrocious conditions exist and that outside action can provide relief to those upon whom inhumane treatment is being imposed. This strand of thought emerged as part of the global reaction to the Holocaust, and it has become intensified since the end of the Cold War because of atrocities in places like Rwanda and Kosovo and more recently Iraq and Syria. This consideration is by no means universally accepted as an adequate reason for using American force within American national security thought, but it does resonate within part of the political spectrum that influences military decisions.

This moral dimension is not likely to go away. If anything, it will become more important, for at least two reasons. One is the growing prevalence of atrocious behavior on the international scene, making the question of what obligations the international community has in the face of moral outrages unavoidable. This concern is likely to be part of the global environment for some time to come. Second, more traditional realist and geopolitical justifications may be on the relative wane. The situations that invite outside interference in the future are decreasingly in places where obvious vital interests are involved or where unfavorable outcomes affect basic geopolitical interests. The likely common denominator of future situations is moral atrocity being committed against a segment of an indigenous population by forces the government either is unable or unwilling to stifle (e.g. ISIS(L) in Syria and Iraq). This influence is examined in Chapter 6.

The reasons that states interfere with armed force in the affairs of others have changed, and humanitarian justifications are now prominent reasons for interference. The age of open imperial justification probably ended with the defeat of the Japanese "Sphere of Co-Prosperity" (the name they euphemistically gave their empire) and the Nazi-led Germans in World War II. There may be traditional imperial sentiment in a few other places, but, by and large, the age of imposing political will in the name of greater dominion has disappeared as a rationale for intervention.

The end of the Cold War accelerated this change. During the 1990s, human atrocities became more frequent (or at least better publicized) matters of international concern, with varying responses that in turn helped to frame the current debate about the use of force. The two most prominent of these were in Rwanda and in the Balkans (Bosnia and Kosovo), both of which have been cited as precedents for the doctrine of humanitarian intervention. In Rwanda in 1994, nearly 800,000 members of the Tutsi tribe in that country were slaughtered during a brief rampage while the world community stood silently by, failing to prevent or cause an early cessation of the atrocity. In Bosnia in the mid-1990s and in neighboring Kosovo during the latter stages of the decade, there was a stronger response to "ethnic cleansing" against the populations of those two former parts of Yugoslavia.

A basic sea change of the post-Cold War period is the rise of humanitarian value-based justifications for intrusion into the affairs of others. This change remains an important element in contemporary discussions, adding a significant subjective, moral base to the empirical questions surrounding intervention. In addition to the empirical question of what *can* physically be accomplished by interfering in the affairs of other states, there is now a second question: what *should* be done in certain cases where moral outrages exist. In *Just and Unjust Wars*, Michael Walzer (2006) dramatically and succinctly phrases the moral concern: "How much human suffering are we prepared to watch before we intervene?" The historic answer is quite a lot. Traditional views even hold that suffering within the sovereign jurisdictions of states is none of the business of outsiders, who have no legitimate right to interrupt human suffering when it occurs within the sovereign jurisdiction of states.

This position has been challenged progressively since the end of the Cold War and has emerged as a position known as the "responsibility to protect" (or R2P). Gareth Evans, the former Australian foreign minister and a leading advocate of this position writing in the Foreword to Thomas

Weiss' 2012 book *Humanitarian Intervention*, summarizes it: "The issue is not the right but the responsibility of every state to play its appropriate role, with the objective not being intervention as such but the *protection* of men, women, and children threatened by the horror of mass violence."

The argument that there is some moral imperative to interfere in the affairs of other states is controversial and not universally accepted. It poses fundamental challenges to orthodox ways of thinking about the dynamics of international politics and particularly international activism in a world where most of the violence and instability occurs in situations where a major part of the rationale for intrusion is humanitarian. Walzer summarizes this changing dynamic. "The greatest danger that most people face in the modern world comes from their own states," he writes, "and the chief dilemma of international politics is whether people in danger should be rescued by military forces from outside." Published five years before the beginning of the conflict in Syria, it is a remarkably succinct description of the debate over international attitudes toward Syria as it has raged and been extended to ISIS(L).

The assertion of a humanitarian imperative to act adds an important normative dimension to the overall discussion of the use of armed force, and one that must become an integral part of discussing future national security policy. To analyze this problem, the rest of the chapter will proceed sequentially. It begins by describing how the rationales for military actions have changed, which is largely a question of attitudes toward international norms regarding the treatment of people. In the process, it raises value questions, answers to which will differ based on people's contrasting values. Humanitarian intervention is then placed in an American context in the form of something called the "do-something syndrome." The chapter concludes with an admonition regarding both the moral and empirical danger of action or inaction in terms of unintended consequences and the danger of producing quite different, far less desirable, effects.

The Changing Rationale for Intrusion: Imperial Glory to Moral Imperative

The idea that states might have some obligation or duty to protect people from harm or abuse in other political jurisdictions with armed force for humanitarian reasons is quite recent. Indeed, the historical record, including philosophical discourse, on the subject does not provide a rich source of information, argumentation, or guidance on moral questions surrounding the question of imperatives to interfere in the affairs of others.

Most of the historical record deals with physical questions of intrusion in a morally neutral sense. People attacked and conquered or repelled others using the force available to them, and the historical record is primarily concerned with who succeeded and who failed. When there was great human atrocity surrounding a particular intrusion such as the brutality of the Mongol hordes or some aspects of the Crusades, concerns were raised that these actions exceeded religious or other moral norms, but even basic moral writings do not address the question of the morality of intrusion per se in great detail. Brutality and horrific violence were simply such a pervasive part of the human condition and so widely practiced by so many human groups against one another that entreaties against them were too abstract to have major meaning beyond the speculation of moral philosophers.

Natural Law and the Principle of Nonintervention

Although it has not been a central theme until recently, there has always been a question of what to do about the commission of atrocious acts within the political jurisdiction of others. One side of this debate is based in concepts of morality that argue, in Terry Nardin's (2002) words, that "the use of force is justified not solely by self-defense but by the moral imperative to punish wrongs and to protect the innocent." He continues that "armed intervention is morally justified when people are mistreated by their rulers." The moral basis of this position is normally derived from natural law and common morality. The competing position is the principle of nonintervention, by which Nardin argues that "states are forbidden to exercise their authority, and certainly to use force, within the jurisdiction of other states." These first premises are not incompatible when states do not abuse their citizens, but they come into direct conflict when such abuses occur.

The natural law position is the historically older of the two positions. Nardin summarizes, "What we now call humanitarian intervention was conceived by moralists, theologians, and philosophers writing before the emergence of international law." The principle of noninterference, by contrast, is largely an artifact of the Westphalian peace that created the modern state system, the bedrock principle of which is the doctrine of sovereignty. Sovereignty also evolved in international positivist law, reaching its zenith of acceptance in the eighteenth and nineteenth century. Gareth Evans (2008) in *The Responsibility to Protect* states the consequences more succinctly and starkly: "the Westphalian principles effectively institutionalized the long standing indifference of political leaders toward atrocities occurring elsewhere. ... Sovereignty meant immunity from outside scrutiny or sanction."

Modern arguments about using force reflect these two positions, often more implicitly than explicitly. The noninterference principle is used to oppose forcefully interceding in countries in two ways. One is that interference in the internal politics of others is, strictly speaking, none of the business of outsiders. In the ongoing American debate, this position is most often, but not exclusively, associated with libertarian attacks on an activist foreign policy. The other objection, which is a more traditional defense of sovereignty, is that interference can be precedent-setting: if one interferes in the affairs of others, then the argument that others do not have a similar right to interfere in your business is weakened.

Humanitarian intervention has emerged as a competing norm. Its precepts are not well known or widely publicized outside academic circles. This connection is both strange and limiting to their appeal. It is strange because the ideas that are involved in humanitarian intervention advocacies have their roots in morality that, according to Bernard Gert (2011), have three generally accepted sources: "religion, tradition, and rational human nature." The religious bases include Judeo-Christian precepts such as the Ten Commandments and the seven Noahide Rules.

At the risk of some oversimplification, the core of the natural law case is found in conceptualizations of morality and, more specifically, common morality, common principles of human behavior that are acceptable and unacceptable in all societies. These are universal enough that they should be honored and enforced in all societies, and rational people in all societies recognize these principles and feel morally obligated to honor them. These principles come from various sources, one of the most common of which is religious, and are found in the western tradition in places like the Ten Commandments and, more generally, the Golden Rule.

The core of these ideas is their universality: common morality suggests that there are standards of behavior that are morally inviolable regardless of differences among human groups. The idea of humanitarian intervention flows from these assertions. The situations in which humanitarian intervention is most clearly applicable are those where natural law is being violated and thus moral transgression is occurring. The most prominent advocacy of this position goes under the rubric of the "responsibility to protect" or R2P.

The competing concept is the principle of noninterference, and it has at least two important implications in the national security realm. One is that the protection of one's own sovereignty is the prime value of the state, its most basic national interest. The other implication is most germane to current circumstances. Sovereignty implies that the state has no authority or interest in what goes on in other states, including instances where states may treat people in ways that clearly violate standards of common morality. For much of human history, this situation was not considered anomalous, and most states routinely mistreated parts of their populations. Thus, to raise objections that others abused *their* citizens was at least to some degree hypocritical and might even invite similar charges against them. Noninterference thus had some of the advantages of a *quid pro quo*, even if it did mean that states had to ignore the immoral actions of other states.

This position was widely accepted until World War II, when atrocious abuses were brought dramatically and unavoidably to the international forefront by revelations of the Holocaust. The systematic extinction of

Jews, Gypsies and other minorities by the Nazis was a moral outrage of such enormous proportions that it could not be condoned as an expression of sovereign prerogatives, and the result was that criminal proceedings were instituted at Nuremburg and Tokyo to try and punish perpetrators of acts that clearly violated common morality. The principle of non-interference was persistent, however. One American jurist who was part of the Nuremburg process, for instance, argued that the Nazis could be tried for atrocities against foreign minorities (French or Belgian Jews, for instance) but not against German Jews, since the principle of sovereignty protected the Nazi regime's right to deal with its own citizens as it pleased. The argument was intended as a defense of the principle of sovereignty and not immorality, of course, but it is an argument that seems anachronistic and would not be seriously put forward today.

The post-World War II reaction to the Holocaust fueled the first general international assertion of the human rights that underpin arguments about humanitarian intervention by asserting the human rights implied in natural law and its adjunct, just war, thought. Genocide, a term invented in 1944, became an international crime, the idea of "crimes against humanity" became a war crime, and ethnic cleansing, an artifact of the 1990s, became unacceptable. As Evans notes, "None of these rights was recognized historically." They are today, even if their full implications still remain debatable.

The 1990s Clash of Competing Imperatives

This section's heading is borrowed from a similar heading in Evans' *The Responsibility to Protect*. The immediate post-World War II period signaled the beginning of a challenge to the paramount claim of sovereignty as the guiding principle of international relations, but that assault was largely sublimated by the Cold War. The period between the later 1940s and 1991 was dominated by realist and geopolitical concerns and imperatives, which were the grist of the Soviet–American relationship.

The discussion changed in the 1990s. During the Cold War accusations of humanitarian violations of common morality were often viewed as propaganda assaults with Cold War motives. Thus, accusations of human rights abuses within the communist bloc were seen as ways to discredit communism in the global competition, as were communist accusations of human rights abuses by some of America's authoritarian allies. Calls for greater attention to human rights were often considered diverting distractions from the central imperative of the communist–anticommunist struggle.

The humanitarian critique begins with a direct rejection of the sovereign claim that political authority has absolute sway over how it treats its people. Evans states this challenge bluntly: "Sovereignty is not a license to kill." Rather, Evans counter-asserts that the rights of humans are superior to that of the sovereign state. Evans asserts this principle in the "Foreword" to Weiss (2012), "When it comes to fundamental issues of human security, the rights of individuals trump the sovereignty of the thuggish states in which they live."

The practical implication of this position is that interference cannot be precluded on the basis that such interference is prohibited by sovereignty. Sovereignty may remain the prime value when its exercise does not include violating more fundamental human rights based in common morality and natural law, but one rarely hears the argument that the United States or anyone else cannot intervene in countries because the inhuman practices of states are protected by sovereignty.

Attitudes toward the *permissibility* of intervening in the affairs of other states have thus changed, and objections based in the illegality of intervening in places like Syria or Iraq on grounds of the principle of non-interference are rarely raised in public debates on intervention. For now, the answer to whether one can legitimately attack and punish human rights abusers seems to have been answered in favor of the interveners. Whether that outcome is shallow and reversible is as yet untested. There is not universal agreement about whether countries—in this case the United States—*should* engage in such activities. That question is still a matter of debate, with its advocates basing their claim in R2P.

How Much Responsibility to Protect?

The 1990s engaged the debate over humanitarian intervention, but the concept has not clearly prevailed as the major legitimate rationale for military intrusion. For one thing, the victory has been implicit: no state has renounced any of its sovereign authority to the moralists. In fact, whenever an intervention is proposed on a humanitarian basis, state governments like that of Syria quickly denounce the proposals on the grounds that potential interveners have no right to intrude on their sovereign territories. For the most part, these objections are ignored rather than denied, presumably because the recourse that states have to sovereignty is not one that they will admit as invalid, because it is a defense of actions they might seek to use themselves sometime in the future. This is particularly true in states with a particularly strong and conservative view of sovereignty as a protection of their own state. The United States is one of the most vocal and consistent defenders of its own sovereign rights against outside intrusion, and anyone suggesting an action that required specific renunciation of American sovereignty would be pummeled within the American political debate. This helps explain, for instance, why the United States refuses to accept the jurisdiction of international agencies such as the International Criminal Court, the mandate of which covers many intrusions on human rights.

At the same time, acceptance of the underlying tenets of the natural law position does not necessarily imply any ironclad obligation to respond to abuses. Humanitarian intervention can, for instance, be justified as a kind of just war, but it is what Walzer calls an "imperfect duty—a duty that does not belong to any particular agent." If humanitarian atrocities indeed constitute a form of moral and legal transgression, who must or is authorized to punish them? The answer is not clear, and as long as it is not, then no particular abstainer can be faulted for not living up to a duty that is not specified. Not specifying who must morally become involved avoids the dilemma of engagement when one does not want to be engaged.

A related loophole is the nature of the obligation of potential agents. A major reason not to intervene in internal conflicts is that such involvements normally fail. If an intervention will fail, is anyone obligated to conduct it? Even among supporters of R2P principle, the answer is negative. Nardin (2002), for instance, argues, "It is consistent with common morality to argue that humanitarian intervention is justified, in principle, in a wide range of situations, but that prudential considerations usually override this justification." He thus adds that "One is not barred from weighing the costs and from deciding not to act if those costs are too high." The formal document endorsed by the UN General Assembly on R2P even includes this hedge among its criteria for intervention under the rubric of "reasonable prospect" of success.

It is within these constraints that advocates have put forward the responsibility to protect construct. The basic motivating concerns of advocates concerned the lack of timely response to humanitarian disasters that occurred in the 1990s and displayed the clear need for some institutional sponsorship or authority (an "agent" in moral terms). One reason that there was no timely international institutional response to the Rwandan outrage was that no international body had a specific mandate or mechanism to respond before the whole horror of the rampage unfolded. This need for a nimble, mandated mechanism was thus framed in terms of the need to stop atrocities before they occurred or in their earliest stages and was needed because, in Alex Bellamy's words in *Responsibility to Protect* (2009), "All too often the world's response to genocide and mass atrocities has been slow, timid, and disjointed."

This concern was expressed at the turn of the millennium by the work of something called the International Commission on Intervention and State Sovereignty (ICISS). One of its most prominent advocates and publicists was Evans, and the Commission issued its report and recommendations for the consideration of the United Nations General Assembly in 2001. At the heart of the ICISS report was the assertion of R2P as a basic principle and the enumeration of six criteria for humanitarian intervention. These criteria are: *just cause* (Is serious harm occurring to people in the proposed target?); *right intention* (Is the reason for intervention to prevent or relieve human suffering?); *final resort* (Is the authorization of an intervention a means chosen only after all other means have or will fail?); *legitimate authority* (Is the intervener appropriately authorized to take the action proposed?); *proportional means* (Is the force proposed adequate to but not excessive given the nature of the problem?); and *reasonable prospect* (Will the action succeed, and the consequences of the act be better than inaction?). The ICISS report was adopted by the General Assembly in 2001, but has never been acted upon by the U.N. Security Council, which has the sole authority to authorize military actions by the world body.

The ICISS report has virtually disappeared from general discussions of intervention. Some of the reasons are idiosyncratic. Champions point out that their timing could scarcely have been worse: the General Assembly acted on the ICISS report shortly before 9/11, and a thorough venting and consideration of the report and its R2P underpinnings was one of the concerns drowned in the tsunami of reaction to the terrorist attacks. The lack of international embrace also undoubtedly reflects the shallowness of support for the notion of R2P. Relieving the suffering of the afflicted is, by now, not an appeal that can be rejected out of hand, but rhetorical support does not necessarily translate into any kind of crusader's zeal for coming to the personal aid of the afflicted. The lack of agency may make it more difficult to mount timely responses, and the same absence means nobody is "on the hook" to respond in any given situation. In the end, sovereignty may not be a license to kill, but common morality is also not a suicide pact.

Summarizing the Situation

The legitimacy, and especially the mandate, for humanitarian intervention are by no means clear or universal. One can argue that its base in natural law, common morality, and just war theory has been explicitly accepted by much of the international community, but that acceptance is hardly operationally complete. A total incorporation of the concept would necessarily include a renunciation of the nonintervention principle and thus the sacrosanct status of sovereignty. Staunch defenders of sovereignty are hardly likely to issue such a renunciation because it would be politically suicidal internally to do so and the act would effectively cut a prerogative to command exclusive control over domestic affairs that the U.S. government has fiercely fought to maintain.

Interestingly, the same kinds of arguments are made, for somewhat different reasons, by many developing world countries where humanitarian intervention might occur. To many of these countries, the weakening of prohibitions on intrusion based in sovereignty is seen as little more than a device for rich and powerful states, including the former colonial powers from whose grasp they have recently escaped, to legitimize their renewed influence. As Bellamy points out, the R2P principle is particularly suspect, because some states believe "R2P is the thin edge of the wedge when it comes to the imposition of basically Western values on the rest."

The nature of the obligation arising from the humanitarian base for intervention is also circumscribed in at least two other ways. The absence of a specified agent to decide where humanitarian intervention might be appropriate relieves potential abstainers of personal moral opprobrium from failing to live up to any moral duty or obligation that do not exist. It also allows consideration of possible forms of intervention on more familiar, conceptually comfortable grounds like realist based national interest or geopolitical calculation. At the same time, empirical determinations that any intervention might fail further weaken any sense of moral duty to engage in what may prove to be Quixotic ventures.

The Yin-Yang of Military Intrusion: The "Do-Something" Syndrome and Unintended Consequences

The Chinese concept of yin-yang (sometimes portrayed as yin and yang) refers to the relationship between two apparently opposite and contrary forces. For present purposes, yin can be thought of as the moral zeal and perceived obligation to relieve suffering when it is imposed on a group of people in a foreign country. Its operational manifestation in the contemporary environment can be described as the "do-something" syndrome. The yang is the danger that intercession might have untoward, unfavorable outcomes. It is a rejoinder within the ICISS criteria ("reasonable prospect") for intervention and can be described as the possibility of unintended consequences. Doing something is the positive urge to act, whereas "unintended consequences" suggests the need for restraint, possibly to the point either of not taking action or not taking the action that seems immediately mandated by the moral aspects of the tragedy.

Applying the yin-yang principle in operation can lead to two outcomes in particular situations. One is that, since they represent competing, contrary dynamics, they lead to the triumph of one or another concept. Thus, the battle between yin-yang could lead either to intervention that might or might not be advisable or to the avoidance of involvement when that might or might not be the best response. At the same time, the yin-yang principles can be complementary, acting in unison to create a more desirable outcome than would occur if one perspective or the other was missing. Thus, an approach that lacks some sort of moral immediacy like situations producing the do-something syndrome can lead to passivity when it is not appropriate, and a response unconstrained by the possibility of an unfortunate outcome could lead to an impulsive, unwise response. Acting as complements, the two may produce the best possible response: moral alert to and concern over atrocities tempered by a cautionary, even skeptical view of what will work and what will not in a particular situation.

Both the yin and yang of intervention fall under the umbrella of common morality and natural law. The impulse to do something in the face of moral outrage certainly flows from the notion that there are conditions of life to which all humans are naturally entitled, and that there is a moral obligation for outsiders to provide relief when those basic conditions are under duress. Restraint, on the other hand, is also part of the calculation of moral obligation since, as already suggested, common morality does not require that people act in ways that can be harmful to themselves to relieve the suffering of others. I am not morally required to jump into deep water to aid someone drowning if I cannot swim, for instance. It does not mandate taking actions that may not improve and actually could harm more than help those it is intended to assist.

These yin-yang constructs also mix moral calculation with empirical concerns. When there are accusations of atrocity in contemporary situations, there will always be claims and counter-claims about whether abuse is occurring and who is committing the abuses. Both the Syrian government and its opponents have accused the other of atrocities, including the recourse to chemical weapons. Modern electronic intrusiveness may make it somewhat easier to reach empirical judgments about such claims, but that process will not be perfect in the heat and chaos of violence and the concerted efforts of perpetrators to obscure the misdeeds they have committed.

At the same time, the impact of various types of response has both empirical and moral content. When outsiders involve themselves in the internal affairs of others, the results are never certain in advance. Outsiders will project a positive impact to gain both domestic and international political support for action, but actual experience suggests that those estimates are virtually always overly optimistic. Outcomes in which considerable sacrifice is made by the outsider occur. The 58,000 American dead in Vietnam, for instance, are testimony. Outcomes unfavorable for those on behalf of whom intervention is undertaken also happen: Vietnam did become communist. The intention of doing morally good acts can result in morally as well as empirically undesirable outcomes.

Both the yin and yang are inevitably present as both moral and empirical influences in virtually any political situation. Political actions are distinguished by the fact that they allocate scarce resources to particular problems with particular outcomes in mind. What leads to political calls for action is thus a value determination that something needs to be done, generally to right some wrong. At this level, there will always be disagreement among moral imperatives, since deciding to do one thing generally implicitly means not doing something else for which the same resources might be used. At the same time, particular forms of action presume certain empirical outcomes, and these projections may prove to be true or false. Thus, both yin and yang are present in all political situations, and because of this, both need to be considered in at least some detail in any situation, and specifically where military force may be involved.

Yin: The "Do-Something" Syndrome

This phrase is a euphemism I devised in the 1990s (see Snow 1997, *Distant Thunder*, 2nd edition) to describe how the United States responded to horrendous events that occurred in the immediate post-Cold War period in the developing world. With the geopolitical criterion of communism-anticommunism crumbling as the rationale for American activism in the world, there was a need for a new standard to guide when the United States would use force. At the time, a firm set of guidelines was not in place—as is arguably true today. In the geopolitical vacuum of a world lacking the Soviet threat, the United States was suddenly faced with vivid images from the relatively new force of global television of human tragedy in far-off reaches in the world. One response was a morally driven shock and horror at great human suffering that beamed itself to Americans and others on electronic outlets like the relatively new Cable News Network (CNN). One response to seeing the horrors that were publicized was the need to "do something" in the face of human suffering, an emotion driven by a human and deeply moral sense of duty.

This emotion was, however, often a knee-jerk response that did not stand up well under close scrutiny. For one thing, the tragedies tended to occur in places outside the Cold War area that was the traditional preserve of American concern and expertise, meaning reliable knowledge about the dynamics of the situations where doing something seemed appropriate was often missing. People were clearly suffering, but who they were and exactly why they were suffering was never so clear. Moreover, clear American realist-based interests were rarely immediately obvious as forces impelling an American response. Ignoring the suffering of others was morally repugnant, but how or whether to act were not clearly obvious either. In some cases, the instinct to do something created an American response; in others, it did not.

The do-something syndrome was applied selectively. Public attention, even moral outrage, focused on those events and those places where the new probing eye of global television media roamed, but not to places where those eyes did not reach. Regimes that are abusing their citizens generally do not publicize their actions, and often they undertake considerable efforts to obscure their horrors from the world. In the early stages of global television, it was still possible to exclude electronic eyes from some places: there were, for instance, no cell phones with cameras to allow those suffering atrocities to record and transmit their fates to others around the world. If journalists could somehow be kept from the scene, then atrocities could be hidden and no one, notably the Americans, would feel the rage to do something about it.

Two events illustrate these distinctions. One occurred in the Kurdish region of Iraq at the end of the Persian Gulf War in 1991, the other occurred in the southern part of Sudan between 1983 and 2005 as an extension of a civil conflict that dated back to the 1960s. The Kurdish case received global media coverage and resulted in a decisive, if arguably ill-considered, American response that ultimately helped lead to the American invasion of Iraq in 2003; the Sudanese case was suppressed by the government in Khartoum, received virtually no worldwide coverage and thus attention, and went on until 2005, when a settlement was reached. Only later did the world discover that roughly 2.5 million Sudanese died in the slaughter.

The catalyst for the American decision to "do something" in Iraq in 1991 was the aftermath of the Gulf War. During that conflict, Iraqi leader Saddam Hussein had been attacked not only by American and allied forces that impelled his retreat from his occupation of Kuwait, but also by rebellions against his regime by Kurds and Shiites at home. Defeated in the Kuwaiti desert, he sought to settle scores with his rebellious opponents within the country. The worst, or at least most publicized, of his acts of revenge occurred against the Kurdish north. The Kurds, a minority group in Iraq with clear desires to break away and create an independent state, were particularly singled out, as they had been during the end of the Iran–Iraq War in 1988, when Hussein had used poison nerve gas to decimate several Iraqi Kurdish villages. Unconstrained by those who had defeated him in Kuwait, Saddam turned his attentions back to the Kurds in 1991; the Kurds, fearing a reprise of the gassing they had endured, panicked and fled to the barren mountainsides of southern Turkey, where CNN found them.

The conditions were appalling and unsustainable. Thousands of Kurds, terrified by the prospect of renewed gas attacks by a vengeful Saddam government, huddled in makeshift camps with little food, water, or sanitation and no means to improve their condition. The Turkish government, with its own Kurdish minority population, neither could nor would offer much assistance and insisted that the Kurds go back across the border to the not-so-tender care of the Iraqi regime. Since the United States had both led the coalition that had evicted the Iraqis from Kuwait and had failed to place restraints on the defeated regime in terms of dealing with its domestic opponents, many Americans felt morally obligated to come to the aid of the Kurds. The United States needed to do something. The question was what?

A solution had to achieve three goals. First, it had to relieve the immediate suffering of the Kurds, which could be temporarily accomplished by a massive airlift of relief supplies into the refugee area. Second, it had to deal with Turkish insistence that the refugees leave Turkey. The Turks were America's prime NATO allies in the region, so it was a demand to which the George H.W. Bush administration had to be sensitive. Third, it had to create a safe place to which the Kurds could migrate, where they would be both secure from Saddam's wrath and could reconstruct their lives.

The solution to the second and third problems was Operation Provide Comfort. Under this plan, the Americans would insist that the Kurds return to their Iraqi homes (thereby satisfying Turkish demands), and once they were there, the United States would protect them from Saddam's military wrath (thereby allaying Kurdish fears). To accomplish this latter goal, the Americans, in conjunction with the British and the French, established a "no-fly" exclusionary zone over the critical Iraqi territory to which the Kurds returned. In that area, which would be patrolled by allied military overflight, no Iraqi military personnel would be allowed.

Operation Provide Comfort thus fulfilled the need to do something to allay the immediate crisis, but it was really a band aid solution with broader long-term implications. The basic problem was that the exclusionary zone kept the Iraqis and Kurds separated as long as it was enforced, but it did nothing to bring about reconciliation between the Kurds and the government in Baghdad. In fact, the operation (which later was renamed Operation Northern Watch as a parallel to a similar protection zone for Shiites in the Iraqi South, Operation Southern Watch) became an open-ended commitment that the United States could not end without the very real prospect that doing so would result in renewed atrocities against those it had been protecting. In fact, the Operation was only ended by the American invasion and conquest of Iraq in 2003 and the consequent overthrow of the Saddam regime. In fact, ending this consequence of the do-something syndrome was one of the relatively few important side benefits of the invasion.

This situation stands in sharp contrast to the southern part of Sudan. Like Iraq, Sudan is an almost totally artificial country with multiple ethnic and religious minorities carved from receding European colonialism. The majority of the population is Muslim and lives in the northern part of the country, with Khartoum as its capital. Since Sudan received its independence in 1956, the Muslims have ruled harshly over the various non-Muslim minorities (and some recalcitrant fellow Muslims in places like Darfur province). Most, but not all, of these are concentrated in the south. These non-Muslims include both Christians and animists, and they were at war with the northern Muslims for most of the period between 1956 and 2011, when an independent Republic of South Sudan was declared with its capital in Juba. More specifically, civil war raged between north and south from 1957 to 1972, at which time a truce was put in place that was eventually dishonored, and between 1983 and 2005, when an armistice created the conditions that led to South Sudanese independence.

In human, moral terms, the suffering of the Kurds pales in comparison with that of southern Sudanese. As noted, estimates are that upwards of 2.5 million, mostly southerners, perished in the 1983–2005 civil war; by contrast, about an eighth of that number (roughly 300,000) have perished in the ongoing but much better publicized rebellion in Darfur province in western Sudan. Yet, few Americans (or other westerners) were even aware of this Sudanese tragedy beyond some vague recognition from a 2003 motion picture, "Lost Boys of Sudan," which was about South Sudanese children (mostly Christians) torn from their families and displaced by the ravages of the disaster.

What is the difference? Part of the answer is that the Sudanese government was able to do a much more thorough job of hiding its atrocities from public view than were the Iraqis. Sudan is in a fairly obscure part of the world in geopolitical terms, meaning there was less general attention paid to it than the oil-rich Middle East, at least until significant oil reserves were discovered and exploited in the latter 1990s, mostly in southern Sudan. During the civil conflict, snippets of information about the atrocities occasionally slipped out of the country—periodic reports of the crucifixion of southern rebels by government troops, for instance—but generally, the leadership in Khartoum was able to keep the lid on. Its basic method was a thinly veiled warning to journalists that they could not be protected in the war zone. Most were imperiled, of course, by the government itself. Thus, with regard to Sudan, the do-something syndrome was never activated, and outsiders never entered the fray. When South Sudanese independence formally occurred in Juba on July 9, 2011, the Americans were represented by then-Ambassador to the U.N. (and later national security advisor) Susan Rice, a lower level official than is normally sent for such a mission.

This selectivity of the do-something impulse is evident in other examples as well. In 1992 in Somalia, the world was alerted to impending starvation and anarchy and responded with an American-led U.N.-sponsored intervention that was ultimately withdrawn not having achieved any of its goals, and Somalia remains in a state of virtual anarchy to this day, a refuge for pirates and terrorists of various affiliations. At the same time, the world did not become aware of the rampage in Rwanda until after it had done most of its savage damage (an estimated 800,000 Rwandans were slaughtered in a matter of weeks) and did not respond before the rampage had run its course.

These pairs of instances illustrate an important point. In those places where the dynamics of the do-something syndrome contributes to action, there are likely to be unforeseen consequences of those actions: the open-ended commitment of American air forces in Operation Provide Comfort dragged on for much longer than those who devised it imagined, and Operation Restore Hope in Somalia utterly failed to live up to its descriptive title. At the same time, the failure to act in situations of moral and physical outrage—doing nothing—allowed human tragedies of enormous proportions in Sudan and Rwanda, outcomes that those who chose to avert their eyes did not intend either. Yin cuts both ways; so does yang.

Yang: Unintended Consequences

It is often said that no pre-war military planning survives the first encounter with the enemy. While an exaggeration in grand terms, this assertion points to a verity of military engagement, including those that may or may not be the result of the do-something syndrome. That truth is that military affairs always have some unanticipated effects under even the best of circumstances, and those effects can result in unintended consequences that may be quite contrary to the initial reasons for which action is contemplated and carried out. Put another way, there is always a degree of uncertainty about what happens when the call to arms is heeded. The ICISS responsibility to protect manifesto makes provision for this factor in its criterion of reasonable prospect by requiring some assessment of the likely outcomes of either action or inaction. The problem is that estimating those prospects is always an uncertain business, especially in the volatile, unpredictable politics of conflict in developing world internal conflicts (DWICs) that are the primary candidates for intercession in the contemporary international system.

Unforeseen outcomes and uncertainty are, of course, intimately related. Some uncertainty arises from the basic disorderliness and unpredictability of warfare. The style of war that has become prevalent in contemporary DWICs, especially when there is intervention by overwhelmingly powerful conventional warriors like the United States, is so-called asymmetrical warfare, a methodology intended to obviate the overwhelming superiority of an outside intervener. This approach to war has the effect of making military outcomes far less predictable than more traditional analyses project. In particular, the adoption of the methodology of asymmetrical warfare results in protraction of conflict well beyond the pre-intervention estimates and expectations of outside interveners. One effect is to raise the costs and sacrifices that the intervener will incur, which affects the tolerance the intervener has for the effort and raises moral questions about the extent of self-sacrifice an intervener is willing to incur.

This uncertainty is also political. One of the thorny problems of developing world interventions is that they are generally proposed in places where the potential intervener has a limited knowledge and understanding of the political actors and dynamics of the situation. Atrocity and inhumane suffering demonstrate there are "bad" guys in the equation, but are there "good" guys who can provide a better alternative to the bad guys? If one does not know, the results may not be what were intended. In Syria, for instance, a source of American reluctance to take partisan sides arose from the perception that the "rebels" were probably not much of an improvement over the Assad government, and that removing the source of inhumanity might not solve the problem but have equally, if uncertain, unfortunate consequences. The perversity in these situations is the possibility that action or failure to act can lead to the emergence of even worse alternatives. In Syria, for instance, it was suggested that had the United States supported "moderate" rebel factions (e.g. the Free Syrian Army) at the beginning, the extremely brutal ISIS(L) might not have emerged or become as strong as it did. This argument involves a counterfactual assertion, of course, that is impossible to prove or disprove.

There are, broadly speaking, two major kinds of possible unintended consequence when intrusion is undertaken, and each poses a different moral, as well as empirical, dilemma. One possibility is that outside intrusion will not improve the situation it was intended to correct. The other is that the results of intrusion will cause greater-than-expected harm to the outsider, testing the moral limits of obligation. In the worst case, both of these outcomes may occur.

The first possible unintended consequence is the failure to achieve the intended result. This possibility has to be taken thoroughly into account, since interventions arguably rarely work in the sense of achieving what they set out to accomplish, as I have argued in *The Case against Military Intervention* (Snow, 2016). In moral terms, this may mean that whatever moral code has been broken may in fact not be rectified, raising the question of the worth of the endeavor in moral terms. In the worst of possible outcomes, the moral situation may actually be worsened, creating a new moral imperative. How does one estimate the morality of actions when these outcomes occur?

The unintended consequence of not improving the situation can occur in one of two ways. First, an intrusion can succeed in overthrowing the source of one set of moral atrocities, but the alternative may provide no improvement. The clearly most probable situations, and the ones most likely in the kinds of societies where DWICs occur, involve removing one national subgroup which was inflicting pain and duress on others and replacing it with an equally malevolent alternative which will do the same thing to the former oppressors. The Iraqi Sunnis under Saddam Hussein, for instance, systematically suppressed Iraqi Shiites, and when the Americans overthrew Saddam and he was replaced by the Shiite majority, they arguably simply returned the favor, oppressing the Sunni majority and leading to the crisis of 2014 in that country. Exchanging one form of moral outrage for another hardly improves the physical or moral situation. Is there any victory in replacing one moral transgression with another?

Second, intercession may actually make the situation worse than it was before. From an American viewpoint, for instance, the moral "scorecard" from its initial foray into Afghanistan in the 1980s is arguably a loss. It did help remove an evil in the form of a brutal Soviet occupation, but post-Soviet Afghanistan quickly plunged into political chaos and an internal civil war in which the Taliban, an offshoot of the Soviet resistance, was and remains a major irritant. Intervention did not solve the problem of Afghan internal instability and any atrocities associated with it. At the same time, Al Qaeda was a direct outgrowth of the foreign *jihadis* who fought the Soviets. It is arguable that some group like Al Qaeda would have been formed without that impetus, but the whole moral evil associated with Al Qaeda is a direct consequence of a morally defensible relief of Afghan suffering at the hands of the Soviet Union.

The fear that intervention to relieve one moral outrage might result in an even greater moral dilemma has constrained the United States in Syria. Continuing fighting there has spawned outside intervention on both sides that has threatened to transform the conflict into a regional, inter-communal imbroglio between adherents of the two major subdivisions of Islam. The Alawites who dominate the Assad regime are nominally Shiite, and they have received assistance from both Shiite Iran and Hezbollah, the leading Shiite terrorist organization. Support for the rebels has come in monetary terms from most of the Sunni Persian Gulf states, and ISIS(L) may have been a major beneficiary of such assistance, in addition to its criminal sources of funds (see Chapter 6). The danger that inhibited the Obama administration was whether American aid might once again find its way into the hands of American enemies.

These prospects create three moral dilemmas. Should the Sunni opponents of the Assad regime prevail, they might well engage in retribution against the Alawites, and the result could be slaughter and suppression that is even worse than what the government is currently visiting on its Sunni opponents. At the same time, if more assistance falls into the hands of ISIS(L), it might be turned against the United States, a morally reprehensible outcome. Third, the fall of the Assad regime could mean its replacement by a regime that would be even more repressive and morally repugnant than what it replaces—one led by ISIS(L) fanatics, for instance. While it was not clear ISIS(L) had the capability to form such a government, it has been a chilling thought.

Nobody can predict with certainty that none of these morally unfortunate outcomes might result from an American (or other) intervention. It is a likely certainty that continued violation of natural law will occur in the absence of such intervention, and the violations may be egregiously immoral enough to demand retribution regardless of the consequences. In any case, a positive outcome is by no means assured. An outside effort that fails is, in the end, at best quixotic, and if it results in an even worse outcome (although the cast of victims may change) is masochistic for those who rise to the moral imperative of trying to relieve suffering. Given these possibilities, what action or inaction is morally most defensible? It is not an easy question to answer.

The other possible unintended consequence is that intrusion to right a wrong will result in a greater-than-expected, intolerable level of suffering for the intruder. If it is generally accepted that there are morally derived limits to the amount of self-harm that can be expected of those who seek to relieve human suffering, then this is a reasonable question to consider. Past experience is cautionary. Greater sacrifice by Americans than advertised in advance has been a regular feature of American interventions in DWICs, and especially on grand-scale interventions like Vietnam, Afghanistan, and Iraq. If the American people are asked to sacrifice to right a human tragedy befalling others, is it not reasonable to expect there to be a realistic estimate of the scope of that sacrifice in advance? But how can one prove in advance what that sacrifice may be?

The uncertainty of war admittedly makes pre-war estimation of negative consequences difficult with any degree of accuracy. In recent and likely future instances of American intervention in DWICs, there have been and will continue to be two reasons for estimates that are lower than actual outcomes. One is that resistance to intrusion is almost always greater than originally estimated—the opponent proves more resilient and resourceful than expected. The simple presence of foreign (e.g. American) troops in the country may actually contribute to this greater-than-expected resistance— no one likes visibly armed foreign troops on their territory. Another source of underestimation is the likelihood that the opponent will adopt a protracted form of resistance when faced with an asymmetrical intruder whom they can only defeat by outlasting it.

The net result of looking at these unintended consequences is to dampen moral enthusiasm for widespread intrusion in the violent affairs of others. Even if one accepts the notion of a responsibility to protect under some circumstances (and not everyone does), the same moral bases on which activism can be justified also contain the basis for caution. The moral dimension is thus not entirely a force demanding greater involvement in the affairs of others. It is indeed not an inviolable suicide pact.

Be Careful What You Ask For: You Might Not Get It!

Outsiders who contemplate and then intervene in humanitarian disasters generally do it for high-minded, morally righteous reasons; they tend to lend an aura of righteousness to the action. That factor colors expectations about how the actions will be viewed both by those who are assisted by the intervention and by the world at large. This nobility of intent includes some sense of moral imperative based in a sense of common humanity or, in contemporary terms, a "responsibility to protect," and those who adopt it inevitably view the sacrifice they make in its name as a noble act on their part. In turn, such an act should be recognized and appropriately rewarded, at a minimum in the gratitude of those who are helped by the action.

Acting morally should, in other words, be appreciated, but this is not always the case, adding to the frustration that surrounds intervention more broadly and provides a cautionary factor when intervention is considered. This dynamic is most poignant and ironic in the case of those on whose behalf intervention occurs.

An initial act of intervention may well be appreciated. The intervener may be able to suppress or squash the direct and immediate source of suffering, and if that is all that is needed and is followed quickly by the removal of the intervener from the scene, then appreciation may follow the benign act. Natural disaster relief often produces this dynamic and outcome. When the problem is a more complex act of internal violence pitting societal groups against one another, as is typically the case in DWICs, those dynamics are more complex and convoluted, and the intervener, no matter how pure the initial motivations, may find itself the object of scorn and hostility, because it does not leave. The appreciation that is expected turns to scorn, even hatred and violent opposition.

The problem arises from divergence in the purposes and expectations of the intervener and those on whose behalf intervention occurs. At first, the purposes are the same: the intervener wants to end suffering, which the recipient also wants. When that occurs (assuming it does), their common motives often end there and come into conflict. If the end of suffering is to last, normally underlying political problems must be addressed and new solutions must be fashioned before lasting peace and stability can take hold (assuming that stability is possible under any circumstances). The intervener has quite likely not considered this problem thoroughly, probably because it does not understand the conditions adequately to have answers that will be acceptable to all parties, including the party on whose behalf it has acted. The intervener will probably seek peace through reconciliation and acceptance of some shared power; the party that has endured the suffering may well prefer retribution and revenge against those who have caused their suffering. Moreover, the parties that caused the suffering will likely recognize that they may be the object of recrimination if an intervener-brokered peace is negotiated and will be reluctant to enter into such an agreement.

If purposes come into conflict—and they almost always do—two bad outcomes can occur that may make the intervener question the wisdom of its benevolent act. One is that involvement becomes protracted. The intervener feels it cannot leave until the situation is resolved, and the parties will not come to a resolution of which the intervener approves. The side against whom intrusion occurred (the original transgressor) opposes the continued presence of the intervener because the intervener is its opponent. That continued presence itself becomes an irritant within the country, and the beleaguered side can use that unwanted presence as a rallying cry for its side. For the side on whose behalf intervention occurred, the intervener's continuing presence may interrupt their final solution, which is the oppression of those who were repressing them. The result is a standoff: everyone wants the intervener to leave, but the internal parties and the intervener cannot agree on conditions that will allow that withdrawal.

This kind of evolution triggers the second negative effect, which is frustration and opposition to the enterprise in the intervener country. As the situation drags on, those on whose behalf it occurred cease to appear grateful and come to resent the continuing presence of the intervener. The evolution of the attitudes of Hamid Karzai of Afghanistan to the long American occupation is a good example. Within the intervener population, those who were helped come to be viewed as ingrates and the original act of benevolence and self-sacrifice seems an increasingly bad bargain. This dynamic is captured in a quote attributed to a returning American soldier coming back from Vietnam in the late 1960s (it may be an "urban legend"): "Here we were a great people trying to help a lesser people, and they didn't even appreciate it." Support for the intervention wanes, and those who supported it in the first place are blamed for their decisions. Noble intentions are punished, not rewarded.

The tortured path of American consideration of intervening in Syria can be understood in this light. There is no question that an early intervention in the civil war could have been justified in terms of common morality—the moral "high ground" was easy to establish. A military intervention would almost certainly, depending on its nature (ground versus air intrusions, for instance) have relieved the suffering of those being attacked by the government, but after that occurred, what was next? The Syrian rebels, incensed by their hatred for government acts, would almost certainly want recrimination against the Alawites and their supporters, actions the interveners would have opposed on the same moral grounds as those justifying their intervention. An impasse between the interveners and the Syrians would almost certainly have ensued, the intervention would have become protracted, and that in and of itself would have created resentment to the continued opposition. The result would almost certainly create frustration and resentment in the United States (and in other countries which intervened) and a political backlash in which there would be no winners. Recognizing these probabilities, is it any wonder that the Obama administration did not respond forcefully in the face of an apparently overwhelming moral crisis until the situation was apparently transformed in threat terms by the emergence of ISIS(L) as a major factor?

The bottom line is that moral imperatives can create a kind of Siren's call to action, but that the morality is usually more complicated than it appears and that morally and physically acceptable outcomes may not be as clear-cut, as easy to achieve, or as universal as they appear. Reality is likely to be much more convoluted, and the result may be something entirely different than what one has anticipated in advance. The saying "no good deed goes unpunished" is not a bad consideration for those weighing the moral dimension.

Bibliography

Bar-Ron, Michael Shelomo. *Guide to the Noahide.* 2nd edn. Springdale, AZ: Lightcatcher Books, 2010.

Bellamy, Alex J. *Responsibility to Protect.* Malden, MA: Polity Press, 2009.

Dagne, Ted. *The Republic of South Sudan: Opportunities and Challenges for Africa's Newest Country.* Washington, DC: Congressional Research Service, 2011.

Donagan, Alan. *The Theory of Morality.* Chicago, IL: University of Chicago Press, 1977.

Evans, Gareth. *The Responsibility to Protect: End Mass Atrocity Crimes Once and for All.* Washington, DC: Brookings Institution Press, 2008.

Feaver, Peter. "The Just War Tradition and the Paradox of Policy Failure in Syria." *Foreign Policy* (online), August 22, 2013.

Garrett, Stephen A. *Doing Good and Doing Well: An Examination of Humanitarian Intervention*. Westport, CT: Praeger, 1999.

Gert, Bernard. "The Definition of Morality." *Stanford Encyclopedia of Philosophy*. Palo Alto, CA: Stanford University Press, 2011.

Homans, Charles. "Just What Is a Just War? Anthropology of an Idea: Responsibility to Protect." *Foreign Policy*, November 2011, 34–35.

Nardin, Terry. "The Moral Basis of Humanitarian Intervention." *Ethics and International Affairs* 16, 1 (March 2002), 57–70.

Natsios, Andrew S. *Sudan, South Sudan, and Darfur: What Everyone Needs to Know*. New York: Oxford University Press, 2012.

Rashid, Ahmed Khaled. "Is Humanitarian Intervention Ever Morally Justified?" *e-International Relations*, March 13, 2002.

Snow, Donald M. *Distant Thunder: Patterns of Conflict in the Developing World*. 2nd edn. Armonk, NY: M. E. Sharpe, 1997.

Snow, Donald M. *When America Fights: The Uses of U.S. Armed Force*. Washington, DC: CQ Press, 2000.

Snow, Donald M. *What After Iraq?* New York: Longman, 2009.

Snow, Donald M. *Concepts in International Relations*. 6th edn. New York: Pearson, 2014.

Snow, Donald M. *National Security for a New Era*. 5th edn. New York: Pearson, 2014.

Snow, Donald M. *The Case against Military Intervention: Why We Do It and Why It Fails*. New York: M. E. Sharpe/Routledge, 2016.

Tabler, Andrew J. "Syria's Collapse: And How Washington Can Stop It." *Foreign Affairs* 92, 4 (July/August 2013), 90–100.

Vincent, R. J. *Nonintervention and International Order*. Princeton, NJ: Princeton University Press, 1974.

Walzer, Michael. *Just and Unjust Wars: A Moral Argument with Historical Illustrations*. New York: Basic Books, 2006 (originally released in 1976).

Weiss, Thomas G. *Humanitarian Intervention*. Cambridge: Polity Press, 2012.

4   The Cold War Paradigm

The contemporary national security environment is uncomfortable to many observers. One of the reasons is that the national security contours of the contemporary world lack clarity. Since so much of national security is premised on threats and responses to them, a prime cause of unease arises from the absence of a clear, identifiable, and relatively constant source of threat and thus a "reliable" content to the threat. Since 9/11, terrorism has provided a certain degree of threat "reliability," but the nature of the terrorist threat is so amorphous and changing that it is difficult to form a coherent focus for threat identification and preparation.

The other source of unease is related: the absence of an overarching framework within which to view the threat universe. As seemingly unrelated threatening events of highly different contents assault our senses and awareness, it is not clear how they should be dealt with. Each problem seems unique, and each seems to be approached and handled in an ad hoc, virtually seat-of-the-pants way. It is not a very satisfying environment in which to make policy.

These two characteristics are, of course, flip sides of the same coin. The fact that events seem both so idiosyncratic and unrelated is compounded by the absence of a framework in which to assess them. At the same time, these events are both very different from one another and less than compellingly threatening. As a result, devising a framework that would accommodate them all—one size that fits all—is both difficult and the need to grapple with it seems less necessary. Almost everyone agrees having a framework would be good; they disagree both about the possibility and feasibility of constructing one.

The situation can be understood in the context of the organizing concepts of interests, threats, and risks. National security analysis is largely about looking for threats to the most important interests the country has and recommending and taking actions to remove or reduce the risks that such threats produce. Generally speaking, there is agreement about what the most important interests are. When those vital interests are in jeopardy, there is usually agreement both on this condition and the need to take risk-reducing actions to deal with it. In those circumstances of what can be called *interest-threat match*, it is normally possible to achieve consensus about a general paradigm for dealing with the threat. The Cold War represents this situation.

The problem occurs when there is an *interest-threat mismatch*. In such a situation, the most vital interests either may not be threatened or there is disagreement about the extent of such imperilment. In this situation, existing threats are generally to less than vital (LTV) interests, and there is disagreement about what, if anything, to do to remove them (risk reduction). When vital interests and threats do not align (are mismatched), it is difficult to agree on what to do in national security terms, including whether or what kind of framework to adopt to organize national security efforts. The interest-threat mismatch describes the contemporary international system. It is historically not unusual, but seems that way to many Americans given the twentieth century experience.

The United States did not have a coherent national security framework—or paradigm—for much of its history, but it did have such a paradigm for the forty years that preceded the end of the Cold War in 1991. Many of those who remain in national security policy positions within the U.S. government gained much of their experience and knowledge during that period, and their experience at least implicitly affects how they view dealing with the quite different contemporary environment.

In the current atmosphere of national dissention about virtually everything in the political system, there is a tendency to view historic periods when levels of disagreement were lower or effectively non-existent much more nostalgically, even romantically, than one might otherwise. Sometimes these recollections are idealized, remembering things in ways that do not hold up under close scrutiny, and this memory selectivity includes ignoring or downplaying less favorable aspects of the atmosphere in which it occurred. It is because of the stark contrast between the present national security environment and the years immediately preceding it that examining the period of interest-threat match is of value in this volume. The Cold War period may have been an historic anomaly, but it is the most recent historic experience, and it was a conceptually orderly period that creates a sense of nostalgia among many of the national security analysts who are products of it.

The Cold War Period and Paradigm

The Cold War years represented a consensual threat and national security response. Once the Korean War removed any real doubt about the ability of the United States and the Soviet Union to continue the wartime collaboration on which hopes for a peaceful postwar environment was premised in the United Nations Charter, the contours of what would become the Cold War had emerged clearly by the time Dwight D. Eisenhower became president in 1953. The national security consensus that was congealing was based more on fear of the military menace the Soviets and their communist allies presented than on any positive image of the post-war order, but the threat seemed so compelling and was so universally perceived that it overcame, or at least muted, other political differences to a degree that seems incredible in today's toxic environment. There were still liberals and conservatives and foreign policy activists and isolationists within the system, but in the public sphere, politics still truly ended "at the water's edge," a phrase that symbolized a bipartisan unity on foreign issues. The threat in the international environment clearly trumped domestic dissention and helped contribute to a non-confrontational, muted tone to domestic politics. That positive outcome was the result of response to an overwhelmingly negative, threat environment, and under-standing the Cold War influence begins with a brief overview of the Cold War experience itself.

The Cold War Environment

The period known as the Cold War spanned a forty-year period after the end of World War II. Since the term Cold "War" is metaphoric, it has no definitive beginning or end date, but it basically spanned the period from the invasion of South Korea by North Korea in 1950 to the final dissolution of the Soviet Union with the last tick of the clock in 1991. This is not the proper space for any detailed examination of the Cold War, as copious histories of the period exist (a personal favorite is John Lewis Gaddis' (2005) *Strategies of Containment*). For present purposes, it is enough to look at it briefly through three lenses: its major characteristics, its evolution, and the circumstances and reasons that it ended. All these are critical to under-standing the evolution of the paradigm that developed to manage it, since these remain the implicit organizational basis for ongoing decisions.

The heart of the Cold War was a confrontation between the West, led by the United States, and the communist states, led by the Union of Soviet Socialist Republics (the Soviet Union). It was an encompassing competi-tion that was the dominant dynamic of international relations during its duration. International events, their meaning, and how to deal with them were considered first in terms of the effect that different courses of action would have on the Cold War balance. That competition, in turn, was considered so important and the outcome of the competition (which side "won") so vital that all other concerns paled by comparison. No one quite knew how it would end or whether it would be perpetual, but no one was terribly optimistic about the outcome.

At the risk of some oversimplification, three characteristics defined the Cold War international system. The first was that it was an *all-encompassing political-military contest for international dominion.* The purpose of the "game" was to turn the world map decisively "blue" (consisting of non-com-munist, preferably democratic countries) or "red" (consisting of communist states). The post-war trend had been for an increasing number of red states, and the problem for the West was how to contain and reverse that trend. The competition could only be considered won when the total map was either blue or red, a potentially apocalyptical event that no one truly wanted to confront. Keeping the Cold War cold was a major priority for all involved.

The instruments for doing so were political and military. Although much was made in the West of the inherent political appeals of communism during the early stages of the competition, the reality of communist rule never matched the attractiveness of the rhetoric of those who made it, and gradually the political element faded. Most of this competition occurred in the developing world, where the niceties of Marxist versus democratic appeal were less cogent.

The real heart of the Cold War, and the basis of most of its legacy for present purposes, was military. Both sides maintained huge, expensive, and lethal military machines under peacetime conditions, a burden on both that eventually helped doom the losing communists. That competition, the centerpiece of which was the growing nuclear arsenals of both sides, was traditional, as both contestants developed and maintained military forces that were thoroughly traditional in the European sense, preparing for the possibility of a highly symmetrical but far more deadly replay of World War II. The military structures and doctrine and practices devised for that period reflected the continuation of a European tradition that had been growing and becoming more institutionalized in the 300 years since the Thirty Years War. That style arguably became obsolete at the end of the war and does not, as already pointed out, work well in dealing with asymmetrical DWICS in the contemporary environment.

The second characteristic of the Cold War was its *deadliness*. The source of that deadliness was the existence and growing size of nuclear arsenals possessed by both sides. As technology made these arsenals more and more capable, largely between the 1950s and 1970s, it became clear that a war between the two sides would be an apocryphal catastrophe that would leave both sides, and possibly the rest of the world an uninhabitable irradiated ruin. The fervent, protracted, and total nature of the political confrontation meant a war would also be total, and the mark of totality in this circumstance was massive nuclear employment, guaranteeing the apocalypse.

This evolution had an ironic byproduct. At the beginning of the Cold War period, the relationship was considered highly *dangerous* (violent conflict between the two sides was considered highly likely, even inevitable). Even without nuclear weapons, such a conflict would have been highly *deadly* in terms of its consequences. Nuclear weapons, however, reduced the calculation of outcomes of this deadly conflict to an implicit agreement by both that everyone would lose such a war, and that both sides would be utterly destroyed in the process. This growing recognition in turn made the outbreak of such a war the only sure way to avoid its deadly consequences. This recognition became institutionalized with the conscious purpose of making the relationship less dangerous as it became more deadly. Eventually, the military competition was reduced to a virtually ritual status that helped lead to the end of the Cold War itself.

This led to the third characteristic, the emergence of a *necessary peace* between the adversaries. The reduction of the military competition to ritual status did not arise from any sense of growing empathy or friendship between them, but rather from the growing realization that war between them was "unacceptable," in language the Soviets used. Peace was necessary, even if the worldviews and issues that divided them remained. Both sides had to learn to get along to survive, and this mutual need circumvented the need for a political accord to end the Cold War. It is not clear how the Cold War could have ended without this dynamic.

The nature and dynamics of the Cold War evolved across time. At the beginning, the heart of the competition centered in wartime central Europe, where the wounds of World War II were rawest. The United States and the Soviet Union came out of the war as the only states with significant residual power, and they quickly gathered like-minded states (or in the Soviet case, states they controlled) around them. Power in the international system was *bipolar* (two dominant states), and the early system was described as one of tight bipolarity, meaning both powers could order matters as they liked.

This situation changed, however. Western Europe recovered economically from the war, became less dependent, and thus more independent of the United States, and heavy-handed Soviet actions like the 1956 suppression of the Hungarian Revolution gave the communists such a black eye that members of the "satellite empire" also were able to exercise some autonomy from the Soviets as well. By the mid-1960s, the system had effectively become one of loose bipolarity. This distinction may have seemed largely semantic at the time, but the loosening of Soviet control would eventually become evident when the Soviet Union was unable to stifle the emergence of dissident movements in Eastern Europe in the 1980s that contributed to the breakdown of the Cold War itself.

The most important change, however, was happening outside the original orbit of the Cold War, in the developing world of African, Asian, and some Latin American states. The force fueling this change was decolonization, as the European empires dissolved in the face of demands for independence. The salient change these new states introduced was that the Cold War concerns did not matter to them—the previously universal competition was irrelevant in increasing parts of the world. The Cold War opponents tried to extend the competition to the emerging countries, but since their priorities centered around political and economic development, these new countries were only interested in the Cold War to the extent they could play one side off against the other for outside assistance. Many of these emerging countries had deep problems that were not addressed in the process. These problems have emerged as the primary sources of violence and instability in the contemporary world.

How the Cold War ended is the final consideration. It is a question that was rarely raised during the Cold War itself because of pessimism about the answer. There were, after all, three ways the competition could end. The first two were that one side or the other would triumph, the possibility that debated "better red than dead" (losing but physically surviving) versus "better dead than red" (reflecting a belief that it was better to perish than to live under a communist dictatorship). As the competition became more deadly, both tended to be disregarded because of the belief that the only way either side could possibly prevail was after a "hot" war that both sides would lose. The third possibility was that the competition would simply continue indefinitely. A "protracted conflict" (to borrow Milovan Djilas classic designation from 1957's *The New Class*) may not have been a happy prospect, but it was better than a fiery nuclear inferno.

What was never seriously considered except by a few like George F. Kennan was that one side would simply quit, which is what happened. The dean of Sovietologists in the United States, Kennan had predicted, first in his famous 1947 "X" article ("The Sources of Soviet Conduct") in *Foreign Affairs* and in books like *American Diplomacy, 1900–1950* (1951), that the Soviet system was fatally flawed, and that if it was contained, it would eventually collapse on its own. His argument was not widely embraced during the Cold War, because Soviet-led communism seemed a vibrant, growing force whose totalitarian control of the instruments of coercion made it appear impervious to change.

As it turned out, the Soviet façade was a true Potemkin village, an elaborate false front that masked an increasingly failing system, most notably in the economic sector. By the time Mikhail Gorbachev effectively threw in the competitive towel, the Soviet Union was perilously behind the West in both productivity and, ultimately more critically, technology. The technological gap was growing exponentially given the nature of the innovative process, and Gorbachev and his colleagues came to realize that the only chance the country had to regain competitiveness was to embrace the West and to seek its assistance. The only way that the Soviets stood any chance of gaining such badly needed help was to cease being the enemy.

The dynamics of the Cold War had also turned against the Soviets. The military competition with the United States was especially ruinous. Starting from a smaller economic base, the Soviets had to devote a much higher proportion of national wealth (upwards of one-third of gross domestic product or GDP by some estimates) to military spending, and one result was to make resources for other purposes—including development and consumer satisfaction—more scarce. Given the military deadlock powered by nuclear weapons, there was little military advantage to be gained from continuing the competition. Ending it made military sense.

International concerns conspired to influence the Soviet decision. The Soviets had engaged in a costly, futile war in Afghanistan between late 1979 and early 1989, and its results had been devastating: the Soviets were forced to withdraw without achieving any of their military goals, and the cost of the effort was highly destructive to the military. At the same time, the Soviets were saddled with Cold War commitments to shore up some Cold War clients who were expensive losers in places like Cuba and Angola, among others. Removing the burden of Cold War competition in the developing world would simply help remove another albatross from around the Soviet neck.

Gorbachev came to realize all these negative factors, and he began in 1989 to allow the Cold War to unravel. He had presaged his strategy for doing so in his 1987 book, *Perestroika*, but its policy statements indicating a very changed Soviet Union were not widely believed in a suspicious West. He began implementing the new strategy in 1989, when he refused to suppress dissident movements in Eastern Europe that eventually over-threw the communist regimes of the Soviet-led Warsaw Pact (the communist counterpart of NATO). From there, the entire edifice of the communist side of the Cold War began to crumble. The Soviet Union itself ceased to exist at the end of 1991, and with it, the Cold War was over. In its wake, only four communist regimes remained in power (China, Vietnam, North Korea, and Cuba), and two of those (China and Vietnam) openly rejected the socialist economic model that was a pillar of communist rule. The Cold War thus ended as the other side simply quit.

The Cold War Paradigm

The end of the Cold War was not anticipated widely in the world. It was decidedly good news in the sense that ending the confrontation greatly decreased the dangerousness of East–West relations, although it remained very deadly because both sides kept their nuclear arsenals. What was different was that there were now no plausible arguments about why one side or the other would launch a military attack: the political dimension, draped in ideological robes, had simply evaporated.

The end of the Cold War was certainly a good thing in terms of lowering the deadliness and much of the danger that national security policy had sought to mitigate. Part of the result was thus a distinct triumph for American policy and the strategic paradigm that had underlain and provided direction for policy and its responses to individual issues that arose.

The victory was not, however, without irony. The success of the Cold War mindset had created a deep, if implicit, attachment to it among national security policymakers, and they were reluctant either to examine its premises and the consequences of a changed environment on the national security calculus. In addition, a large and elaborate set of institutions devoted to implementing and influencing Cold War national security policy evolved, and people within these institutions had a vested interest in their continuation and prosperity. All of these factors have produced an inertial drag on orderly and systematic examination of the premises and dictates that should be part of a post-Cold War national security paradigm. It is useful to look both at the premises of the Cold War paradigm as preface to its lingering consequences and legacies, their impact on the current environment, and what should be done to adapt the paradigm to the contemporary situation.

An examination of the Cold War paradigm must begin with the Cold War environment, both because that was its spawning ground and the predicament it was supposed to manage. As already noted, the Cold War was an extremely intense, dangerous, and all-encompassing competition between the systems of communism and anti-communism. It was certainly perceived as a life-or-death, zero sum confrontation, the political bases of which were so irreconcilable that the only apparent way for one side or the other to prevail was through a violent military clash that would be destructive to an unprecedented degree and which, as nuclear arsenals grew to cataclysmic proportions, would almost certainly be civilization-threatening. In the early years before arsenals reached these proportions, there was much brave talk, especially within a professional American military that still remembered World War II, about actually fighting this war, regardless of the consequences. As consensus grew that nuclear weapons had transformed such a conflict into a likely Armageddon, agreement that avoiding such a war (deterrence) was the primary, if not sole, purpose of military force increased as well.

The crucial event in this conceptual transformation was the Cuban Missile Crisis. As numerous accounts have shown, the 13 days of the crisis were a remarkably tense period in which the world teetered arguably closer to nuclear war than it ever had before or has since. Beyond the substantive outcome of the crisis itself (the removal of Cuban missile installations in Cuba in exchange for the removal of some obsolete American installations in Turkey), the retrospect was extremely sobering for all concerned. Both sides looked seriously at the probable outcomes of a nuclear war, realized such results were unacceptable, and began efforts in areas like arms control aimed at lessening the prospect in the future.

It was not widely recognized at the time, but the missile crisis was the seminal event of the Cold War. Prior to the confrontation, crises between the two sides with escalatory possibilities to direct confrontation were not uncommon. After the Cuban crises, these confrontations either ceased to occur altogether or were diffused quickly. The Cuban crisis did not reduce the deadliness of the Cold War: in fact, advances in nuclear weapons and delivery technologies already underway actually increased arsenal sizes and thereby made the potential deadlier. The dangerousness of the relationship did, however, decline gradually until the end occurred.

The consensus that nurtured and sustained the Cold War paradigm was forged in the early postwar years before the Cuban crisis. The confrontation between the Soviets and the American-led West began in Western Europe and leapfrogged to northeast Asia (Korea), areas that were of indisputably vital interest to the United States. The threat was grave and primarily military in nature, and the vitality of the interests threatened meant there was no question that heroic measures including national self-sacrifice were mandated to reduce the resulting risks.

This consensus was the seedbed of a remarkable agreement on national security that composed the Cold War paradigm. Its heart was realist, the idea that military force should be marshalled in support of the most vital national interests. In a condition of fundamental interest-threat match, the realist mandate clearly held. Further, it was agreed that the threat was quintessentially military in nature, meaning the heart of risk reduction was the development and support for a military establishment adequate to dissuade the enemy from attacking vital American interests, and if deterrence failed, of engaging and defeating that opponent. This idea that military force could be the primary instrument in helping shape the international environment matured in this atmosphere.

Implementing the response was made easier by the military nature of the opposing force. The Soviet and American military machines that emerged from World War II were basically mirror images of one another in terms of composition, organization, and doctrine regarding preparation for and conduct of war. The military task for American risk reduction was thus a continuation of the symmetrical effort against European fascism, with the major difference being the ideology confronted. The task was daunting given the size and capability of the Soviet forces, but it was also conceptually comfortable in a military sense. World War III with the Soviets would be a more violent reprise of the recently concluded war. Knowing that added to military comfort with and support for the paradigm.

The result was a massive harnessing of American resources for military purposes. It was unprecedented in the United States in peacetime, and represented a basic reorientation of American priorities. The anti-communist consensus meant this essential militarization of American foreign policy was almost entirely unchallenged; indeed, anyone who might question it was deemed as suspiciously unpatriotic. Consensus bred unity, but it did not nurture critical self-examination or dissonance.

Managing the Cold War's military challenge became the priority goal, and it required the development of a massive governmental and private sector effort to assure the Americans kept up. On the political side, the result was the emergence of a "national security state" of military bureaucracy and support functions (e.g. intelligence) that effectively militarized much of government effort and established implementation of the dictates of the paradigm as the most central concern of government. In the private sector, the wartime military industrial base not only was not dismantled (as it customarily had been in the past) but actually grew in size and power, as elements of the competition were diffused around the country in ways such as military bases and defense industrial installations.

In his 1960 farewell address, President Dwight Eisenhower dubbed this sector "the military-industrial complex" (MIC) and warned of its potentially insidious effects.

While the Cold War was a costly, stressful environment due to the consequences of its failure, it was a heyday of sorts for those who were part of it. It was, for instance, a period of unprecedented prosperity for the U.S. military, as the political system provided it with the most fulsome peacetime resources in its history and thus nurtured the emergence of a large career military force that gained much greater prestige than peacetime militaries in the country ever possessed before. The experience created a large coterie of national security "intellectuals" to meet the crisis, and they permeated the bureaucracy and support mechanisms (e.g. research organizations or think tanks). Especially in the burgeoning aerospace industry, defense producers enjoyed unprecedented prestige—and profits.

The Cold War paradigm also produced some comforting intellectual conditions. It was an orderly period, a characteristic intellectually valuable to military thinkers. The enemy was there, and his basic challenge did not change much. Responding to his menace mostly meant adapting to new forms of weaponry he might develop. It was also predictable. Even if the burgeoning of nuclear capability had rendered plans for actual direct confrontation problematical, the planning problem remained largely the same. As late as the middle 1980s, for instance, the U.S. Navy was aggressively developing and implementing a "forward maritime strategy" to sink most of the Soviet Navy and then to steam north around the northern tip of Norway to attack Soviet staging areas. These actions would have almost certainly precipitated massive war, but the exercise and the problem remained. It is not difficult to understand how military planners wax nostalgically on this period.

The seeds of dysfunction were also present, but were largely unrecognized or ignored. This dysfunction had two implications. As independence spread through the European colonial empires, a new category of international actors emerged on the scene. These new states were not terribly interested in the Cold War competition, whose bases were largely irrelevant to their more basic concern with development. At the same time, the Cold War principals saw these new states as fertile places in which to conduct the continuing pursuit of their competition to turn the map blue or red. The implications of dysfunction flowed from this situation.

First, it was not at all clear that the United States had important interests in most of these countries, and especially interests important enough (vital) to justify the use of American force. Subsuming them as instances of the Cold War competition arguably raised American interests in these countries, which was necessary. Second, these countries were among the most violence-prone states in the world, and warfare in the developing countries tended not to be European in conduct. It was asymmetrical warfare, and the Americans in Vietnam and the Soviets in Afghanistan both discovered that their Cold War forces did not adapt particularly well to the new environment. While the Cold War was still ongoing, these problems were dismissible in the context of the overarching problem. When the Cold War dissolved, these implications remained as the principal challenges to applying a Cold War paradigm that had already been shown to be marginally successful in dealing with them.

Consequences and Legacies of the Cold War Paradigm

The Cold War may be a quarter-century old fading memory, but much of the mentality and physical attributes of the era remain a live influence on how Americans, including policymakers, think about and act in the world. Much of that influence is virtually by default. The Cold War environment may have evaporated, but it has not been replaced by a clearly articulated, well rationalized alternative environment around which policymakers and planners can wrap their conceptual efforts. At the same time, an impressive physical edifice was developed during the Cold War to deal with the specific threats it created. Part of this edifice is human, in terms of a large coterie of Cold War actors, many of whom are still active, and ways of thinking about things. Part of the legacy is also physical, in terms of an elaborate national security state apparatus designed to organize efforts against the threatening monolith of Soviet communism and still largely intact, and a massive military structure and force designed for the deterrence and confrontation of Soviet force.

Some of this has changed, mostly at the margins. No one asserts that there is a central threat as imposing and life-threatening as the Cold War menace, but the rhetoric that regularly arises when some new threat—ISIS(L) in 2014, for instance—appears. The Cold Warriors are retiring or dying, and their ranks are thinned in decision circles, but they have not disappeared altogether, and they tend to be present in particularly senior councils. The national security bureaucratic structure, centered on the institutions created by the National Security Act of 1947, remains in place, and where it has changed, it is largely through addition of structures to deal with new challenges (the Counterterrorism Task Force, for instance), not by replacement. The military has been made leaner by reducing manpower and material weapons resources, and additions have been made in places like the creation of a Special Operations Command, but there is also a high level of continuity as well.

Many of these consequences and legacies are implicit in how the United States attempts to move from the highly structured national security environment of the Cold War to the much more fluid, ambiguous present. The result is often confusion and apparent indecisiveness, as the country's leaders attempt to respond to threats for which there is not adequate general consensus and advice that can guide appropriate reactions. The result is an apparent adhocracy about policy actions that pleases virtually no one and is exacerbated by the extreme contentiousness of American politics generally. It is unclear both if it is possible at all to forge a new post-Cold War consensus on national security policy at all under current political circumstances and what the content of that paradigm might be given the nature of the international threat environment.

Working through these problems begins with assessing the effects of the Cold War past on the present. One way to sort out that influence is to break it into two categories, the physical consequences and artifacts of the past and how they prejudice dealing with the present, and conceptual legacies that color the way people think about contemporary realities.

Physical Consequences and Artifacts

As already suggested, the physical leftovers of the Cold War experience are prominently manifested in two ways. One of these is a very large institutional network of government and government-influencing structures that have some vested interest in viewing the world in terms of familiar patterns with which they have familiarity, expertise, and not infrequently, personal interest. The other, related artifact is a large, highly lethal military structure that, while making some adaptations to the new environment, is still largely structured and most functionally proficient at planning for and conducting the kinds of symmetrical military operations for which Cold War dictates prepared it.

The remaining structures are familiar and have been introduced. One of the first reactions that policymakers had to the looming clouds of a mounting Cold War was to realize that government was inadequately organized to cope with this new kind and size of threat. Its initial major response was to pass and implement the provisions of the National Security Act of 1947. That landmark piece of legislation produced the institutional nexus around which the Cold War paradigm was implemented. Among other things, it created a single cabinet-level agency, the Department of Defense, to oversee and manage the country's national security efforts. It also created the National Security Council (consisting of the President, Vice President, the Secretaries of State and Defense, and others who might assist them to advise the Commander-in-Chief on national security matters), the country's first peacetime intelligence effort in the form of the Central Intelligence Agency, and an independent United States Air Force. That structure has evolved, adding new agencies and functions (but rarely dismantling any old ones) as necessity dictated. The Defense Department (military and civilian personnel) is the largest agency in the federal government, and at its zenith in the 1950s, nearly half the federal budget was funneled through it.

The result was to elevate the centrality of national concerns within government to unprecedented levels, creating what is sometimes referred to as a "national security state" wherein national security considerations achieve paramount status, especially in foreign policy matters. This change is seen most dramatically in the changed status of the Department of State, which historically had the premier position in international concerns, to a position of equality (some would argue at best) with the Defense Department. This change was certainly appropriate when the national security menace of the Cold War, clearly a predominantly military, national security problem, reigned supreme. Whether the predisposition to military solutions that the national security state leans toward is so appropriate is an open question in the contemporary environment, but the continuing importance of the national security edifice prejudices that debate to some degree. As an example, as the debate over what the American response to the activities of ISIS(L) in Syria should be during the summer of 2014, hardly any of that discussion was phrased in the language and concerns of diplomacy, the historic preserve of the State Department.

There is also a considerable structure of influences outside government that continue to operate in and to influence the policy process. There are, for instance, a wide range of private organizations, often known as "think tanks" that provide copious (if often conflicting) advice on a whole range of national security policy areas, and their members often flow into and out of government depending on which party is in power (for a discussion, see Donald M. Snow and Patrick J. Haney, 2013, *American Foreign Policy for a New Era*). At the same time, whole industries exist or have their primary sources of revenue deriving from their supply of military equipment of one kind or another. These defense industries are located strategically around the country in a maximum number of Congressional constituencies, thereby assuring vested Congressional support for their sustenance. Government facilities from military bases to Veterans Administration hospitals are also located in places where their cancellation would have highly negative political consequences.

The large network of these private organizations, often in concert with counterpart elements of the governmental bureaucracies—the military services and armament manufacturers, for instance—form the core of Eisenhower's military-industrial complex. The reason Eisenhower raised the MIC phenomenon was because it exerted, in his view, an excessive and pernicious influence on the country. Chief among his concerns was the vast and apparently insatiable appetite it had for funding, a drain on a national budget that he felt only contributed to the country's security when it was in balance, a condition he felt imperiled by the voracious appetite of the MIC structures for funding for defense contracts. At a minimum, this maze of private influences has a vested interest in a robust national security enterprise that can sustain its members and industries, and this interest is best served by a compelling threat environment to which it can respond intellectually (through policy advice) and physically (by providing the instruments of war).

The other, related element is the military itself. The Cold War was, after World War II, the heyday of the United States military. It grew to its largest peacetime size in history, it achieved the highest priority within the government in terms of funding, and it was accorded a level and quality of prestige that was unprecedented in its history. This favorable attention and support was certainly appropriate given the primary task assigned to it in managing the Cold War confrontation: the military had to be so formidable as to dissuade the Soviet foe from contemplating aggression, and it further had to be prepared to meet that opponent on the battlefield should dissuasion fail.

Given its past experience and the military nature of the opponent, it is absolutely unsurprising that the U.S. military approached its task as a continuation of the World War II model of symmetrical warfare. Their approach was conditioned by rapidly changing levels of military technology virtually across the board, but the challenges were to be met in kind, because the two opponents were philosophically so similar to one another. The Soviets, for instance, always possessed a massive tank capability, and the American response was to develop military technology to lessen this advantage. The United States had a sizable advantage in naval assets, especially submarines, which the Soviets countered with a technological effort in the anti-submarine warfare (ASW) field. The result was to reinforce and perpetuate traditional, conventional ways of thinking and acting conditioned by the patina of technological innovation. The approach was so apparently successful that it largely survived after the problem to which it had been assigned was over.

That approach was, however, influenced by seminal events, although the reaction was often intellectually timid. The Cuban missile crisis of 1962, for instance, demonstrated the decisive difference that nuclear weapons made to thinking about military matters. One response was to raise deterrence in the hierarchy of conceptual tools of the Cold War, but the military establishment was very slow to recognize the more profound impact of rendering obsolete the actual use of military force as a solution to the differences between nuclear-armed opponents, a realization that occurred more quickly to civilian analysts and politicians.

The Vietnam War was similar in impact. That war became intensely unpopular, far more so than America's other Cold War foray into Asia in Korea. Part of the reason for this unpopularity was the seemingly endless, indeterminate nature of a conflict in which the prospects of prevailing seemed ephemeral at best. Traditional military thinking taught that military actions by democracies require popular support to be sustainable. President Richard Nixon realized more quickly than the military that continued involuntary conscription of young Americans for a feckless conflict was undermining that support, and moved to end the draft, replacing it with an all-volunteer force (AVF) concept that had great political support but which has shown signs of stress in dealing with post-Cold

War conditions such as providing adequate manpower for simultaneous military efforts in Iraq and Afghanistan. This problem is discussed in Chapter 5.

The end of the Cold War itself has been met by similar resistance to change. In the immediate period after the collapse of the communist threat, change in structure, approach, or mission was resisted on the grounds that the collapse of communism could create a power vacuum in Europe that could explode into unpredictable violence, thus creating a need to "keep our powder dry" (resist change). The 9/11 attacks and emergence of terrorism as the major national security problem has also reinvigorated interest in the national security area, even if it is uncertain whether the old structures, concepts, and ways of doing business clearly apply in the changed environment.

Conceptual Legacies

The Cold War not only created an elaborate, enduring, and stubbornly persistent set of institutions and organizations. It also produced ways of looking at national security problems that flowed from the Cold War paradigm's assessment of the threat environment and what risk-reducing actions were necessary to cope with it. It also created or reinforced distinct ways of thinking about national security matters that remain quite resilient and constantly recur in ongoing discussions.

Two aspects of that conceptual legacy, both of which have been mentioned in passing, bear emphasis. The first of these is a military solution mindset that suggests that military options are likely to provide the solutions to complex politico-military situations. The other is a persistent belief that these apparently militarily actionable situations can be confronted in largely conventional military terms.

The Cold War solidified and enhanced the position of the United States military as the centerpiece for implementing national security policy. This enhancement was predictable. The military had performed admirably in helping win World War II, the Cold War competition was analogous to the structure of political conflict in the global conflagration, and the military received much of the credit for persevering and prevailing in the long confrontation with the Soviet Union. In addition, both World War II and the continued mobilization during the Cold War produced a large number of veterans for whom an enhanced view of the military provided some afterglow.

All this added to the self-image and mythology that surrounded the military institution. Like virtually all countries, Americans have a generally heroic set of ideas about the military that emphasize both its valor and its positive accomplishments. The result is a kind of strategic culture that almost always inflates to some degree the glory of the military past and thus the expectation for its performance in the future. The United

States is no exception to this rule, and the primarily military assessment of the situation on which the Cold War paradigm was constructed simply added to the positive image of the military.

This set of dynamics had two consequences that arguably haunt the post-Cold War assessment of how the United States should deal with national security problems. The first is a belief in the primacy of military solutions to global difficulties. Military activism had taken a lead role in reducing Cold War risk. If the activation and recourse to military means could be effective in as difficult an environment as the Cold War, it was not unreasonable to extrapolate that experience to the lesser problems of the post-Cold War environment. This presumption was an implicit extension of the Cold War assumption of the *lesser included case*, a belief that if the military could deal successfully with the worst possibility (the confrontation with the Soviets) then it should be able to deal with smaller instances of challenge as well.

There was, however, a flaw in this logic that was demonstrated but largely ignored in the Cold War context. For the lesser case to be *included* as solvable by prowess in the worst case, the nature of that lesser case needed to be similar—a smaller version of the worst case. Thus, a capability and strategy that could confront and defeat the symmetrical Soviet threat could presumably be effective against a smaller version of that same sort. If one could defeat the Soviets, in other words, one should also be able to defeat the Bulgarians.

The difficulty emerged when one attempted to apply the logic of the lesser case to dissimilar situations, ones that were very different from rather than isomorphic representations of the worst case. The classic instance during the Cold War, where it was presumed that an American military armada that could successfully blunt the mighty Soviet challenge should easily be able to brush aside a third-rate power like the Democratic Republic of Vietnam (North Vietnam). The problem was that Vietnam was not like the central confrontation in Europe. In Southeast Asia, the American forces faced an enemy that conducted asymmetrical warfare, a style wholly unlike what they were prepared for and against which they consequently did not fare as well as the lesser included case analogy predicted. In this situation, the famous American "can do" military tradition—the idea that when faced with even the most difficult problem, suggests the Americans will somehow prevail. The "can do" tradition survived the Cold War as the second aspect of the misleading legacy of World War II and the Cold War.

What also somehow survived was the American military preference for large, heavily equipped military forces designed for European-style symmetrical warfare. The "American way of war," to borrow the title of Russell Weigley's seminal 1973 study of the American military tradition, was premised on the European model, and it had been dutifully applied in virtually all American military endeavors. In the major conflicts in which the United States had confronted similarly prepared and intending opponents, this model was applied successfully. The model did not work so well in isolated brushes with what would now be called asymmetrical opponents, such as the Seminole Indians in Florida in the 1820s, the various campaigns against the plains and western Indians, or even the campaign in the Philippines at the turn of the twentieth century. In all these encounters, superior American mass eventually prevailed, but it did so virtually in spite rather than because of the way the country prepared for and conducted war.

Vietnam should have been the wake-up call for the American military, since American size and overwhelming power could not defeat a smaller, less well equipped force that employed strategies and tactics specifically designed to thwart and negate American advantage and where the enemy's political will and devotion exceeded that of the Americans. There was much soul-searching within the American military about why they had failed in the Vietnam War, but its conclusions missed the point, which was that the style of warfare enshrined in the Cold War approach and paradigm simply did not work in situations where the enemy would not cooperate and fight according to American stylistic preferences. The lesson that was learned from Vietnam was that the military should avoid these kinds of conflicts in the future, not that it should change fundamentally enough to be able to deal successfully with this style of warfare. As a result, the military legacies of the Cold War paradigm—the can do tradition and the belief in the efficacy of a traditional military prepared to fight symmetrically—lived on after the Cold War disappeared. The problem was that the era where the Cold War military model was appropriate ended with the demise of the communist challenge, and the post-Cold War period has offered a set of problems much more isomorphic to Vietnam than to World War II. The Cold War paradigm's influence lingers on into a contemporary era for which it is not clearly relevant or in which it can be successful.

Looking Forward: The Cold War Paradigm as Model or Albatross

On August 27, 2014, President Obama held a press conference on U.S. plans for dealing with the growing crisis over ISIS(L) actions in Syria. His candid response was, "We don't have a strategy yet" for dealing with the problem. This admission created a firestorm of negative reaction from across the political spectrum regarding the administration's national security strategy, mostly centering on accusation of irresolution on the President's part and calls for a more forceful, assertive policy (the actual contents of which were noticeably not forthcoming). The problem was that Obama's statement was entirely correct and reflected the state of American national security essentially since the Cold War ended in 1991.

The reason there is—and has been—no coherent national security strategy or paradigm is because there has been no national consensus around what that strategy should be. President Clinton tried to tie American actions around humanitarian disasters (in the Balkans and Haiti but not in Rwanda), and President George W. Bush tried activism that resulted in large-scale interventions in Iraq and Afghanistan that the public ultimately rejected. In both cases, the commanders-in-chief tried to guess at a policy around which strategy might congeal, and they guessed wrong. Obama has tried to chart a middle course between activism that features diplomatic assertiveness with an unwillingness to commit American forces to DWICs. That approach is also apparently unacceptable, but no one has put forward a real alternative. To criticize Obama for irresolution and a lack of direction is really an indictment of the political system more generally. Until there is consensus on these matters, the discussion cannot move forward, and politics as usual in the contemporary context means everybody criticizes everything but offers no better alternatives.

Does the mission definition and force that the United States currently possesses best serve managing the current national security environment, or are the situation and American thinking and means inappropriate for the contemporary world? Both the paradigm that organizes American thinking and the force currently in place are artifacts of the Cold War and the paradigm and force developed for its conduct, although officials often deny this connection. Is that inheritance functional or dysfunctional for handling the current problems facing the country? Is the inheritance, in other words, a model for the future? Or is it an albatross weighing heavy around the American intellectual neck and impeding American success in dealing with current realities?

Even a cursory look at the contemporary world scene strongly suggests that the fit is less than perfect. Most of the situations that challenge the United States (and the world at large) are located in the developing world, with particular emphasis on the volatile Middle East. Almost all the sources of violence and instability in that part of the world have their bases in domestic political differences among groups, some of whom are not committed to the state structure in which they are contained and most of whom have deep and abiding disagreements with other groups within their states on ethnic, religious, or other grounds. These conflicts frequently do not remain confined to the political jurisdiction from which they spring, spilling over to their neighbors and endangering regional stability. When this happens, the United States often perceives its own interests to be affected and believes it should "do something." The question is "what" should the United States do in these kinds of situations, and the national security paradigm is supposed to provide guidance regarding appropriate responses. The deep level of dissention within the United States about whether or how to react belies any claim that the current, implicit Cold War paradigm does a very good job of that.

The situation as it has evolved in Syria and spread to Iraq, centering in 2014 on ISIS(L), illustrates the problem and provides an introduction to a more detailed analysis in Chapter 6. It is a complicated problem. At the time civil war broke out in Syria in 2011, that conflict was viewed as part of the short-lived Arab Spring uprisings against tyrannical governments in the region, of which there was no short supply. Hardly anyone argued that the United States had important specific interests in this instance of the Arab Spring: the United States had no significant interests in Syria. There was a general American preference for the success of democratically inclined regimes that extended to the Syrian situation, but there was nothing that suggested a particularly active role in its resolution.

The situation changed when it became apparent that the underlying cleavage between the Assad regime and its opponents was sectarian and ethnic. The ruling group in Damascus was from the minority Alawite tribe (less than one-fifth of the Syrian population), and they were adherents to a form of Shiism. The majority of the population was Sunni and Arab, and the alignment between the regime and the majority had been effectively destroyed. As Syrian forces began to attack the emerging threads of the rebellion, this sectarian/ethnic cleavage became more evident, as urban areas like Aleppo, with a large Sunni majority became the primary focuses of an increasingly brutal repression. Allegations of chemical weapons use against citizens brought world—and hence American—attention to this growing humanitarian disaster. The initial American assessment was that the Syrian civil war was none of the business of the United States; the humanitarian crisis bred a strain of support for American response on humanitarian grounds. The question was what should the United States do? The national security paradigm should have provided some guidance, but since the consensus on which such a paradigm is built was absent, it provided no real help.

Any American national security analysis of this complex must begin with the question of interests and threats. Traditional realist philosophy, of course, counsels the use of force only when vital interests are involved, a condition that was clearly met during the Cold War but that was not evident about Syria. The only basis of vitality in the early going was the humanitarian basis, and although there was some support for American response on that ground, it was never very deep or widely accepted. During Cold War forays into the developing world, the problem was solved by declaring that the competition with global communism and its impact on the global blue-red power map elevated these conflicts in otherwise peripheral situations to meet the criterion. If one did not accept the vitality of humanitarian concerns, American security responses could not be rationalized within the realist construct. The considerable suffering of the Syrian people met with great angst but no action from the United States.

That situation gradually changed as the composition of the opponents of the regime evolved. One of the early problems of any American interference was finding the "right" anti-Assad rebel groups to back. Policymakers were understandably fearful that aiding the "wrong" side could end up badly as it had in Afghanistan in the 1980s, when the United States helped sponsor groups that evolved into the Taliban and Al Qaeda. This impasse solved itself in a sense in 2014 with the active ascendancy of ISIS(L) among Sunni opponents of the regime. These fanatical fundamentalists swept with breathtaking ferocity across parts of Syria and Iraq, and their rhetoric expanded to include direct threats against the United States. Suddenly, an American interest appeared to emerge. By mid-2014, some Americans were arguing that ISIS(L) posed a direct, arguably vital threat to the United States, thereby justifying an American interest and risk-reducing response that included direct assaults on ISIS(L) in Iraq and Syria. Given the divisive nature of American politics, not all Americans agreed.

Elements of the implicit Cold War paradigm influenced the debate. From the start, the principal form of debate was over what kind of *military* action the country should contemplate, a direct extension of Cold War paradigm logic untroubled by the very spotted record of American military involvement in DWICs. The introduction of American ground forces was ruled out on political bases (the presumption that the public would not support such a course), and the question was whether American airpower could decisively decimate the newly anointed enemy.

This reaction put the United States in an anomalous political position. The Iraqi government, whose own forces had buckled under the ISIS(L) assault, readily approved American air strikes, but the opponent was operating both out of Syria and Iraq (basically ignoring the boundary between those two countries). An air campaign would clearly have better prospects of success if Syrian targets could be attacked as well, an idea the Syrian government instantly and vehemently rejected. This position was based both in the international illegality of violating Syrian airspace and by the practical concern that the United States was its enemy and had been trying to overthrow it—which was true. Here the anomalies enter. To attack ISIS(L) in Syria, the United States would have to reach some kind of accord with the regime it was trying to displace, a delicate problem at the least. In the absence of such an accord, American air strikes would effectively put it in opposition *to both sides* of the Syrian civil war.

The result has been an impossible situation for American policy. It is important because much of the dynamic is played out in one way or another in most DWICs, and these are the main kinds of situations where American force may be called into action in the foreseeable future. It would be very helpful if the United States had some kind of paradigmatic agreement about what to do in these situations, but it does not. Each of these situations is sufficiently idiosyncratic that it is probably impossible to reach any overarching, encompassing agreement, but some guidance would be helpful.

Is the mindset and structure of the Cold War paradigm helpful or deleterious in approaching and organizing for these contemporary situations?

At one level, it clearly is not helpful, because the two environments are very different. The Cold War environment featured a traditional, symmetrical military confrontation between two blocs of sovereign states led by the United States and the Soviet Union. The political structure of that relationship was entirely Clausewitzian and traditional, and the symmetry of the relationship extended to the military balance between two heavily armed opponents designed and crafted in the European tradition for conventional interstate war in Europe. With the exception of the novelty of nuclear weapons and their impact on the relationship, nineteenth and possibly even eighteenth century political and military leaders would have been comfortable with the construct.

The post-Cold War environment turns that structure on its head. The dominant source of violence, instability and threat has moved from Europe (which has become remarkably stable and conflict-free) to the old peripheries of the developing world. The reasons for and structure of violence are rarely state-against-state, but almost always between factions within states, and as civil conflicts always are, they tend to be intense, very personal, and profound. The military outcome is influenced by the military conduct of hostilities—who prevails on the battlefield—but that calculation is less important than the battle for political loyalty in the population. Speaking of Vietnam, President Lyndon Johnson labeled that struggle "the battle for the hearts and minds of men." It creates an entirely different aura than does the conventional conflict for which the Cold War paradigm is fashioned.

The conduct of these conflicts is also fundamentally different than warfare fought on the European model. The whole idea of asymmetrical warfare, after all, is for a weaker military contestant to find a way to negate the combat superiority of a larger, stronger opponent and to devise ways either to frustrate that enemy to the point it gives up the pursuit or, in the best of circumstances, to reverse the balance of power between the two sides. The conventional military advantage of the United States against developing world internal movements is so great that such opponents cannot even contemplate reaching a point where they can successfully defeat American forces on the battlefield, so they do not even seriously try. What they can hope to do, however, is employ unconventional measures that frustrate the Americans sufficiently that *they* cannot achieve the decisive triumph that is the major objective of asymmetrical warfare. This approach is what American opponents consistently employ as the heart of their asymmetrical strategy; if the United States has devised a successful counter-strategy to negate this frustration-producing approach, it has not been evidently successful.

From the western perspective on which the Cold War paradigm is based, the basic approach to all warfare is to bring such superior conventional firepower to bear upon the opponent to cause it to buckle and eventually to capitulate, which is the very situation asymmetrical approaches are intended to negate. Americans operating out of the western symmetrical worldview have had great difficulty in adapting to this strategy, because one of its implications is that the premises from which they have operated are simply wrong, or at least irrelevant. Military forces, and specifically those operating from the "can do" presumption, have great difficulty accepting the idea that their unquestioned conventional prowess may be indecisive, even irrelevant in the more political battle for "hearts and minds" that is the focus of the asymmetrical warrior. When Americans, for instance, were amazed that a clearly numerically smaller ISIS(L) force was wreaking such havoc in Syria and Iraq and mused that American force could be decisive in defeating the insurgents, they were basically missing the point of conflict from the enemy's perspective. Among other things, the American paradigm was getting in the way.

Is the Cold War paradigm a model for the future or a conceptual albatross weighing heavily around the intellectual necks of the country as it faces a very different environment? The sideshow of Ukraine in 2014 notwithstanding, kinds of threats on which the Cold War paradigm was based and for which its application was most obviously relevant are the perils of the past, not the future. The future of threat and challenge is in the kinds of violent, combustible witches' brews of internal conflicts and terrorism so clearly evident in the contemporary Levant from which ISIS(L) has emerged as the threat *du jour*. These are the kinds of situations with which national security decision makers will have to deal in the near and probably midterm futures, and it is not clear that all the premises and implications of the past apply to that present and future. Before turning to specific questions and options for an alternative paradigmatic approach to the contemporary dilemma, however, it is first necessary to look both at some contemporary influences and limitations on policy considerations and more specifically at the current worst case in Syria and Iraq.

Bibliography

Allison, Graham. *Essence of Decision: Explaining the Cuban Missile Crisis.* Boston, MA: Little Brown, 1971.

Allison, Graham, and Robert Blackwill. "America's Stake in the Soviet Future." *Foreign Affairs* 70, 3 (Summer 1991), 77–97.

Ambrose, Stephen E.. *Rise to Globalism: American Foreign Policy, 1938–1970.* Baltimore, MD: Johns Hopkins University Press, 1970.

Brzezinski, Zbigniew. "The Cold War and Its Aftermath." *Foreign Affairs* 71, 4 (Fall 1992), 31–48.

Claude, Inis. *The Changing United Nations.* New York: Random House, 1967.

Djilas, Milovan. *The New Class: An Analysis of the Communist System.* San Diego, CA: Harcourt, Brace, Jovanovich, 1957.

Gaddis, John Lewis. *The United States and the End of the Cold War: Implications, Reconsiderations, Provocations.* New York: Oxford University Press, 1992.

Gaddis, John Lewis. *Strategies of Containment: A Critical Appraisal of Postwar American National Security Policy during the Cold War*. Revised and expanded edn. New York: Oxford University Press, 2005.

Gorbachev, Mikhail. *Perestroika: New Thinking for Our Country and the World*. New York: Harper and Row, 1987.

Jervis, Robert, and Seweryn Bialer (eds). *Sino-American Relations after the Cold War*. Durham, NC: Duke University Press, 2012.

Kennan, George F. *American Diplomacy, 1900–1950*. New York: New American Library, 1951.

Kennan, George F. *Memoirs*. Boston, MA: Little Brown, 1976.

Kennan, George F. "The Sources of Soviet Conduct." *Foreign Affairs* 25, 4 (July 1947), 566–582.

Kennedy, Robert F. *The Thirteen Days: A Memoir of the Cuban Missile Crisis*. New York: W.W. Norton, 1999 (originally published 1963).

Mearsheimer, John J. "Why We Shall Soon Miss the Cold War." *Atlantic Monthly* 266, 2 (August 1990), 35–50.

Simes, Dmitri. "The Return of Russian History." *Foreign Affairs* 73, 1 (January/February 1992), 67–82.

Snow, Donald M. *The Necessary Peace: Nuclear Weapons and Superpower Relations*. Lexington, MA: Lexington Books, 1987.

Snow, Donald M., and Patrick J. Haney. *American Foreign Policy in a New Era*. New York: Pearson, 2013.

Weigley, Russell F.. *The American Way of War*. New York: Macmillan, 1973.

Yergin, Daniel. *Shattered Peace: The Origins of the Cold War and the National Security State*. Boston, MA: Little Brown, 1977.

Part II
Influences

5   Factors in the New Environment

The basic international environment in which national security policy competes has changed in two ways since the end of the Cold War. Each of these changes has an impact on the appropriate form of such a policy, but neither has been entirely incorporated into how the United States deals with the quite different set of problems which the country faces now and in the foreseeable future. Although both have been introduced before, they bear emphasizing as context for considering new and different possibilities and limitations on policy in the contemporary circumstance, which is the major burden of this chapter.

The first major change is the nature of the threat that faces the United States. Part of this change has been the result of structural change in the composition of international actors. Before the end of the Cold War, virtually all the potential threats to American national security were assumed to come from so-called *state actors*, or, more simply put, from the national governments of states, and the major operational threat that national security risk-reducers had to counter was the threat posed by the organized armed forces of all those states. Those opposing forces were, with few exceptions, organized and led in manners similar to American forces, and the challenges they posed were traditional *raisons d'etat* (reasons of state). Certainly, the structural Soviet threat was of this nature.

The basic change has been that state actors have been replaced almost entirely by *non-state actors* as the source of opposition. Non-state actors, by definition, are groups that do not represent the recognized governments of states and do not fight for the traditional reasons that states wage war. Some of these groups represent insurgencies against the continued rule of state governments: the National Liberation Front in Vietnam and the Taliban in Afghanistan are examples. In these cases, the United States has occasionally found itself in opposition to such movements because it supported existing governments for one reason or another. In other cases, non-state actors may be effectively *transnational*, meaning they have memberships and usually purposes that transcend state boundaries. ISIS(L) and many contemporary terrorist movements (e.g. variants of Al Qaeda) are obvious current examples. These groups may form for religious, ideological, ethnic, or other purposes, and they tend to be particularly troublesome, both because of their frequent fanaticism and because the changes they seek are so fundamental. Non-state actors are arguably the most prominent kind of threat facing the United States today.

The second change flows from this structural change. Both the kinds of national security opponent and the form of the threat they pose are different now than they used to be. With the possible exceptions of the Persian Gulf War of 1990–1991 and the first phase of the Iraq War in March–May 2003 (the conquest of Iraq), the United States no longer fights traditional interstate warfare conducted under the conventional rules of war—and neither does anybody else. Contemporary military challenges tend to be different. DWICs, the major form of military challenge with which the United States is now confronted, are unconventional. Most are broadly asymmetrical wars where the opponents use unconventional methods. They tend to be fought in comparatively primitive, topographically challenging physical places where the traditional symbols of American military might cannot operate. American overwhelming armored (tank) superiority has been of no real use in Afghanistan, for instance, because the country's geography and lack of roads and bridges mean they cannot get to most places where fighting occurs (a condition which opponents know and exploit). Moreover, many of the challenges are only semi-military in terms of conduct and response. Anti-terrorist activities have a military component, for instance, but they also have significant intelligence, law enforcement, and even political components that may be equally or even more important.

These changes are evident in other, noticeably non-traditional ways as well. One of the more novel forms of contemporary threat, for instance, is something called *cyberwar*. There are conflicting views about whether the term cyber "war" is meaningful, since the activity and its purposes are certainly non-military. *Wikipedia* defines it as "politically motivated hacking to conduct sabotage and espionage," and suggests it is really a form of information warfare. It can affect more traditional national security activities if cyber "warriors" can interrupt military communications or communications between political and military leaders or if it allows the compromise of military capabilities or operations. In the contemporary world, attacks on electronics are frequent and can be quite serious. They are not, however, traditional national security concerns, and it is not clear how or if they fit into national security calculations. As such, they primarily illustrate the much more complex environment in which such concerns must take place.

This changed environment can be translated into familiar interest-threat-risk terms, all of which have been arguably changed in the current environment. The primary question of interests arises from where the challenges occur and the peril they pose. Almost all of them occur in the developing world (especially the Middle East in the recent past) in places where the level of American interests is not clear-cut. In places like Syria, Iraq, or Afghanistan, for instance, the United States has historically lacked vital interests for which robust national security defense would be unambiguously appropriate to justify upgrading situations of less-than-vital (LTV) interests to vital interest (VI) status that would clearly justify a military response. Humanitarian justifications have generally proven inadequate to elicit such an upgrade, and thus the rationale for moving across the LTV/VI frontier has been on the nature of threat in particular circumstances.

The nature of the threat is also more opaque in contemporary situations. The most unambiguous form of threat is a direct, tangible, physical threat to national existence—an existential threat—and contemporary threats never rise to that level. Indeed, only the Soviet nuclear threat during the Cold War was clearly of this nature, and there is no stretch of the human imagination by which Middle Eastern terrorist groups, for instance, pose or could pose such a threat, their own inflammatory rhetoric notwithstanding.

This means that the actual threats posed to the United States in developing world crises are in the *psychological* realm, where judgments are not intersubjective and reasonable people can and do disagree on the degree of peril involved. There is, for instance, no question that a number of Middle East-based terrorist groups do not wish the United States well and would like to inflict damaging and suffering on Americans. How much mayhem are they capable of committing? How much should Americans worry about this potential danger, especially given that there are competing threats in the world? People legitimately differ on their assessments, and those differing conclusions also affect their assessment of the risks that attach to different responses.

A central dilemma of risk assessment and risk management is that risks always exceed the resources necessary to negate all of them. This deficiency is partly true when one moves into the psychological realm of threat, which can be virtually infinitely expandable, depending on who constructs any particular list of risks. These disagreements clearly extend to any priority ordering one can construct about which risks must be countered and on which one will take a chance that they will not be challenged. People will disagree on those risks that are intolerable, and there will always be a tendency for the rhetoric to become increasingly heated when particular risks are assessed. The intolerability of any risk is, after all, a direct extension of its importance as an interest. By definition, a vital interest is one where an unfavorable condition would be intolerable, and if one is passionate about negating a particular risk, there will be a natural tendency to inflate its vitality. Even a cursory examination of the evolution of any national security situation reveals this proclivity.

If there is change and disagreement about the core questions surrounding national security issues, there are also other, more specific difficulties with which the contemporary national security decision maker must cope. For illustrative purposes, three of these issues will be examined to demonstrate the range of influence they present. The first is *military manpower*, a matter of concern and a potential constraint given the Iraq/Afghanistan experience. The second is *unmanned aerial vehicles* (UAVs or drones), pilotless means of flight that offer reconnaissance and attack options not previously available but which contain potential dangers. The third is *terrorism,* a historical and continuing concern that has created considerable dilemmas for the national security community. Individually and collectively, these three phenomena help define the operational universe in which the national security enterprise currently operates.

The Delicate Problem of Military Manpower

For many Americans, including most of their military leaders, referring to a military manpower "problem" seems curious, even anomalous. At the end of 1972, the Nixon administration formally shelved the historic method by which the United States "manned" the armed forces, the Selective Service system, a euphemism for conscription, or the draft. In its place, the administration instituted the All-Volunteer Force (AVF), wherein only those individuals who voluntarily agreed to serve in uniform would do so. At the time, the AVF was largely a political response to growing criticism of continuing American military involvement in Vietnam, which at that point was approaching eight years. The criticism was sharpest among young American males 18–25 years of age, who were subject to conscription, and their families. Ending the draft dissipated much criticism of the war and helped provide the political cover behind which the Nixon administration could negotiate American withdrawal from Southeast Asia. The AVF largely worked in this regard.

After the war ended, the expedient of the AVF gradually evolved as a virtue. During the middle 1970s, the jury was still out. Conscripts and some others fled the armed forces at the first possible opportunity after the war was over, and the military had a difficult time replacing both the quantity, and especially the quality, of personnel leaving. By the end of the decade, however, the trend began to reverse, and adequate numbers of well qualified young Americans began to fill the AVF ranks.

The military in particular became enamored of the AVF concept. The key factor was the fact that members were indeed *volunteers,* people who joined the military because they *wanted* to do so, not because they were compelled to serve. Involuntary service members (draftees or conscripts) create morale and disciplinary problems simply because they do not want to be in uniform or to do the things the leadership requires them to do. When the force consists entirely of volunteers, these problems disappear, and the military can spend its time training and educating its members to reach higher levels of performance rather than whipping them into shape and keeping them out of trouble. The result has proven to be a more proficient—the military itself likes to refer to it as "professional"—force that is more capable and proficient than its conscript-laden alternative. The AVF force is both a better and a "happier" force than the alternative. Because of this situation, the military itself is among the strongest opponents whenever the possibility of a return to some form of conscription is raised. As a sidelight, since it has been over forty years since it has had to deal with the kinds of problems endemic to a non-volunteer force, it has also largely lost the capacity to do so.

For the most part and for most purposes, the AVF has been a remarkable success, and it has very strong support, especially within the political system. The military clearly likes it because of the quality of force it has produced. Politicians of virtually all persuasions also support it strongly. Political figures are, of course, much better at giving people things—from tax breaks to government programs—than they are at taking things away or making people do things they do not want to do. Forcing young Americans into uniform and especially into harm's way in war is an especially distasteful responsibility, and one the AVF allows them to avoid altogether. The public also supports the concept, because it means there is no danger they or their loved ones will be compelled to a military duty they would rather avoid. War has become someone else's problem. No American under the age of 60 has ever had to fear compulsory service, so there is very little collective memory about what the threat or reality of that compulsion feels like. Americans like it that way.

The American experience with the AVF has been almost uniformly positive, but the experience of the American military in the 2000s, when it was simultaneously given the tasks of engaging in two major military excursions in Iraq and Afghanistan, raised concerns about the adequacy of the AVF to meet the future national security needs the country may incur. These sources of strain are not widely recognized or acknowledged, but they are nonetheless present and cannot be ignored as the country faces an uncertain future. The simple fact is that the Iraq–Afghanistan experience tested and stressed the quantitative capabilities and potentials of the American military in the future. The unacknowledged 800-pound gorilla in the manpower room is whether the AVF system can produce as many forces as the United States may need in the future. The question that no one wants to answer because it might involve modifying or abandoning a cherished concept, is what to do about that problem.

Manpower Questions

The military manpower question can be conceptualized in terms of four related questions. They cover the range of personnel concern: recruitment, retention, qualitative performance, and quantitative adequacy. The concerns are also related: success at retaining the force that is recruited, for instance, eases the burden of future recruitment efforts, and qualitative proficiency can be a substitute for sheer numbers of personnel. Each concern, however, merits some individual attention.

Recruitment: Who will serve? This, of course, is the keystone question and the concern that led to the conversion from a conscript-based force to the AVF. In one important sense, this question has been answered politically in such a satisfactory manner that it is effectively a non-question within the dialogue over national security. It is an unnecessary question as long as the recruitment system produces a personnel base that is adequate and politically satisfactory in fulfilling the other concerns. If, however, it does not or changes in the other factors (lower retention rates, for instance) affect the adequacy of its performance, it does become a matter of debate.

As noted, there are two bases on which military manpower can be brought into military service: voluntarily and involuntarily. Both kinds of systems are used in different countries of the world and are emphasized at different points. Almost all of the countries that participated actively in World War II conscripted service members during the war to produce adequate numbers of personnel for the fight, but relatively few of them retain conscript-based forces today, when very large forces are not needed. In the United States, the traditional pattern was for all-volunteer forces during the prolonged periods of relative peace that marked American history prior to World War II. In times of major war, conscription was introduced with varying success: it worked well in World War I, but had a checkered record in the American Civil War on both sides. World War II was the first war of true national mobilization, and most of those who fought were conscripts, very few of whom resisted the call to arms. After the Korean War, the United States maintained large forces in peacetime for the first time as part of the Cold War mandate. This system, which mixed voluntary accession with conscription of adequate numbers to meet quantitative requirements, remained in place until 1972, when the system was suspended (but not rescinded) and replaced by the AVF.

Despite its immense popularity, any all-volunteer force faces two obstacles that recruitment efforts must seek to mitigate. The first is that such systems are more expensive to maintain than conscript-based systems. The main reason is personnel costs. Since conscripts are compelled to service, there is no need to provide inducements such as competitive salaries and benefits to them. As a result, first-time conscripts are generally very poorly paid. AVF members, on the other hand, must be recruited in competition with other institutions that utilize young Americans—notably entry level jobs in the private sector and higher education. To compete, the military must pay a wage and provide benefits competitive with what the recruit could earn "on the outside," and this pushes up personnel costs considerably above the pittance paid to conscripts. Defenders of the AVF point out that recruitment of volunteers produces a "better" soldier who requires less ancillary costs like discipline, and that volunteers are more likely to be retained in future re-enlistments, thereby lowering training costs. These rejoinders are true, but only partially mitigating: the average cost of employing an AVF member in the U.S. armed forces is well over $100,000 a person.

The other limitation is on size. Military service is, after all, a special form of occupation that puts unique stresses on its members and subjects them to dangers such as those incurred in combat that do not attach to other forms of endeavor. Not everyone will voluntarily choose military service because they are unwilling to endure the dangers and privations that can be part of military life under any circumstances, including those of competitive compensation. Add to this the fact that young people currently entering the age of potential service almost all have parents and even grandparents who also have had no military experience, and the tradition of service is diluted as well. For most Americans who have meaningful opportunities in the job market or reasonable access to higher education, the military service choice is simply not a meaningful option. The only group of young Americans who are not deterred by these dynamics tend to be the offspring of veterans.

The result is that there are very real limits to how large an all-volunteer force ever can or will be, and that size is well below anything like large-scale national mobilization. Current international conditions do not pose many likely scenarios where a force larger than can be recruited by voluntary means will be needed, but there are ominous signs that the limit was approached and possibly even breached during the period when large-scale operations were still ongoing in both Iraq and Afghanistan. Whether this is acceptable in the future is a national security policy issue.

There are methods to increase recruitment effort and outcomes, but they are controversial. One is to lower standards—either admitting individuals with lower scores on standardized testing or people with spotted pasts, such as some categories of felons. Another is to move aggressively to reduce gender inequality by recruiting larger numbers of females to the service. Each has its drawbacks. Admitting less intellectually gifted members could lower qualitative performance that is a proud hallmark of the current force, and recruiting individuals with questionable backgrounds raises the prospect of greater disciplinary problems the solution to which was a major byproduct of the transition to the AVF. Greater gender equality raises physical questions (e.g. jobs a woman cannot physically do) as well as cultural difficulties (e.g. the reluctance of males to subject females to certain combat situations and roles). All these are perennial ongoing concerns.

Retention: How does one convince people to continue to serve? Recruitment and retention are bookend concerns. The more people who are retained within the military through re-enlistment, the fewer new people must be recruited to maintain particular numerical or skill needs.

Conversely, the fewer people who "re-up," (re-enlist), the greater is the need for successful efforts to recruit new members.

The tension between the two activities is greatest in a conscript force. Since many of the junior members (in terms of service) are draftees who did not want to be in uniform in the first place, re-enlistment rates tend to be much lower than in an all-volunteer force, where those who willingly joined are more likely to remain in service. Moreover, a force composed of large numbers of retained personnel is likely to have higher skill levels among its members, contributing to job satisfaction and reinforcing the proclivity to remain on the job. The result is a more contented and able force than a reluctant and more inexperienced conscript force composed of members who will get out at the first opportunity.

The key element in this equation is clearly the ability to retain members. For most of the history of the AVF, retention has not been a problem, as the military establishment has been able to make itself attractive enough to those who belong to keep them in uniform. For the first time during the Iran–Afghanistan period, however, significant strains became apparent and retention rates threatened to fall to unhealthy levels. The culprit was the great demand for deployment of large numbers of forces in the two theaters. These demands strained and even exceeded the ability of the military to furnish adequate forces in the field while maintaining rotation schedules that did not unduly tax their members through repeated and prolonged exposure to combat operations. Initially, manpower demands were augmented successfully by activation of reserve units in the various services and committing them to active line duty. As demands grew, however, these units began to be integrated into normal rotation schedules, leaving less and less forces for temporary, relieving duty. The result was increased rotations of troops to the theaters of operation through increased deployments for longer periods with decreased intervals between these tours of duty. Particularly but not exclusively among the reserves, dissatisfaction began to grow, and it threatened retention rates within a force the adequacy of whose numbers was already being tested. This problem was becoming especially great in 2007–2008, as the "surge" in Iraq and increases in levels of action in Afghanistan were stressing combat capabilities.

The military response was to invoke a provision of the contract military members sign (paragraph 9c) when they enlist or re-enlist. It is known as "stop-loss," and its provision is to prevent a military member from leaving the force once his or her contracted period of service has ended. Stop-loss orders can be extended for up to six months under the contractual terms of service. The provision was included in legislation that authorized the AVF and was first used in the Persian Gulf War of 1990–1991 and again during the middle 1990s. Its intent is to insure the military does not lose critical expertise during wartime; its effect is to create a period of semi-involuntary service. Its invocation is also an indication that during times of military stress—the need for larger number of forces that can be recruited and retained under the AVF concept—some alternative may have to be considered.

This situation corrected itself after 2008, as the United States began to reduce the size of its forces in Iraq in anticipation of their total withdrawal in 2011. Although there was an increase of commitment to Afghanistan in 2009, those numbers leveled off and have gradually declined. The crisis passed as demands on the recruitment-retention system declined. Under some circumstances, they could return.

Quality: Does the system produce a force of adequate quality to meet the country's needs? The quality of the AVF has been one of its chief selling points, a major reason for satisfaction with it within the professional military, and a source of national pride. In the sense of producing a quality force that is arguably the world's finest and most proficient at its trade, there have been no arguments about whether the AVF works. It does. Any qualitative questions are indirect, peripheral, and largely beyond the scope or capability of the military.

One aspect of the issue of quality is how well the military can compete with the civilian sector for those who have or can be taught sophisticated skills. Highly trainable, educable young people are in greater demand than those who lack such skills in both the competitors for the entry-level target audience (essentially high school graduates). As noted, the major competitors are the private job market and higher education, and the military's ability to compete is inversely proportional to the health and vitality of those sectors. Especially since the recession of 2008, opportunities within the competitor sectors have been limited, and so military recruitment and retention have comparatively flourished despite national war weariness. Conversely, a dramatic improvement in the country's economy could make it more difficult to get and keep military members. The military obviously cannot control this.

The nature of the military environment is also a factor in assessing quality. The sophistication associated with a high quality force is most clearly demonstrated in military situations where that sophistication can be brought militarily to bear, and developing world situations are often difficult places to apply technological superiority, a hallmark of a quality force (in fact, part of the point in DWICs is to negate such advantages). A high quality force is clearly most applicable to situations requiring a sophisticated response. Traditional European-style military confrontations are the most obvious application. It is not the military's fault there are not any of those available.

Quantity: Does the force produce adequate numbers for the country's needs? If quality is not an issue with today's force, quantity is—or could become—such an issue. It is not a problem that AVF proponents, especially within the military itself, like to talk about, but the simple fact is that the Iraq–Afghanistan experience was more traumatizing than is publicly admitted. Succinctly stated, these two simultaneous large-scale deployments came very close to overusing the quantitative capacities of American combat forces (mainly conventional ground forces). Had one or both of the wars not been wound down by the Obama administration, that strain might have become unbearable.

The reasons for this strain are simple enough, coming from sources already introduced. There are limits to how many young Americans will volunteer for military service, and more specifically, for the so-called "combat arms" during wartime when there is not a crisis that warrants a massive national commitment on the scale of the world wars. The AVF concept is not conducive to a large standing American military in other than dire circumstances that do not exist. In the absence of situations that constitute consensual wars of necessity, American forces are about as big and capable as they are likely to be. The only ways to remedy this situation are unacceptable to large portions of the population (making convicted criminals or women eligible for direct combat roles, for instance), or by offering even greater monetary incentives for people to join. Unfortunately for the latter solution, the AVF is already expensive, and the political climate is not favorable for spending more money on the military.

Those who are most supportive of and invested in the AVF concept are numerous, powerful, and recognize the dilemma they face. The chair of the study that proposed the AVF was former Secretary of Defense Thomas Gates, who served in that capacity under President Eisenhower from 1959–1961. Almost all high ranking military since the AVF's inception have tied their careers and reputations to it. All at least implicitly realize that limits on the concept reflect on their legacy. They all know the quantitative limits on the AVF, but there is not much they can do about it.

As long as its size is not stressed beyond abilities it cannot possess, the AVF has been a great success for over 40 years. Its structure has provided a rousing recruitment pedestal that produces a force that it is by and large able to retain. Qualitatively, it has produced an exemplary record of which its leaders are understandably proud. The military loves it because of the force it produces that they get to lead. The politicians also love it, because it releases them from having to make negative decisions that affect their young constituents and their families. The American public likes it because it frees them from any military obligations—war is now someone else's problem, not theirs. The AVF thus admirably meets three of the four standards raised in this section (recruitment, retention, quality); it is the fourth that is the problem.

The AVF as a Limit on National Security Policy

One way to evaluate the success of the AVF is by comparing its tenure to other periods of American history. In essence, the United States has had an implicit reliance on voluntary forces for most of its citizen-soldier history, and in the second half of the nineteenth century, fulfilling the country's "manifest destiny" of populating and "taming" the continent was carried out mostly by Civil War veterans fighting against under-manned Indian opponents. Between the world wars, the U.S. Marines (a volunteer outfit except in times of dire crisis) enforced the American "good neighbor policy" south of the U.S. border.

The all-volunteer concept has not proven adequate at times of national military stress, when large numbers of Americans were needed to fight the country's wars. The American Civil War had conscripts fighting on both sides, and both the world wars required pressing Americans involuntarily into military service. The post-Korean Cold War continued this pre-cedent, and it remained as long as involuntary service seemed a necessity to protect the United States from harm. The mold broke when many Americans came to believe that the Vietnam War was a conflict of choice in which they chose not to take the risk of personal sacrifice.

There is a simple and obvious truth in this historical pattern. Something like the AVF is an adequate concept on which to base military forces as long as the demands placed on those forces do not exceed the capabilities they possess, but it is inadequate when crises exist that require commit-ments in excess of what those volunteers can accomplish. Historically, the characteristic that has required abandoning or augmenting volunteer forces has been the quantitative inadequacy of those forces for the tasks at hand. Has anything really changed?

In historical terms, the four decades since the end of the Vietnam War have not been militarily stressful. As long as the Cold War continued, there was a perceived need for large forces, but these were scaled back after 1991 to more or less current levels. The force levels currently avail-able under the AVF have essentially been adequate to deal with the threat environment, although the middle 2000s tested the quantitative limits of current force size. Those who designed the AVF, beginning with the Gates Commission, recognized this dynamic. It is no secret. As Crawford H. Greenewalt, a member of the commission wrote to the chair in 1969, "While there is a reasonable possibility that a peacetime armed force could be entirely voluntary, I am certain that an armed force in a major conflict could *not* be voluntary." This assessment simply reflected past American experience. The country may only have engaged in conscription for 36 years of its existence, but those were also the most militarily stressful years of its existence.

This point may be obvious, but it has also been largely lost in con-temporary discussions about the use of American force that implicitly operate from the assumption that the AVF will produce a force that is adequate for any military task to which it might be assigned. For the most part, such an assumption is true, but it is not immutably true. Were the United States to be faced with a very large military commitment (admit-tedly not a great possibility), the AVF might face a situation it could not surmount, in which case its existence could prove a hindrance, even a preclusion, of the ability of the United States to pursue its national security interests.

Two observations can be made here about this possibility, each of which is further explored in Chapter 7. The first is whether this situation is recognized, either in the current policy debate or in thinking about longer-range strategy. The public record does not seem encouraging. Current discussions about American proposed or ongoing operations in the Middle East are frequently stated in terms of their very long-term needs, and the question of the stress such commitments could place on the manpower system are never publicly addressed on the implicit assumption that such concerns are not relevant and that the current system can handle all the demands that might be placed on it. Is that assessment correct? No one publicly says or suggests they are looking at it.

The other observation surrounds what can be done if the country potentially faces situations where the current system cannot provide adequate personnel to meet prescribed requirements. There are two basic possibilities. One is to scale back requirements to meet the capabilities of the current force. If demands remain at or below the levels that have existed since 1991, the current system works fine, and plans are in the works to reduce force size even more. Scaling perceptions of threat, which means manipulating the psychological dimension of threat perception, to convince the public that there are no threats the system cannot accommodate, is thus one possibility. The other is to alter the method of manpower recruitment to allow for accession of larger numbers of personnel. That means reinstituting some kind and level of involuntary service, or conscription. That has, of course, been the traditional method for expanding the armed forces.

Neither of these solutions is likely to be acceptable in the current political climate. The current debate seems to emphasize, even amplify, the extent of crises and their dire potential consequences, not to dampen such suggestions. There is a conundrum at work here. To convince a war-weary American public to support post Iraq/Afghanistan military involvements, it is necessary to convince them that such actions are necessary—that vital interests make these conflicts of necessity, not choice. Since such assertions are debatable, the only way to do so is through heated advocacy, which has been the staple of the current political climate. The result is to inflate, not to deflate, the situations that might invoke American military responses.

The other possible response would be reactivation of the conscription system (which was suspended, not dismantled, in 1973). The problem is that proposing to do so in the absence of some truly major, even cataclysmic threat would be politically suicidal for anyone who proposed it. Beyond political expediency (dampening opposition to Vietnam), there were good reasons to suspend the draft (too many eligible participants, which meant only some would serve). Moreover, the AVF *is* over-whelmingly popular. Aversion to conscription has been possible in the last few decades in the face of overwhelming threats the direness of which was consensually accepted. In the absence of a World War II-sized threat, the draft has been resisted. Are there any threats on the horizon that could cause the return of a consensus that would embrace a return to involuntary military service?

There is one other possibility that speaks directly to the American penchant in such matters. Another way to make the existing force capable of larger tasks is to enhance the capabilities of its current members. This process is known as *force multiplication*, and it refers to actions that can be taken to increase the lethal capabilities of individual members and thereby to increase their ability to fight. Replacing soldier single-shot rifles with machine guns is an example. The process that produced this outcome is technological innovation, which is an important part of the American way of life—and war. The latest example of this phenomenon is the use of unmanned aerial vehicles (UAVs) in modern warfare.

The Siren's Call of Drone Warfare

The use of small, unpiloted aircraft has become a central part of Amer-ican military strategy in dealing with some of the difficult military pro-blems associated with conducting military operations in developing world countries, and specifically in the Middle East. From a strictly military point of view, drones are a classic force multiplier, allowing the United States to do things it could not do easily or at all in their absence, and their multiple utilities have created a considerable support base for them within military and other national security sectors. There is no question that they present military opportunities that have the added virtues of not requiring the dedication of considerable manpower resources to the tasks to which they are assigned. In addition, they do so without putting American lives at risk, since they fly to their targets and back with no human operators on board.

Despite their clear military virtues, UAVs have become increasingly controversial. Some of this controversy is the direct result of their flex-ibility. Drones can fly to destinations that are extremely remote and can do so in a virtually undetectable manner, which are among their virtues, but this also means there is a temptation to use them in circumstances and in places where the host government of the territory may be reluctant or opposed to their use. This has been the case of Predator use in both Pakistan and Yemen. Their ability to provide precise surveillance of tar-gets is also a double-edged sword of sorts, as the military technology has been applied to domestic uses by law enforcement and other authorities in ways that some feel are unduly intrusive and even threaten basic privacy standards. The "stealthy" quality of UAVs will undoubtedly induce technological efforts to obviate their effectiveness, thereby creating yet other difficulties. The future of drones may be bright and promising, but it is not without problems.

The technological thrust behind the efforts that have produced capabilities such as the Predator UAV that has carried out extensive bombing raids in a number of Middle Eastern countries—Pakistan, Yemen, Iraq, and Syria, for example—is by no means anything new. The research that has made these aircraft feasible and useful is decades old and has come to maturity as numerous technological elements from quiet and long-distance propulsion to satellite-aided guidance have matured. At least as far back as the argumentation over whether to build the F-22 fighter-bomber first used over Syria included arguments that the plane was unnecessary, since future aircraft would all be pilotless.

UAVs are thus part of the current and future national security environments, and their utilities, limitations, and outlook are part of planning for the future. Any discussion must operate within some parameters of uncertainty, since technological developments are dynamic, creating new possible applications not all of which can be confidently predicted.

The Uses and Advantages of UAVs

Pilotless aircraft are a classic example of the force multiplier. These small vehicles do not require large expenditures of manpower or labor beyond the maintenance necessary to keep them airworthy, and since they do not require an on-board pilot, they do not run the risk of pilot casualties; their "pilots," instead, are located at computer consoles far from the places they are used (often in the United States itself). They are apparently highly reliable, as there are very few publicly available reports of UAVs either being shot down or crashing, especially over hostile territory, where such events would be widely publicized.

The use of drones has been particularly attractive in the contemporary environment, for two basic reasons. The first is that they are a very useful tool for dealing with DWICs. These kinds of conflicts by definition occur in countries where the infrastructure is deficient in terms of things like roads and airfields, and they are typically geographically challenging in one way or another: the rugged, forbidding mountains of some Middle Eastern countries like Pakistan, Afghanistan, or Yemen, or the tropical rain forests and swampy terrain of parts of Asia and Africa. The result is that these countries have historically provided excellent physical sanctuary areas for insurgent movements (asymmetrical warriors) safe from the reach of stronger government or outside forces. Drones erase these impediments and leave asymmetrical warriors, and especially their leaders, vulnerable to attack and destruction. The 2011 killing of American-born Al Qaeda leader Anwar al-Awlaki in the rugged mountainous hinterlands of Yemen was a signature example of this capability, and it has also been brought to bear against ISIS(L) leaders and cadres in Syria and Iraq as well. Before drones, these kinds of missions could only be attempted by human elements like Special Forces teams, the success of which was much more problematical in many cases.

The other great virtue of UAVs is that they can be sent into combat without running the risk of putting American personnel, notably pilots, at risk. In the atmosphere of war-weariness and war-wariness after Iraq/ Afghanistan, it has become politically hazardous to suggest military operations that put Americans at risk in hostile environments. This reluctance is most prominently present in aversion to "putting muddy boots on the ground" (inserting ground forces), but it extends to sending manned aircraft over war zones. In places like Syria, where active anti-aircraft systems exist over parts of the country, it would simply be a matter of time until an American pilot is shot down and captured. Eliminating the pilot from the attack equation removes that obstacle.

UAVs thus have considerable attraction militarily. In addition to the virtues already mentioned, there are other capabilities they create or enhance. They are, for instance, excellent reconnaissance platforms. This characteristic arises from the fact that they use little fuel, meaning they can be in the air for long periods, and they can "loiter" over areas in more or less stationary positions for extended periods of time. This latter capability has been useful in watching the comings and goings of terrorist suspects at their headquarters, who are unaware of the observation that is occurring, because the UAVs generally hover at altitudes of 10,000 feet or more, where they cannot be detected by the unaided human eye. Because these vehicles are equipped with excellent cameras that can instantly upload images to satellites, the result is to produce a real time level of intelligence otherwise unavailable, and this kind of information has been critical in pinpointing and eliminating terrorist leaders from organizations like Al Qaeda and ISIS(L).

Their long-range capabilities both allow their dispatch from far distant locations that are more secure than forward basing near theaters of operations and enhance the element of surprise in attacks by very accurate and lethal munitions. This accuracy also contributes to the ability of those directing drone attacks to limit—if not eliminate altogether—civilian casualties, so-called collateral damage. The fact that unintended deaths cannot be prevented altogether, however, is one of the primary objections to the use of drones against developing world targets. This is especially true since one of the standard ploys of those under threat of UAV attacks is to imbed themselves in civilian populations, where they know they cannot be targeted without civilians inadvertently losing their lives, an outcome the United States seeks to minimize.

The attraction of UAVs is that they combine a number of technologies into a military capability that enhances the lethality and effectiveness of the force without having to expand physically. Instead of training as many pilots to fly combat aircraft that are decreasingly used, for instance, the Air Force (which has primary operational responsibility for most military UAV activities) can instead train more operators of drone aircraft. In fact, in recent years, the Air Force has put more drone "pilots" through training than manned aircraft pilots.

Not only are UAVs force multipliers, they also permit the armed forces to conduct military operations that were heretofore impossible or highly risky or problematical. Effectively removing sanctuaries for terrorist and other leaders removes one of their sources of safety and one of their advantages as asymmetrical warriors. Terrorist groups, for instance, have become quite adept at electronic means to coordinate and communicate among themselves, and those very capabilities (cell phones, for instance) now allow western opponents to locate them and to dispatch drone and other capabilities to eliminate them. The result has been to make life much more uncertain for developing world opponents and has even caused them to quit using many of the communications devices that have allowed them to prosper in recent years.

For all these reasons, drone capabilities have become one of the true "darlings" of the modern military in its attempt to deal with DWICs. Certainly at the tactical level, UAVs have proven to be a valuable asset—in some ways a game changer. Technological advances are almost certain to allow the development of countermeasures that will render them less decisive, and it is central to the philosophy of asymmetrical warfare to develop means to obviate their effectiveness. Drones are the wave of the present, but their impact will undoubtedly change and probably decrease somewhat over time. While their effectiveness is basically unchallenged, however, they will remain a major part of operational response to the international threat environment.

The Limits and Disadvantages of Drones

Unpiloted aerial vehicles are currently in vogue for all the reasons already suggested, but they are also not without critics. The major criticism of drones is political, and it has both an international and a domestic political component. These components are separate, both in content and in import, but they do overlap enough to merit consideration.

The primary national security concerns about drone warfare come from the foreign countries in which their use is proposed or conducted. These objections tend to be of two sources, and while some of their content may be as largely for domestic consumption in the countries raising them, they are nonetheless consistent and not inconsequential.

The first objection is that many of these attacks are carried out without the permission of the host governments of the countries where they occur. Launching a Predator drone carrying active munitions at a target in Pakistan, for instance, can occur from almost anywhere. In this real example, the UAVs are *always* initiated from outside Pakistani territory, for the simple reason that the Pakistan government forbids stationing UAVs on their soil and would object vociferously if the U.S. military were to initiate drone strikes against Pakistani targets from Pakistani bases.

The official objection that these foreign governments have is that these attacks represent direct violations of Pakistani sovereignty, because the weapons fly through sovereign Pakistani airspace without the permission of the government of the country. This objection is entirely valid under international law, and were another country to attempt similar actions in the United States, the reaction of the American government would be overwhelming. Part of the context of these objections is that many developing countries, not that long removed from colonial bondage, are extremely sensitive about issues of their sovereignty, as are their people. Indeed, when the United States has carried out drone strikes in the remote territories of Pakistan along the Afghan border to attrite Taliban and Al Qaeda elements enjoying sanctuary among fellow Pashtun tribesmen, it has been political opponents of the government (and the United States) that have been most vocal in their criticism of these violations of sovereignty.

There is a certain amount of disingenuousness, even hypocrisy, in some of these representations that both the U.S. and Pakistan governments recognize. In some ways, the "sovereignty card" is little more than an act of political cover: the Pakistan government would also like to eliminate the targets of the drones, but it lacks both the physical capabilities to do so (many of the rugged locations are barely accessible on the ground, making them ideal drone targets). They may covertly support what the United States is doing, but cannot admit it in public. Much of the same dynamic has been true in Yemen, where the government has officially condemned but unofficially applauded much of the drone campaign the United States has waged against Al Qaeda in the Arabian Peninsula (AQAP) in the inaccessible mountainous outback of that country.

This objection is worth noting partly because of its applicability to the situation in Syria. When the United States first proposed the air campaign against ISIS(L) in Syria, one question was the reaction of the Syrian government. Would the U.S. propose some form of cooperation with the Assad regime to deal with this threat? Would the Syrians permit American intrusion into their air space, or would they oppose incursions? The short answer (elaborated in the next chapter) is that the Syrians did not trust the United States (which had, after all, been trying to overthrow them for three years at that point) and said they would consider American incursions over Syria a violation of Syrian sovereignty. This rejection implied that the government might try to interdict American military aircraft, but this possibility was rejected because Syrian air defenses, formidable where they are in place, are basically non-existent in the eastern regions facing Iraq, from which most of the attacks were launched.

The more serious foreign objection to American UAV activities has surrounded the collateral damage that inevitably is a byproduct of these forays. Aerial attacks in the form of dropping precision munitions on enemy targets are the heart of the active military uses of these weapons. The United States goes to great lengths to identify and discriminate target areas to avoid attacking non-hostile objects in the target area, but such attempts are imperfect. The inevitable result is that some bombs land in places they were not intended, and the result is civilian deaths and the destruction of property. Using the antiseptic term collateral damage to describe these unintended, unintentional events does little to assuage those who happen to be the unwitting victims of these attacks.

The collateral damage phenomenon creates several problems. First, it enrages the governments where it occurs, because it means the United States is killing their citizens, and those citizens express their outrage to their governments. Former Afghan president Hamid Karzai was particularly vocal in expressing this concern. Second, one of the effects of the resulting deaths is to make enemies of the surviving family and friends of those inadvertently killed. There is an old Pashtun proverb (the Pashtuns are the largest ethnic group in Afghanistan) that says, "Kill one enemy, make ten more." The result of attacking and killing some of the enemy (the purpose of the attacks) may, in other words, create more opponents than it eliminates. Third and related, collateral damage is tremendous propaganda fodder for those the United States opposes, and since the U.S. is often aligned with the government in power, the criticism may extend to added opposition to the government and the creation of even more enemies than one already had. Fourth, one common response to those who are targeting by drone attacks is to imbed themselves within the population, making it even more difficult to attack them without incurring civilian casualties.

Proponents of drone warfare do not, of course, see these problems as insurmountable. They tend to point to increasingly rigorous attempts to reduce levels of collateral damage and to argue that despite the admitted occurrence of some unintended civilian suffering, on balance the effects have been overwhelmingly positive. Almost all of the criticism on these grounds, moreover, come from governments in the countries involved and thus do not tend to make it very loudly into American debates on the subject. Nonetheless, the collateral damage problem will continue to remain at least a minor thorn in the side of drone planners.

Some of the suspicions and rejoinders about the use of drones have spilled over into the domestic sector. Most of these are concentrated on alleged violations of civil rights by invading the privacy of American citizens who are subject to suspected drone surveillance, and these objections have some national security implications. The reason is that many of these alleged activities (most of them are classified and clandestine) are conducted by federal agencies with national security responsibilities and with national security purposes. Until the latter part of 2014, when the Obama administration issued guidelines regulating the use of drones within the sovereign territory of the United States, these activities have remained essentially unregulated.

Most of the suspicions about the use of UAVs by government inside American territory come from issues of potential invasion of privacy. A variety of federal agencies already have drone-based programs, including the Department of Defense, the Justice Department (mostly the Federal Bureau of Investigation), and the Department of Homeland Security, all of which have national security mandates. In addition, the National Aeronautical and Space Agency, the Interior Department, and the Commerce Department have smaller programs involving UAVs.

Arguments about applications of drones to domestic uses parallel broader concerns raised about efforts undertaken as part of the national response to 9/11. The lightning rod for such concerns was the so-called PATRIOT (an acronym for Provide Appropriate Tools Required to Intercept and Obstruct Terrorists) Act of 2001, which granted wide powers to the federal government to collect clandestinely obtained information and to interrupt the activities of Americans suspected of terrorist-related activities. These activities included intrusive invasions of privacy without obtaining authorization from judges, and safeguards against such questionable activities are included in the guidelines for their use over American sovereign territory.

The use of pilotless aircraft remains an alluring and yet partially controversial national security topic. UAVs clearly have utility as force multipliers, and technological advancements will undoubtedly make them even more effective in the future. They do allow the military to perform tasks that were heretofore difficult or impossible to accomplish without them, and they do so without endangering the lives of American military personnel. These advantages provide them with strong support within the military arms of national security. At the same time, foreign governments over whose territories they operate have strong, legitimate issues with American drone activities, and their increasing domestic use raises questions of their impingement on fundamental American rights. For the time being, the advantages seem to outweigh the disadvantages, and drones will continue to be an active component of the American national security arsenal.

The Continuing Long Shadow of Terrorism

The specter of terrorist attacks on U.S. soil has hung ominously over Americans since the awful assault by Al Qaeda on New York and Washington, DC on September 11, 2001. Dealing with that threat has been the central concern of the American national security community ever since, in some ways occupying a conceptually unifying replacement for the communist threat of the Cold War. The terrorist enemy, however, is more elusive and ephemeral than its Soviet predecessor. There has not been a successful terrorist action on American soil since the assaults on the Trade Towers and the Pentagon, although some smaller attacks have been attempted. Moreover, the content and immediacy of the threat have proven elusive: Al Qaeda as it existed in 2001 essentially is gone, but it has been replaced by other permutations, some arguably as formidable as the original foe.

The emergence of ISIS(L) and the Al Qaeda offshoot Khorasan Group in 2014 returned the terrorist threat to the highly public agenda and to center stage of the national security agenda. Without a terrorist component potentially aimed directly at the United States, it is likely that the emergence of both ISIS(L) and Khorasan would have been treated as lesser threats (less-than-vital) to the United States, and that debate about what to do about them would have been more contained in abstract geopolitical or humanitarian terms. The fact that both espoused ambitions to do direct harm to the United States elevated their importance as national security questions.

Terrorism is both a very old and complex problem, the roots of which are generally dated back to Biblical times. As a phenomenon, terrorism has been a part of the fabric of international relations for over two millennia, but its impact has neither been uniform nor identical. A large body of literature has developed on the subject (some of which is included in the bibliography at the end of the chapter) and cannot be adequately summarized here. Rather, the rest of this section will be devoted to a brief overview of the nature of the terrorist threat and some attempt to summarize the current terrorist predicament facing the country.

The Nature of the Terrorist Threat

Prior to September 11, 2001, terrorism was barely on the American public radar. It received some attention among specialists within the national security community (who had, among other things, been warning about Al Qaeda for some years before the attacks), but their warnings were generally duly noted but not acted upon particularly. There had been a few instances of terrorist activity in the United States (e.g. the assassination of President James Garfield by anarchists in 1881), and the actions of Timothy McVeigh in attacking the Murrah Federal Building in Oklahoma City in 1995 were a recent reminder, but these attacks were generally by small, isolated groups of so-called "lone wolves," and were treated as aberrations within the system.

The 9/11 attacks sent the public and its government into a frenzy of activity about terrorism that continues to this day. In the immediate wake of 9/11, there was a great deal of national fear and confusion about the nature of the threat, and this prompted a great deal of governmental actions, from the passage of the PATRIOT Act to the establishment of a Department of Homeland Security purportedly to coordinate and lead the ensuing "war on terror" declared by President George W. Bush.

Understanding the terrorist problem requires taking a step back from the immediate cacophony that surrounded the reaction to 9/11. After that fateful day, the terrorism threat seemed ubiquitous, and a confused governmental response did little to allay this confusion. Everything that happened was suddenly viewed as potential terrorism, and the most drastic measures were considered and in some cases adopted to deal with it. The hurried, arguably ill-conceived rushes to war in Afghanistan and Iraq are examples.

What exactly is terrorism? Definitions abound, and reiterating them goes beyond present purposes (some discussion is found in the various editions of Donald M. Snow, *Cases in International Relations*). For present purposes, terrorism can be defined as *the commission of atrocious acts against a target population, normally to gain compliance with some demands the terrorists insist upon.* As such, terrorism is a political act not dissimilar to acts of war, which share a common goal of accomplishing some political end. They differ mainly in that they generally consist of illegal acts of violence and mayhem that are not sanctioned by any society and that they are committed by small, generally weak groups lacking either the popular support or strength to accomplish their goals in any other way. Terrorism is not the tool of the powerful; rather, it is a particularly unconventional tactic of asymmetrical warfare. It has been generally true throughout the history of terrorism that although powerful political units—governments, for instance—may from time to time resort to acts of terror, systematic uses of terror tend to be evidence of the weakness and lack of broad appeal of terrorist groups, not of strength. It is also true that terrorists rarely act "for the hell of it" (to borrow from 1970s activist Abbie Hoffman's description of revolution) but because they seek some tangible political outcome. That outcome may be obscure and not easily recognized, but generally successful efforts to combat terrorism take this fact into account.

Terrorism has existed as a method for a long time. Historians of the subject generally refer to the Zealots, who opposed the Romans in the first century AD and who martyred themselves at Masada, as the first recognizable terrorist group, and terrorism has been a recurring phenomenon ever since. Modern terrorism (including the use of the term) is normally associated with Robespierre's "Reign of Terror" during the latter stages of the French Revolution. Terrorism has been carried out both by sectarian groups for religious purposes by followers of all the world's major Western religions at different times, as well as by strictly secular groups with secular agendas. Terrorism is a method, even a methodology, not an ideology.

What this suggests is a relationship between terrorism as a phenomenon and terrorists and the organizations they represent. Terrorism as a method has endured through time for a simple reason: it works. For groups with a radical goal that is not widely accepted, it may be the only way that they have to be heard and possibly to succeed. In fact, terrorists are rarely successful in achieving the ultimate goals they espouse, but terrorism does provide them a method by which they can publicize and pursue their goals when no other method would permit even that. Terrorists and terrorist organizations, however, are rarely enduring. Terrorists do not succeed, and generally they are either suppressed or wear out. While they may commit considerable mayhem when they are active, individual terrorists come and go. Only terrorism abides.

Contemporary terrorism is, of course, mostly associated with adherents of radical interpretations of Islam. In most cases, their stated purposes have included religious purification and the political establishment of a truly Islamic order—the Caliphate. In addition to being directed at non-Muslim outsiders (heretics), their actions have also been directed at adherents of other sects of Islam considered impure or misdirected. This internecine aspect of the phenomenon adds to the difficulty outsiders have both in understanding the movements and, most importantly in terms of combating it, in terms of picking "goof guys" and likely winners in particular terrorist-based conflicts, such as that being waged currently over Iraq and Syria.

Because some of the terrorist rage is directed at the United States and Americans, it has been the object of a concerted effort by the United States government, which correctly identifies the problem as a national security concern. The activities undertaken to combat terrorism fall into two conceptual categories: anti-terrorism and counter-terrorism. The two terms are sometimes used more or less interchangeably, which confuses both concepts. Both have some conventional, military component, but the problem of terrorism is a semi-military problem, not a threat that can be reduced or destroyed by military means alone.

The first means is *anti-terrorism*. This term refers to primarily defensive efforts to reduce vulnerability to terrorist attacks and to lessen the effects of attacks when they do succeed. Efforts to make it more difficult for terrorists to enter the country—strict enforcement of regulations on entry through airports or reinforcing borders—are examples. Making public buildings bomb-resistant by requiring that they not be built near streets (where bomb-laden vehicles might park) is another. Most of this effort is non-military and is assigned to law enforcement or customs officials. Securing the Mexican border is a semi-military task. The other means is *counter-terrorism*. This term refers to offensive and military efforts against terrorists or their sponsoring agencies to prevent, deter, or respond to terrorist attacks. Counter-terrorism is more proactive than anti-terrorist actions and can include significant military involvement. The entire drone campaign in the Middle East is largely counter-terrorist, although it is a responsibility shared by the military and the Central Intelligence Agency.

Efforts to deal with individual terrorist threats necessarily combine military and non-military components. Terrorism is philosophically a form of asymmetrical warfare, and like other variants, it has a sizable political component. One can try to beat such a movement into submission, but one of the purposes of asymmetrical warfare is to avoid such decimation. The heart of any successful terrorism suppression must combine the degradation of terrorist violent capabilities with undercutting of the appeal of the terrorists to whatever political base they have. As campaigns against other asymmetrical foes have shown, military force in and of itself is not an efficient or effective way to accomplish this latter task. Indeed, it is not at all clear that outsiders can convince those fanatical enough to engage in terrorism to surrender their causes and methods.

The Current Predicament

The terrorist threat today is different than it was in 2001, and it will continue to adapt and change in the future. That fact is important because it helps sharpen the contrast between the Cold War period that remains the basis for the current national security paradigm and because it means that whatever framework that replaces the Cold War construct will have to take a changing environment and the need for flexibility into account.

One of the comforting simplicities of the Cold War period was that its major dynamics did not change much. The interests that came into conflict remained basically constant, and the threat tended to change at the tactical margins (particular categories of weapons balances, for instance), whereas the underlying menace remained constant. This meant that the risk reduction equation did not change fundamentally either. The result was stability and constancy, but it came with a price. Since change was not built into the worldview, it was not conceptually prepared for nor particularly capable of adapting to the fundamental change of the collapse of operational communism.

The contemporary environment stands in sharp contrast to the recent past. Since 1991, change has been the most prominent element in the national security environment: the interests, the threats, and responses to those threats seem constantly to change. Yesterday's Soviet threat was also today's and tomorrow's during the Cold War; predicting future sources of threat in the current environment is much more daunting.

The changing nature of the national security predicament is nowhere more obvious than in the terrorism area. Prior to 9/11, terrorism was a minor, peripheral part of national security planning, and it was dramatically thrust into a centrality for which national security mechanisms were largely unprepared. The threat posed by the original Al Qaeda terrorist organization has effectively been destroyed, most prominently illustrated by the successful assassination of its founder, Osama bin Laden, in May 2011. Beheading the beast did not kill it, however. Instead, spinoffs (sometimes call franchises or affiliates) have appeared elsewhere: Al Qaeda in the Arabian Peninsula (AQAP) in Yemen and Al Qaeda in Iraq (AQI), to cite two prominent examples. American counter-terrorism efforts managed to remove both these leaders "from the board" (American-born Anwar al-Awlaki in Yemen and Jordanian-born Abu Musab Zarqawi in Iraq), but both of their organizations live on. Most prominently, ISIS(L) and the Khorasan Group have both been linked to Zarqawi and AQI as their roots in public discussions since 2014.

Most terrorism experts now refer to the current terrorism threat as being more "diffuse" than it was in 2001. What this basically means is that there is no single group as large and well organized as Al Qaeda was, and thus as capable of direct action against the United States. The fact that no outside terrorist attack has occurred since 2001 (although a few "lone wolf" attacks have been tried) speaks both to this structural change in the threat and to the success of American terrorism suppression operations since 2001. Whether ISIS(L) can and will grow to pose a direct threat on American soil is a question currently driving American consideration of military actions in Iraq and Syria.

The terrorist threat will continue to change and thereby make national security planning more complicated than it would be otherwise. The current focus of national security planning, examined in some detail in the next chapter, has been the Levant area, and although that focus may shift somewhat, the Middle East is likely to remain the seedbed of much of the terrorist and other concerns the country will face and with which it must come to effective grips. If the center of the terrorist challenge moves away from the intersection of access to the petroleum reserves of the Persian Gulf region and American attachment to Israel, the calculation of American interests may require rethinking as well: are American interests as affected by terrorist instability and violence in eastern Africa as they are with the same kind of violence in the Middle East? If the answer is no and is accompanied by a reduced American physical presence near terrorist hot spots, will the United States not seem as much of a threat to the terrorists, meaning they will feel a reduced need to confront the United States? If the latter is the case, will the risks that the U.S. encounters and with which it must deal be simplified or reduced? All these questions are, of course, largely speculative and unanswerable in a state of great change within the terrorist problem itself. They are, however, critical questions with which an adequate framework to guide American national security efforts must come to grips in the future.

Influences on National Security Planning

The three factors having an impact on how America thinks about and plans for its national security future are not the only factors that will influence how a new framework emerges. As noted, there are other candidates that could have been included, including such things as information and cyber warfare, the emergence of China as a major military counterweight to the United States, even an increasingly cutthroat competition for natural resources like energy or changes in global ecology. The three raised, however, are immediate and concrete variables that are both illustrative and arguably among the most important external influences on the shape of policy to come.

The first of these, military manpower, is the one over which the American political system has the most power, if not necessarily political will. If flexibility emerges as a major priority for the future, one area where that might be most obvious will be in the ability to expand or contract the size of the armed forces with which the United States faces current and future crises. Clearly, the all-volunteer system has its advantage in terms of the quality of the personnel it recruits and maintains, and it has overwhelming political support, since it relieves elected officials of potentially making the extremely unpopular decision to conscript young men against their wills.

The great disadvantage is flexibility: the AVF can be made smaller (although doing so would force kicking people out of the force who want to stay and potentially adding to national unemployment statistics), but it cannot be made much bigger than it is right now. As long as America's military tasks remain constrained enough to accommodate the present size, manpower is not an issue. If the United States faces a situation where it might require a larger force than can be raised voluntarily, there is a problem with only two solutions: abandon the mission or abandon the sanctity of an all-volunteer force. It is not a prospect political actors or national security planners want to confront, but it is a parameter on what the United States can do. It is also a matter that should be decided before one is confronted with an urgent situation that raises it.

Unmanned Aerial Vehicles used as bombers or for reconnaissance missions have become the weapon *du jour* in the war against terror and in DWIC situations where it is impossible or too hazardous to conduct either of those missions in other ways. Finding and getting to AQAP in the rugged, forbidding Yemeni Mountains probably cannot be accomplished by any other currently available method, and the use of drones in hostile areas like Syria removes the danger of U.S. pilots being shot down, captured, and displayed on global social media. The problem of collateral damage remains and is probably unsolvable in any absolute way that avoids civilian deaths altogether, so they will remain points of contention with the governments in whose territory they are employed. It is probably just a matter of time until counter-UAV technologies will permit the discovery, tracking, and interdiction of these weapons, at which point warfare against asymmetrical foes will require some new technological fix to re-establish advantage.

Terrorism endures. As a method of asymmetrical warfare, it will continue to be chosen by those with no other alternative as long as it is effective. After 2,000 years of trying, no foolproof method of destroying those employing it has been devised, and until there is, the fanatic and desperate will, in some cases, continue to turn to the methodology. The best one can do is to try to contain the effectiveness of actors employing the method, attrite them as best possible, and wait for particular groups to wither and disappear, knowing they will be replaced at some point by others.

What these three influences all illustrate is the complexity and complication surrounding recourse to military solutions to contemporary situations. Were the threat and the need to counter it as compelling today as they were in 1941, none of these would matter. The manpower problem would be solved by simply requiring all the able-bodied men needed to provide an adequate force to serve; the difference would be that women would be included this time. No one cared much about anything like collateral damage during World War II, since it was assumed everyone in the enemy country was a hostile, and thus most means to subdue them were acceptable. Acts of terror would have been suppressed ruthlessly. A few might have objected to some of the measures taken, but fighting a war of necessity removes ambiguity about national purpose.

There are no situations like 1941 on the present agenda or on the horizon. When was the last war of necessity fought by the United States? Situations today are dangerous, and they potentially have high stakes, but how often are vital interests engaged to the point that drastic measures could be taken and accepted? Would Americans accept a return to conscription to eradicate ISIS(L)? How many civil liberties are Americans willing to accept in the name of combatting terror? The situational universe is more complex and the problems less consensually compelling than they once were. Other influences are bound to enter the conversation and to place real constraints on policy responses.

Bibliography

Anderson, Martin (ed.). *The Military Draft: Selective Readings on Conscription.* Stanford, CA: Hoover Institution Press, 1968.

Bacevich, Andrew J. *The New American Militarism: How Americans Are Seduced by War.* New York: Oxford University Press, 2013.

Bailey, Beth. *America's Army: Making the All-Volunteer Force.* New York: Belknap Press, 2009.

Baskin, Lawrence M., and William A. Strauss. *Chance and Circumstance: The Draft, the War, and the Vietnam Generation.* New York: Random House, 1978.

Brusard, Jean-Charles. *Zarqawi: The New Face of Al-Qaeda.* New York: Other Press LLC, 2005.

Burke, Jason. "Think Again: Al Qaeda." *Foreign Policy,* May/June 2004, 18–26.

Clarke, Richard A. *Sting of the Drone.* New York: Thomas Dunne Books, 2014.

Cronin, Audrey Kurth. *How Terrorism Ends: Understanding the Decline and Demise of Terrorist Campaigns.* Princeton, NJ: Princeton University Press, 2011.

Cronin, Audrey Kurth, "Sources of Contemporary Terrorism." In Audrey Kurth Cronin and James M. Ludes (eds), *Attacking Terrorism: Elements of a Grand Strategy.* Washington, DC: Georgetown University Press, 2004.

Dershowitz, Alan M. *Why Terrorism Works: Understanding the Threat, Responding to the Challenge.* New Haven, CT: Yale University Press, 2002.

Evangelista, John, and Henry Shue (eds). *The American Way of Bombing: Changing Ethical and Legal Norms, from Flying Fortresses to Drones.* Ithaca, NY: Cornell University Press, 2014.

Flynn, George Q. *The Draft: 1940–1973.* Lawrence, KS: University of Kansas Press, 1973.

Foley, Michael Stewart. *Confronting the War Machine: Draft Resistance during the Vietnam War.* Chapel Hill, NC: University of North Carolina Press, 2003.

Gardner, Lloyd C. *Killing Machine: The American Presidency in the Age of Drone Warfare.* New York: New Press, 2013.

Gilroy, Curtis L., Barbara A. Bickster, and John T. Warner. *The All-Volunteer Force: Thirty Years of Service.* Washington, DC: Potomac Books, 2004.

Hoffman, Bruce. *Inside Terrorism.* 2nd edn. New York: Columbia University Press, 2006.

Howard, Russell, and Bruce Hoffman. *Terrorism and Counterterrorism: Understanding the New Environment, Readings and Interpretations.* New York: McGraw-Hill/Dushkin, 2011.

Jenkins, Brian. "International Terrorism." In Robert J. Art and Kenneth N. Waltz (eds), *The Use of Force: Military Power and International Politics.* New York: Rowman and Littlefield Publishers, 2004.

Kaag, John, and Sarah Kreps. *Drone Warfare (WCMW—Warfare and Conflict in the Modern World).* New York: Polity Press, 2014.

Kaplan, Fred. "The U.S. Military's Manpower Crisis." *Foreign Affairs* 85, 4 (July/August 2006), 97–110.

Marmion, H. A. *Selective Service: Conflict and Compromise.* New York: John Wiley and Sons, 1968.

Medea, Benjamin, and Barbara Ehrenreich. *Drone Warfare: Killing by Remote Control.* New York: Verso Books, 2013.

Nacos, Brigette. *Terrorism and Counterterrorism: Understanding Threats and Responses in the Post-9/11 World.* New York: Penguin Academics, 2006.

Rogers, Anna, and John Hill. *Unmanned: Drone Warfare and Global Security.* London: Pluto Press, 2014.

Rostker, Bernard. *I Want You: The Evolution of the All-Volunteer Force.* Santa Monica, CA: RAND Corporation, 2006.

Singer, P. W. *Wired for War: The Robotics Revolution and Warfare in the 21st Century.* New York: Penguin Books, 2009.

Sloan, Stephen. *Beating International Terrorism: An Action Strategy for Preemption and Punishment.* Montgomery, AL: Air University Press, 2000.

Snow, Donald M. *September 11, 2001: The New Face of War?* New York: Longman, 2002.

Snow, Donald M. *Cases in International Relations.* 6th edn. New York: Pearson, 2014.

Stern, Jessica, and J. M. Berger. *Terrorism in the Name of God: Why Religious Militants Kill.* New York: ECCO Books, 2003.

Stern, Jessica, and J. M. Berger. *ISIS: The State of Terror.* New York: ECCO Books, 2015.

White, Jonathan R. *Terrorism and Homeland Security.* 7th edn. New York: Cengage, 2011.

Whittle, Richard. *Predator: The Secret Origins of the Drone Revolution.* New York: Henry Holt and Company, 2014.

Williams, Brian Glyn. *Predator: The CIA's Drone War on Al Qaeda.* Washington, DC: Potomac Books, 2013.

Zenko, Micah. *Reforming U.S. Drone Strike Policies* (Council Special Report). New York: Council on Foreign Relations, 2013.

6 The Syrian Microcosm

The Middle East has come to represent the perfect storm of all the instability and violence in the developing world. It is a maelstrom of internal blood feuds and fighting that are so fundamental and deep that it is not clear how or when they will end. Except for those doing the actual fighting and killing, virtually everyone else peers over the edge of the whirlpool, unwilling or unsure about whether to become involved, what form their involvement might take, and whether their involvement might make a positive difference.

The maelstrom has been building for thousands of years. Within the region itself, many of the blood feuds are tribal, between groups who have been fighting and killing one another at least since Biblical times, and the inability of these groups to work out their differences makes it virtually impossible to bring political order to the region. Layered on top of these cleavages is the pernicious effect of sectarian differences within the dominant religion of the region, Islam. The bases for bloodshed are ancient and deeply held by the various faithful, and religious explanations rationalize many of their animosities and legitimize their blood lust. Artificial political boundaries imposed by the retreating European colonial powers exacerbate the situation.

The current vortex of the storm centers on the Levant, a historically contentious body of land that encompasses most of contemporary Syria, and parts of Turkey, Lebanon, Jordan, Palestine, and Israel, and it has been extended to Iraq in recent years. The term was not frequently invoked until recently, when the source of the most egregious irritation, the Islamic State, announced its intention to establish a caliphate there, a religious state headed by a "successor" to Mohammed (the term "caliph" means successor). The IS movement has eclipsed the Syrian Civil War as the epicenter of international concern in the region, mostly because the success of this traditional terrorist group turned territorial state aspirant has been so striking and accompanied by such spectacular, repulsive violence.

The crisis in the Levant is worth examining in some detail in this introduction to American national security policy for at least two reasons. First, it is the prototypical, even stereotypical DWIC, exhibiting all of the characteristics that make involvement in such conflicts so tempting, intriguing, and forbidding. The confusion over how the United States should respond, especially to the IS aspect of this crisis, has been partly the result of the fact that this country has no real conceptual lens through which it can assess how, as a general or specific situation, the United States should view potential involvement. In other parts of the crisis in the Middle East in places like Iraq and Afghanistan, the United States has basically made up its response on the fly, and it may well again. What it decides and how that works out will influence the future. Second, this crisis is such a perfect storm that its resolution (at least from an American standpoint) could provide valuable lessons for dealing with the DWIC maelstroms of the future.

The examination will proceed in two chronological steps. It will begin with the Syrian Civil War. That conflict began as part of the largely now-forgotten Arab Spring. In 2011, when the Arab Spring spread through the region, there was great hope that it would turn to a bright summer of expanding, modernizing national, even democratizing, self-expression in the region's countries. In places like Syria where the influences of the ancient past made such an emergence problematical at best, it instead turned into a winter of tribal and sectarian bloodletting that, while not so well publicized currently in the public spotlight as the successor concern with IS, goes on abated.

The second step is the emergence and threat posed by the IS. The two are loosely related. IS, the successor of Al Qaeda in Iraq (AQI), became involved in and an increasingly powerful part of the Sunni opposition to the Shiite Assad regime in Syria, and that opposition proved fertile recruitment grounds for IS. A not insignificant part of the caliphate is IS-controlled territory in Syria. At the same time, the outcome of the war with IS could easily affect the eventual outcome in Syria as well.

Syria and Iraq are the bookends of the physical crisis. In some ways, their centrality is symbolic of the divisions of the region, the bases for many of the DWICs in the world, and the dilemmas facing the United States as it tries to understand and cope with these threats to world stability. These differences can be conveniently grouped around three observations: their internal bases are ethnic and religious; they occur in artificial states that are the product of decolonization; and these conflicts were neither created by nor can they be solved through the application of American force.

First, internally, the countries are virtual mirrors of one another in terms of causes of conflict. Most of those bases are ethnic and religious, and both are present in both countries. In Syria, the minority Alawite tribe, a group that practices a form of Shiite Islam, rules over the Sunni Arab majority (although that majority itself is tribally divided). In Iraq before the American invasion of 2003, the government was run by the Sunni minority whose leader, Saddam Hussein, came from a tribe located in and around Tikrit, and they ruled over the Shiite majority and Kurdish minority. In both mirror-like cases, the substantive heart of conflict is ethnic/tribal and religious.

Second, they occur in artificial states. They are artificial in the sense of containing multiple groups with more loyalty to their ethnic/tribal/religious group than to the state. In both the cases of Iraq and Syria, their imperfection was largely the result of how the victorious allies of World War I (principally Britain and France through the Sykes Picot Agreement) carved up the Ottoman Empire. The divisions resulted in interwar occupations and post-World War II independence for political units which, in the form they gained independence, did not make much sense.

Third, the United States was not a prominent part of any of these problems and cannot "solve" them for the parties. The ethnic/tribal roots of conflict go back to antiquity, and the religious bases date back to the aftermath of the death of Mohammed in 632. Both are deeply ingrained in the psyches of the people of the region, and they represent differences that only the internal parties can possibly address or solve. American armed force, the often-suggested "solution," can offer no more than a temporary respite in the violence or tip the military balance temporarily in the direction of one side or another. It cannot heal the major schisms that give rise to the violence.

Syrian Origins of the Current Crisis

In 2012 and especially in 2013, the tragedy in Syria became a caricature of the world's dilemma for dealing with global instability in the global system. It was a distillation of many of the worst conditions that have led to DWICs in the contemporary world, thereby spotlighting and concentrating all the dilemmas and temptation such situations create both internally and for outside parties like the United States. In a specifically American context, it reflected both the deep and apparently abiding divisions within the American body politic and how those fissures make fashioning either a coherent domestic or foreign policy virtually impossible. The Syrian crisis seems destined to continue for a long time with uncertain outcomes. It has also proved the nurturing ground for broader instability in the Levant, specifically the IS crisis.

At the risk of some oversimplification, the Syrian civil war began as a tribal and ethnic conflict with religious overtones that has become something wider, more profound, and much more deadly. Since Bashar al-Assad's father Hafiz came to power in 1968, the Shiite Alawite minority (about 10 percent of the population) has effectively ruled Syria. Members of this tribe, who come from the northern coastal part of the country, have positioned themselves in places of authority and power in both the military and the government. For decades they ruled with the tacit approval of the Sunni business community that controls most of the economy. That coalition began to break down after the ascent of Bashar following his father's death in 2001, and in 2011, inspired by the Arab Spring, civil war broke out as unhappy Sunnis objected to Bashar's rule and he responded by unleashing the military against Sunni strongholds like the city of Aleppo. This in turn produced the development of a series of resistance movements that operated mostly in isolation from one another; IS became the most prominent of these.

Attempts to quell the uprising have been harsh from the beginning and have received ample international condemnation. Supporters of both sides emerged from outside Syria to assist the side they favored. Shiite Iran quickly came to the Assad regime's assistance, followed by Iranian-influenced Hezbollah. Russia, Syria's historic patron in the region (it is the only country to host a Russian military base outside Russia), has guaranteed a supply of arms and a shield against potentially painful UN Security Council penalties. Sunni neighbors like Saudi Arabia, Turkey, and Jordan came to the aid of different rebel factions, and along the way, the rebels attracted the participation of supporters of Al Qaeda in Iraq that became the core of IS.

These events become a problem for international politics, and thus for American foreign policy, when internal violence spirals out of control, as it did in Syria. Civil conflicts often reach such proportions: the division between population segments becomes so deep, or is fanned to the point that violence becomes desperate and often hideous. Civil wars are inherently desperate affairs, because the fate of the losers is often problematical and predictably bleak—the stakes are very high. When civil wars occur between population groups with no positive interpersonal or intergroup ties to moderate their actions, that violence can lose all restraint, and the result is often human horror of gross proportions. That level of desperation and resultant atrocity has been part of the Syrian situation virtually since war broke out in 2011. It accelerated with the use of chemical weapons against the Syrian population in 2013.

When violence reaches such atrocious proportions, it becomes an unavoidable international problem in the modern world. Atrocity often manifests itself in inhuman acts by contending groups against one another, and specifically against parts of the population incapable of defending themselves. This atrocity is increasingly clear in an electronically transparent environment where crimes against humanity are increasingly difficult to hide. Prior to World War II, such actions were viewed simply as regrettable. That is no longer true. The massive attempts by the Nazis to extinguish the Jews, Gypsies, and others transcended human sensibilities and helped give rise to moral considerations that asserted there are certain human conditions which are inviolable and against which transgressions cannot be tolerated under any circumstances. International expressions included the various UN declarations on human rights, the outlawing of genocide, and expansion of definitions of things like the laws of war to forbid new categories of violence. Among the more recent additions to international prohibitions against atrocity is the Chemical Weapons Treaty of 1995 that forbids all employment of chemical weapons.

The internal conflicts in numerous developing world countries clash with these new norms. Generally speaking, these wars are fought between irregular fighting units or between national forces and irregulars, and one side or the other does not honor conventional norms of behavior in war, often routinely resorting to methods and actions that grossly violate international rules and understandings about acceptable fighting. They are, in other words, asymmetrical conflicts. The actions of terrorist groups are a caricature of this illegality, but terrorist organizations are not alone in practicing illegal acts of terror; in some cases, governments themselves may engage in these kinds of tactics as well. The Syrian government's use of chemical agents is case in point.

The International Dimension

The international problem is how to deal with this new category of breaches of the world order, and it comes down to a clash of the values of the traditional and more contemporary world orders. The traditional vantage point, reflecting the notion of inviolable sovereignty within states, is that even the grossest violations of humanity are not enough of the business of outsiders to warrant outside interference unless some specific interest of the outsider is affected by the outcome. Possible interference is a matter of determining the importance of outsider interests. In most developing world situations, those interests are less than vital, and stretching national interest claims in places like Iraq and Afghanistan has made many Americans leery of interest-based calls to intercede. The assertion of humanitarian reasons for intervention has become an alternative form of justification.

This distinction has been reflected in both the international and domestic debates over whether to interfere in the affairs of Syria, and has been extended to IS. The strongest arguments that have been made against outside involvement in the Syrian civil war have been based in national interest, a derivative of the sovereignty position. In essence, they maintain either (or both) of two points: that national interests are not sufficiently engaged to justify outside intervention in the outcome of the struggle; or that intervention is wrong, a violation of Syrian sovereignty. These negatives are reinforced by uncertainty about what the outcome, even with outside interference, might be (in other words, questions about whether intervention would work). Those who advocate interference, particularly after the documentation of Syrian government chemical weapons use against its own people, argued the moral position that such actions by the government violated such fundamental and overriding rights of the citizenry and represented crimes against humanity that can only be corrected by punishing the guilty parties—in this case the Assad government.

Deciding which argument had the greatest merit has been difficult. The realist, self-interest position is the traditional standard by which states have decided on courses of action, and that argument militates both against the violent violation of Syrian sovereignty and toward the assessment that not much in the interests of those who might interfere would be accomplished. It has become virtually a universal evaluation that there have never been any good options in Syria, only varyingly bad options and outcomes, none of which clearly serves the national interest of outsiders. Getting rid of Assad may be good; his replacements might be different but no better (or even worse). Similarly, even if one acts to relieve the humanitarian crisis in the country, it is not clear that a successor regime might not engage in the same kinds of atrocities against their former oppressors. The result could simply to switch the cast of war criminals and victims. The possibility that IS might replace Assad illustrates this concern in Syria.

Deciding which argument was persuasive would have been much easier if elements of both arguments did not have merit. Unfortunately, both do. Even the most ardent defender of sovereignty does not argue against interference on pre-World War II grounds, but the national interest extension of their position has merit. As has been widely argued and documented, it is not at all clear that any successor regime from the highly fragmented opposition would represent a real triumph for any outsider in the sense of becoming a reliable partner in which the interferer could take pride. More likely, the fall of Assad would result in the various rebel factions falling upon one another with one or another eventually prevailing. Whether the winner would pass the "smell test" is at best problematical. Overthrowing Assad would likely relieve the humanitarian suffering of Sunni victims, but it is not at all clear that the successor would not turn its wrath on the Alawites and other Shiites who have been associated with the atrocities.

The two positions are mutually exclusive conceptually, but in fact they have been intermingled in almost all advocacies on one side or the other of the issue (intervention or nonintervention). Virtually no one, for instance, argues exclusively for or against action on purely moral grounds, even though the moral basis is arguably the strongest basis for some form of action. At the same time, some opponents of action have argued close to the pure national interest position that the United States has essentially no interest in the outcome, but even these arguments generally concede the need for some assistance to those suffering on moral grounds. More generally, the positions are a mixture of the two arguments, with those who favor intervention generally emphasizing moral grounds but selectively adding national interest grounds that support their contention. The limited action taken by the UN to force Syria to divest itself of chemical stockpiles addressed both concerns. The moral atrocity of chemical weapons usage provided the impetus for some kind of action, but negative geopolitical determinations constrained those actions below levels that would have dictated a physical intervention to enforce.

If all of this is not confusing and difficult enough on its own, neither position has been unassailable. Both were derived in part from assessments of the empirical situation on the ground in Syria, about which there has been disagreement (the most frequent of which has been the existence or strength of a "moderate" component of the opposition). At the same time, assessments are extrapolations from their understanding of the facts, and these extrapolations added their own, subjective values, about which people can legitimately disagree. The level of activism one supports, for instance, reflects to some degree both the level of activism one feels the United States should adopt in the world, which is a subjective judgment. Finally, each of the arguments that are made both within moral and national interest arguments is arguable, not a matter of black and white clarity to all observers. The result is a witch's brew of bases of disagreement.

The arguments and permutations must be understood in this confused and confusing context, both because of their impact on resolving the issue and on why otherwise reasonable people disagreed so strongly on what to do about Syria. Having said that, the two arguments can be presented and laid out in the major forms in which they are found. Of the two, the moral argument is the more compact.

The Moral Argument. This argument is based on two premises; one of these is generally accepted and the other is contested. The first premise is that the most extreme acts committed in Syria, notably the use of chemical weapons against defenseless civilians, represent an unacceptable moral outrage that violates the most basic moral premises on which all societies are based. The second is that these moral outrages demand an international response to punish those who committed them and to insure the end of suffering by the victims.

Virtually no one disagrees that the use of chemical weapons represents a "moral outrage," to borrow a phrase used by U.S. Secretary of State John Kerry in an August 26, 2013 speech on the Syrian use of chemical weapons. The Chemical Weapons Treaty of 1995 (of which Syria is a non-signatory) specifically forbids the stockpiling of such weapons, let alone their use, which is generally included in descriptions of crimes against humanity, a war crime that can be prosecuted at the International Criminal Court (of which the United States is not a member). At a more general level, essentially all moral codes prohibit outrageous violence against defenseless civilians, an affront that falls under the category of general morality.

The second premise is more controversial: who, if anyone, has an obligation to punish those who violate moral norms? The question is more than academic, since if nobody has such an obligation, then moral standards do not represent consequential prohibitions because they cannot be enforced. Even among those who accept the existence of moral precepts, opinions vary regarding enforcement.

The strongest positive answer is found in something known as the "responsibility to protect" (R2P), a position taken by strong supporters of international obligation and described in some detail in Chapter 3. The heart of R2P is that the international community has an undeniable obligation to correct such situations. As a moral question, the reason for such an obligation was summed up by Kerry in an August 29, 2013 statement: we must act, he said because of "who we are."

Hardly anyone takes issue with this formulation in the abstract, but adopting it as a *personal* imperative is more difficult. One can, after all, accept that wrong-doing has occurred without accepting personal responsibility for righting the wrongs. Most moral codes require that one respond to violations of moral standards, but that such a demand does not extend to the situation where one may put oneself at personal risk to relieve the suffering of others. Both the Syrian and IS cases are of this nature. Actions by each have clearly violated standards of morality and deserve punishment, but it is questionable whether such a sacrifice is morally required or would be effective.

The Geopolitical/National Interest Argument. The moral arguments are straightforward and relatively unambiguous compared to arguments made about whether the United States should have intervened in Syria based on national interests. The general conclusions of national interest arguments have mostly opposed involvement, but there are arguments on both sides of that conclusion. Moreover, all arguments require judgments reflecting the values of the person making them and thus are subjective and the source of disagreement.

The negative arguments based in national interest have been more numerous than the positive arguments. In no particular order of importance or frequency of advocacy, there are at least six of these. The first and most fundamental is that the United States has no important interest in the outcome in Syria, a country in which the United States has had little historic influence or involvement. This position can be colloquially described as the United States has had "no dog in the fight" in the Syrian civil war. The major counter argument, described below, is that even if the U.S. has no direct interest, the outcome could radiate in negative ways to surrounding Middle Eastern countries like Jordan and Turkey where the United States does have national interests that could be adversely affected. The emergence of IS adds steam to this counter argument.

The second argument is that it is not clear there are parties (especially parties with any reasonable prospect of succeeding) that are worthy of American support. The constant search has been for so-called "moderates," a category largely undefined (what is a Syrian moderate?) or, more expansively, pro-democratic. Experience in Egypt has demonstrated that the search for groups with either of these pro-western characteristics may be very difficult to fulfill. Since there are also clearly radical, anti-western groups within the opposition (e.g. groups like IS), the final impact of assistance is questionable at best.

The third argument is closely related to the second, contending that the absence of compatible groups within the opposition means there are also probably no good outcomes to the conflict from an American vantage point. It has become axiomatic in discussing Syria that all options are likely to lead to bad outcomes and that choosing a policy option is looking for the least worst alternative. After Iraq and Afghanistan, is the American public willing to go to war to achieve the least bad outcome?

This dismal assessment of prospects extends to the assessment of close American allies, including adjacent powers like Turkey and European NATO allies with past involvements in pre-independence Syria like France and Great Britain. The lack of enthusiasm among others with greater geopolitical interest in what happens in Syria is a fourth geopolitical source of opposition. American behind-the-scenes attempts to create support among others have not produced obvious results, so why should the United States do what others will not? Some of this reasoning also applies to IS.

This reluctance is reinforced by the fifth argument, which arises from the precedent of the consequences of the American aid effort to Afghan rebels in their 1980s resistance to Soviet occupation. That assistance had the dual purposes of aiding the *mujahideen* in their anti-Soviet resistance and of causing geopolitical difficulties for the Soviets. It did contribute to the downward spiral and eventual disintegration of the Soviet Union, but it also had the undesirable effect of contributing (in generally unspecified ways) to the creation and sustenance both of the Taliban and Al Qaeda, since both were offshoots of the resistance. Given the uncertainty about the detailed intents of the various opposition groups in Syria, the possibility that assistance could end up in what might prove to be the wrong hands cannot be ignored or dismissed out of hand.

The sixth negative argument is that the United States simply could not "win" in Syria, regardless of what it did and how the conflict may end. The bases of this argument are extrapolated from the United States' experience in the three major military incursions in developing world internal conflicts (DWICs) since World War II: Vietnam, Iraq, and Afghanistan. The United States has a better record inserting itself in very limited ways for limited times and purposes (places like Panama, Grenada, and the Balkans) than in grand interventions, but no one believes that a successful U.S. operation in Syria or against IS could be short and limited. The United States hardly needs another similar failure on the heels of Iraq and Afghanistan.

National interest arguments have also been used to support some form of generally limited American action. There are three of these arguments worth mentioning. What is notable about all of these but the last is that they focus not so much on the outcome of Syria per se and its influence on American interests as they do on the negative effects different Syrian outcomes could have on other American interests.

The first argument is the precedent that American action or inaction in Syria will have in the region and elsewhere. This argument has become a virtual chestnut to justify actions that otherwise might seem less than compelling. Its core is that if Syria can flout American interests and threats, others will be encouraged to do so as well. The failure to act in Syria in 2012 or 2013 may have encouraged IS to believe it could act without fear of American reprisal.

The second argument is that what the United States does in Syria is a way of measuring American resolve in the world. It can be argued that some countries like Iran and North Korea might be tempted to conclude that American decision making resolve is so paralyzed by the gridlock of American politics that they can freely act, a perception that American inaction in Syria reinforces. Since the Obama administration has been subject to withering criticism on virtually anything it does on any issue, American enemies might be led to believe that American action or inaction in Syria is symptomatic of American reaction to actions they might take. Secretary Kerry has made this argument to bolster efforts to demonstrate American resolve.

The third argument is that the failure to take decisive action in Syria will lead to the Syrian violence spilling over and evolving into a regional conflict. One can argue that this has already occurred with the spread of the IS caliphate, although it is not at all clear that active American military efforts in Syria would have dampened the growth of IS. Since the presence of foreign forces can be an exacerbating influence on a basically internal conflict, the reverse may actually be the case.

All these geopolitical arguments have merits and drawbacks. Each represents an assessment of a factual situation that is imperfectly understood and an extrapolation into hypothetical futures of varying subjective concern depending on the personal assessment of the interpreter. A reasonable person can advocate any of these positions with some justification, and another person can equally reject each one of them reasonably as well. No matter what position one takes on Syria, it is likely to be attacked from both extremes, and there is simply no single position that is likely acceptable to all observers.

The Domestic Dimension

The domestic American political debate has generally been negative about a direct American military involvement in Syria, reflecting public sentiment. Much of the debate has begun from the poles of humanitarian obligation or geopolitical imperative. This distinction is rarely made starkly: hardly anyone proposes or opposes U.S. involvement in Syria strictly on one ground or the other. Rather, arguments on either side tend to be framed more in terms of one emphasis or the other, using the other argument as support for the basic contention.

Moral arguments, for instance, tend to emphasize the R2P logic that one must respond to human moral disasters in order to avoid revealing the applied vacancy of moral rules. These arguments, interestingly, tend to be reasonably pro-involvement. National interest-based rationales tend to reflect the negative side of the policy spectrum. At the extreme, moral entreaties disappear and negative assessments are based on the notion that the United States has no national interests, and especially the vital interests most realists maintain are necessary to justify the use of force, involved in the outcomes.

There are a few people who argue one extreme or the other as sole justification. Libertarians like Kentucky Senator Rand Paul have argued that involvement is to be avoided because what goes on in Syria is none of America's business, a very restrictive statement of the vital interests argument and one from which Paul has retreated. In practice, advocacies tend to mix moral and geopolitical arguments with varying degrees of passion and different levels of positivity or negativity. As a general rule, those who are opposed will argue most strongly one or more of the negative national interest arguments combined with one of the limitations on a moral obligation as a secondary consideration. Those who argue for some form of action will normally combine a moral basis with one of the positive arguments attached to a realist analysis.

Nothing resembling a consensus has emerged around any particular argument or policy position. When asked simple "yes-no" questions about whether they favor American intrusion in Syria, the American public consistently says they oppose involvement, especially military action on the ground. They voice no strong agreement on the basis of opposition other than a combined sense of war-weariness after Iraq and Afghanistan and a belief the United States could not accomplish much by involvement—two reasons that are, of course linked by the presumption that any effective action would likely become protracted and probably inconclusive.

There is thus no consensual view of what the United States should do about the Syrian crisis, and this disarray is strongly reflected in the often strongly phrased positions of American policymakers and influence shapers. The practical implication is that no matter what position any public figure makes, and especially if that figure is the President, it will be opposed by loud and concerted objection from both extreme ends of the argument spectrum. Whether this predictable level of cacophony compromises the ability of the president to make and implement coherent policy (regardless of content) is arguable, since those at whom that policy is aimed know the President has opposition to anything he may propose. The simple fact, however, is that the President will be condemned regardless of what position he adopts, and the only way to avoid such criticism is to avoid making definitive policy pronouncements at all.

Syria as Microcosm

A final resolution of the Syrian crisis that ends the civil war and establishes some sort of internal stability and order may be years or even decades away. In the end, a stable Syria within the artificial boundaries that mark the current state may prove impossible, and the country may somehow be physically reconfigured in some manner other than its present form and composition. Certainly there is reason to question whether Syria as it emerged from colonial rule has ever made sense, like so much of the developing world that has emerged from mostly European colonial rule. This problem and possible solution are not entirely unlike the dilemma of neighboring Iraq.

The point is not how or even whether peace and stability return to the troubled Syrians, although one can only hope that they do and that things eventually work out well for the beleaguered Syrian people. From the present perspective, it is more important to realize that probably there was very little meaningful positive outcome that would have been served by any significant level of outside interference, and especially physical intervention. The situation was, and is, so complex and mysterious that it is not clear what could have been done to change things and whether any changes would have been for the better. Certainly, military interference could have altered and in some cases even likely attenuated the short-term situation, including the suffering of some groups, but it is not clear that interference would not have resulted more in a change in who was suffering rather than in whether people were suffering.

Cooler international heads have so far prevailed in Syria. Certainly there was partisan behavior on both sides: the interference of the Russians and Iranians in support of the Assad government and, to a less decisive extent, the material assistance of the Sunni Gulf states to various insurgent groups, including some to IS. Whether that outside interference did more than prolong the suffering and delay an internal resolution that was ultimately the only way the civil war could end is debatable.

The West, and specifically the United States, ultimately decided not to join the greater interference in the Syrian crisis per se, and the decision was almost certainly the right one for them. It was correct for the United States because involvement, and especially overt intervention, almost certainly would have served no useful interests of the United States and would have run the risk of entangling the country in another open-ended conflict with no resolution. It was probably just as well for the Syrians themselves, because such interference would almost certainly have upped the violent ante and increased greatly the likelihood the conflict became regional and even bloodier than it was anyway. It also meant that at the end the Syrians did not have to figure out how to get the Americans to leave, a desire that seems a universal part of the outcome of outside interference.

In the end, the outsiders did what they could do that was in their clear interests and avoided doing what they could not do and that was not so clearly in their interests. Convincing the Syrians to forfeit their chemical weapons under international supervision, while a difficult and controversial process, clearly served the interest of an international community that seeks to limit and eliminate the possession and especially the usage of chemical agents. The Syrians clearly crossed the "red line" of international values when they employed these weapons, and international moral and legal values would have been undermined by not acting to punish that behavior. The punishment would have been more satisfying had those who authorized and carried out the attacks been identified and brought to justice, and this may eventually occur. To have insisted upon such a condition at the time would have made it virtually impossible to reach any agreement with the Syrians at all, since the regime would certainly have been implicated and was hardly likely to turn itself in. Doing so would have almost certainly implied a regime change, which sponsors like the Russians would have strongly opposed on their own self-interest grounds.

The international community settled for half a loaf rather than holding out for the whole loaf or risk settling for no loaf at all on the chemical weapons issue. Syria agreed to comply with international norms, which meant that the chemical weapons ban was sustained, but did not admit guilt and thus force the issue of war crime prosecution. Destroying Syria's chemical weapons *and* punishing those who had used them would have been the most satisfying outcome from an American viewpoint, but it was simply not one that could be achieved without ratcheting up an intervention the international community was wisely unwilling to mount and the American public would have opposed.

The Syrian "settlement" of the chemical weapons issue did not resolve the Syrian civil war either. Certainly a "just" resolution that ended suffering and established a consensual stability would have best served humankind and the cause of peace, but the ability of outsiders to achieve such an outcome was always highly unlikely at best. The conditions for peace and stability may simply not exist in Syria, and outside views of what such an outcome should look like probably do not align very well with the sentiments of the Syrians themselves—at least to the extent it can be said that the Syrians as a whole share any real common vision for their country after the last shots are fired. In the end, only the Syrians themselves can resolve these questions, and how they will is quite beyond the decisive influence of outsiders. Standing aside may implicitly mean accepting a great deal of human suffering, but there is no accepted formula for making it better. As the violence spread to Iraq and the emphasis shifted to IS and its caliphate ambitions, the singular tragedy of Syria somehow got lost in the shuffle. Ultimately, however, it will return to center stage.

The Syrian episode is a clear microcosm and an instructive contrast to the American experiences in Iraq and Afghanistan. It is a microcosm both because the situation in Syria was not dissimilar to what was faced in Iraq and Afghanistan and of future situations in unraveling countries of the developing world in the future. The lesson of Iraq and Afghanistan should be not to repeat the mistakes that were made intruding into situations that are unclearly understood and beyond the resolution of outsiders—the same lesson learned and forgotten in Vietnam a generation ago. It is not clear whether the lesson was learned and applied in Syria because Americans finally figured this out or because the country was too sick of war to jump into another quixotic quest so close on the heels of the latest misadventures. It is a worthwhile dynamic to try to understand, however, because Syria will not be the last place where the temptation to become involved in other people's violent business will manifest itself.

The IS Complication

Prior to 2013, the participation of Al Qaeda and its various offshoots was a peripheral aspect of the crisis in Syria. The Syrian civil war was tragic and regrettable, but it was primarily a DWIC, an *internal* conflict that piqued the world's humanitarian interest but did not greatly threaten the region. The Syrian conflict exemplified the problems underlying Middle Eastern DWICs—it was partly a tribal affair between the Sunni Arab majority and the ruling Alawite minority, and it had a sectarian facet pitting Shiite Alawites and Sunni Arabs and Kurds. These characteristics gave it some international potential if either source of cleavage spread dangerously to other regional states. Unless that happened, however, the vital interests of outsiders, notably the United States, were not affected enough to justify action, and such sentiment as existed to "do something" about the civil war was primarily confined to humanitarian concerns.

The emergence of IS in 2013 and 2014 changed fundamentally the nature of the problem. The IS threat and the Syrian conflict are connected both because the Al Qaeda forebears of IS were part of the diverse Sunni resistance in Syria and because many initial IS supporters and recruits came from the ranks of elements of that resistance. The problem that IS posed within Syria and Iraq, the greater Middle East region, and the international system—including the United States—was fundamentally different than that posed by the internal struggle in Syria.

As it has evolved, IS is a very different "animal" with which to deal. Its roots are in Al Qaeda in Iraq as a classic religious terrorist group, but it has gone far beyond those humble beginnings. What principally distinguishes IS from other terrorist organizations is its territorial ambitions—its desire to recreate the Islamic caliphate in large parts of the Levant, including Sunni sections of Syria and Iraq, but also Jordan, Lebanon, and Palestine. This makes it a qualitatively different phenomenon that goes beyond the challenge posed by the civil war in Syria: Syria is primarily an *internal* problem; IS represents an *international* threat. Moreover, it has become a more traditional military threat as its loose "army" spreads across and seeks to control territory. No other contemporary terrorist organization has been so ambitious or posed this level of quantitative dilemma. IS represents something new on the international horizon. Whether it is an aberration or the harbinger of threats to come is uncertain.

The IS problem is rapidly changing, making definitive analysis of what it is, what it may become, and what threat it poses hazardous. With that rejoinder in mind, the rest of this section will look at the IS threat from three vantage points. The first is trying to define IS: what it has been and what it is or may become. The second is to examine the uniqueness of IS as an organization and a threat: how it has evolved from its "modest" roots as an Al Qaeda spinoff to a virtually new kind of menace. The third is to examine the options for dealing with it, emphasizing why it has been so difficult to decide how and on which side of a multi-sided conflict to come down and about what actions would most likely help the situation: what are the dilemmas and pitfalls of involvement by outsiders like the United States?

What is IS?

By its very nature, the Islamic State is a clandestine organization which does not widely publicize details about itself, other than its goals of creating a new caliphate, continuing its battlefield successes, and demonstrating its harsh punishments of infidels. Its roots are as a terrorist organization that first appeared in Iraq in 1999 and became the Al Qaeda affiliate, Al Qaeda in Iraq (AQI) under the leadership of a Jordanian freedom fighter by the name of Abu Musab Al-Zarqawi. AQI first came to prominence in 2003 as one of the groups resisting the American occupation. Its major base of operations and support was in Sunni-dominated Anbar province among Sunnis who had been displaced from rule by the Americans. Its popularity was based in adopting and channeling Sunni discontent with the occupation as part of the Mujahideen Shura Council, which consolidated its various parts under the banner of the Islamic State of Iraq (ISI).

AQI/ISI gradually fell into disfavor. It lost some of its momentum in 2006 when Zarqawi was killed in an American bombing raid. By the time of the so-called Anwar Awakening in 2007–2008, many former Sunni supporters had been alienated by its harsh, violent style and joined the American-sponsored Sunni resistance to its presence. After 2008, the organization effectively went underground, but it did not disappear.

In April 2013, IS returned to public view under the leadership of Abu Bakr al-Baghdadi, who declared the organization to be ISIS (the Islamic State of Iraq and Syria). On June 29, 2014, Baghdadi announced the creation of the Islamic State (IS) with himself as the caliph (Arabic for successor to Mohammed). As ISIS, it joined the Sunni resistance to the Syrian government of Bashar al-Assad, gradually increasing its role and prominence as it recruited members and support from the loose Sunni array of resistance organizations. Its numbers swelled from general estimates of around 4,000 fighters in June 2014 to estimates of around 40,000 by the fall of 2014. The stated goal of IS is to extend the caliphate to include Sunni-dominated areas of the Levant generally, although its military activities through 2014 were confined to large swaths of Iraq and Syria.

At heart, the Islamic State is a fundamentalist, revivalist Sunni organization that represents an important minority following within the Sunni community. Its orientation is broadly Wahhabist (the unofficial state religion of Saudi Arabia), jihadist and Salafist. It teaches a fundamentalist return to the values and virtues of the original caliphate of Mohammed whose tenets include the strict observance of sharia religious law, and it enforces sharia codes in places it occupies. It believes that everyone who does not accept its teaching—including more moderate Sunnis, all Shiites, and non-believers in Islam—are apostate and subject to righteous and harsh sharia judgment and punishment. These codes and their enforcement have led to numerous atrocities against outsider groups like the Kurds and are most notoriously illustrated by the electronically documented beheadings of western, including American, hostages.

These characteristics are important to note, because they do represent an extremist strain of Islamic thought as practiced by Sunnis (Shiites have their own fundamentalist traditions) that has some support, especially among some wealthy Wahhabists in some of the Gulf States—places like Saudi Arabia and Qatar. These wealthy Wahhabists have provided some of the financial support for IS and its campaign, and they are also powerful enough within their countries that their governments are reluctant either to join international efforts to eradicate IS or completely to shut down the conduit of funds to IS. The Sunni base of IS also means that Middle Eastern governments at odds with Shiites on grounds that include religion are also reluctant to join wholeheartedly in IS suppression for fear doing so will indirectly aid their Shiite enemies. The position of Turkey has reflected this ambivalence. The Turks are repulsed by the actions of IS, but they are also at odds with the Kurds who, as apostates, have been the subject of IS wrath, and the Shiite government of Syria, which they fear would have its position in the civil war strengthened by the elimination of IS.

How Is the IS Challenge Different?

IS has exploded on the international scene as a whole new breed of organization. Its roots may have been as a classic terrorist group, an offshoot of Osama bin Laden's Al Qaeda, but since the death of Zarqawi and the rise to power of al-Baghdadi, it has clearly been transformed into something more closely resembling an insurgent movement. It retains some of the characteristics of its terrorist roots—its penchant for spectacular, atrocious violence and its fiery rhetoric, for instance—but it has clearly become more. In the process, it has come to represent a larger, more profound threat to the countries of the Middle East, and arguably to the United States and Europe as well. At the same time, its growth and the subsequent changes in its structure and methods may ultimately make it more likely that it will be destroyed.

There are at least four things about IS that make it stand out from other revolutionary groups that have operated in the Middle East or elsewhere. The first is the sheer scale of its success to date. The roots of IS in AQI were traditional in membership size, reach, and effectiveness, but IS has surpassed those quantitatively and qualitatively by orders of magnitude. The supposed competitor faction within AQI that it supplanted, the so-called Khorasan group, may remain small, generally considered less than 100 effective terrorists, but the human resources available to IS now measure in the thousands and have been growing. The reason IS has become a territorial threat, for instance, arises from the simple fact that it has the human resources to field what amounts to an army in the western sense, a level of action no other terrorist organization has been able to achieve in recent years. The number of active fighters in its forces numbers in the tens of thousands, and this has provided it with a physical reach quite beyond that which other terrorists have been able seriously to contemplate. That size had made it remarkably more effective than other terrorist organizations, but it has also probably transformed it beyond the roots from which it sprang. That change has been a virtue as it has spread across Sunni areas of Syria and Iraq, but it may also make it a more "conventional" opponent in military terms, which can lead to its demise.

Second, it is a terrorist group, but it is also a highly successful, wealthy criminal enterprise. Criminal behavior does not make it sui generis among terrorist organizations: one of the key characteristics of terrorist acts as described in Chapter 5 is that they are illegal. Killing people and destroying property is the basic way they get the world's attention to air their demands and to gain compliance by promising that others may be subject to the same mayhem if they fail to comply with terrorist demands. At the same time, acts like kidnapping have long been part of the methods by which terrorists raise money, in Africa particularly. Nigeria's Boko Haram is one of the masters of this technique.

It is the scale and effectiveness of criminal behavior that sets IS apart from others. Precise, reliable data is impossible to come by, but it is estimated that the criminal acts of IS largely finance its ongoing campaign, bringing in several millions of dollars daily. The sources include traditional activities like kidnapping and human trafficking, but they have been extended to include robbery (when IS forces take a town, for instance, they routinely confiscate the money from all the banks), theft (stealing everything of value from citizens in the locations they conquer), extortion (demanding protection money from businesses in towns they occupy), and charging outrageous tolls for things like people using roads in places under their control.

The sophistication and effectiveness of IS criminal activities have made them essentially self-sustaining, and this fact has made attempts to weaken the movement by cash-starving it largely ineffective. The other major sources of IS revenue have been illegal sales of petroleum produced in places they occupy and donations from wealthy benefactors. The oil refineries in Syria where the oil is turned into the fuel IS sells (largely in Turkey) have mostly been suppressed by bombing refineries and stepped-up efforts by the Turkish government to stop smuggling across the border, and the United States has brought pressure on the governments of the states from which donations come—largely from wealthy Wahhabists—to suppress that flow by pressuring their donor citizens to halt contributions. These efforts have undoubtedly reduced the amount of funds available to IS, but as long as its Mafia-like activities in occupied parts of Iraq and Syria continue, IS will survive. The only real way to suppress this activity is to liberate the fertile grounds in which the crimes occur, which would effectively require defeating and destroying the threat. That is, of course, the ultimate objective, but not one likely to be achieved soon.

Its resulting wealth is part of what sets IS apart from other terrorists. Many terrorist groups have been funded in various, including criminal, ways, but not on the scale of IS. Limited financial resources have historically been a source of limitation for most terrorist organizations: they may have grandiose plans and ambitions, but they lack the resources to carry them out. This is especially true of ambitions that may include extending their violent reach to the United States, but this is not necessarily a barrier for IS. For now, they are preoccupied with establishing the caliphate, but if that is accomplished, they would have the potential capability to engage very ambitious terrorist campaigns.

The problem that extending IS terrorist activities overseas represents may, however, be somewhat attenuated by its third unique characteristic. Unlike other terrorist organizations, IS both has and is realizing territorial ambitions. The major goal of the organization is to create a sovereign territorial state, and this is a far more ambitious goal than most terrorist organizations espouse or particularly attempt to realize. Al Qaeda and other movements have talked of territorial ambitions—vague promises of a caliphate—but none have gotten so far as to occupy territory and to set up governance like a normal state. The establishment of safe havens or sanctuaries in places like the territorial regions of Pakistan or in parts of Yemen outside the effective control of the government has been about as much as any have tried.

The transformation of IS from terrorist organization to insurgency has been the result of its phenomenal growth and success. A ragtag group that numbered in the hundreds when it entered the Syrian fray in 2013 had grown to a force approaching 50,000 in late 2014, IS succeeded in conquering and occupying large parts of eastern Syria and the Sunni regions of Iraq (mostly Anbar province). This growth and success have astounded most outsiders, but both must be placed in context that helps understand why and also aids understanding the IS problem.

The growth of IS must be attributed to its Sunni roots. In both Syria and Iraq, Sunnis have been the politically displaced segment of the population, which makes them vulnerable to the appeal of movements promising to lift their oppression. In Iraq, many of the former military leaders of the Hussein regime have signed on with IS, because it opposes what they view as the Shiite tyranny of the government in Baghdad (an opposition that was not unjustified under the regime of Shiite Nouri al-Maliki). It was, after all, Anbar Province, the only part of Iraq with a distinct Sunni majority, in which there was a major uprising against the American occupation between 2004 and 2007, when the United States was able to organize (some argue bribe) Sunni tribal elements into opposing the resistance, which included leadership from AQI. Many reports have indicated that, at least initially, IS forces have been viewed as liberators by Anbar Sunnis. When combined with the ineptitude of the largely Shiite Iraqi armed forces and the reluctance of Shiite soldiers to defend Sunni territory, there is a clear recipe for success of IS.

This context helps explain the success of IS in Iraq and suggest what may be done to counter it. For IS in Iraq, a Sunni population that either supports or at least does not oppose IS acts as a kind of force multiplier for IS forces, since it means they encounter minimal resistance to their advances in Anbar. To reverse this situation, the Sunnis must somehow be convinced to turn on IS, just as they did in 2007. Fortunately, many Iraqi Sunnis find the crude and brutal administration of *sharia* offensive, and will, with any luck, turn on their "liberators," just as they did their American counterparts a decade ago. The emphasis of American policy has been on convincing Maliki's successors to reach out to and curry the support of the Sunnis, and until (or unless) they do, IS will remain strong in Sunni territories of the country. Probably the last way to further this cause would be the introduction of American ground forces into Anbar, since it was the American intrusion after 2003 that helped to spawn the original uprising.

The situation in Syria is different. Sunnis are the vast majority in Syria, but they are ruled by Shiites. That majority has been a blessing and curse, however, because it has lent itself to a fractious, splintered resistance to the Assad regime. In an October 2014 op-ed in the *Washington Post*, Fareed Zakaria cites American official sources as estimating that there are as many as 1,500 separate elements of the Syrian resistance, and IS has exploited this disarray, recruiting members of some of the competing groups into their own ranks and using others as sources of weapons and equipment (one of the reasons the United States has been reluctant to send weapons to opposition groups). When IS entered Syria in 2013, they were simply regarded as a competing element that was part of AQI. Their superior organization has helped them enlarge their ranks.

Their effectiveness has been further magnified by the fact that most of their territorial gains have been in eastern sections of Syria, rather than in or around major urban centers. The areas they have annexed to the caliphate are among the least populated and poorest parts of the country. A simple political map of Syria distorts their impact: they have occupied a large physical part of the country, but only about 30 percent of the population in late 2014 (the government controls about 50 percent and other resistance groups about 20 percent). The Assad regime does not hotly contest these regions, preferring to concentrate on its population and economic base in the western parts of the country. Moreover, the Syrians are not particularly concerned with atrocious IS activities in their occupied areas, since they have mostly been committed against Sunni Kurds who oppose the regime anyway. IS will be difficult to dislodge from many of its occupied areas in Syria basically because it is not clear who cares enough to make the effort.

IS has been spectacularly successful, but some of its apparent success may, in other words, be slightly overblown and the result of fortuitous circumstances. This very ambitiousness and success, however, make IS vulnerable in ways other organizations have not been, in at least two ways. The first vulnerability comes from the transformation of IS into a more conventional military organization. It may not be a traditional, western-style armed force, but as it sweeps across Iraq and Syria using tactics that Edward Lawrence (Lawrence of Arabia) would have approved, it is forced to concentrate its forces in ways terrorists do not, and when it occupies places, it become a stationary target that can be targeted and attacked by more conventional forces—and especially air forces. Being a territorial aspirant means having both to conquer and then to administer land areas and population centers, and this makes them both static and potentially vulnerable to conventional response.

Second, being territory possessors creates a conceptual problem for an organization with terrorist roots. One of the advantages terrorists have is that they do not have physical territory to defend. At the practical level of counter-terrorism, this means that there are no automatic targets against which to unleash retaliatory vengeance. Instead, terrorists tend to imbed themselves within populations that are either sympathetic to them or whom they can effectively terrorize. These areas are within the sovereign jurisdiction of countries that do not themselves engage in terrorist activities (Pakistan or Yemen, for instance), and reprisals against terrorists on their soil are also attacks on their sovereign lands. Moreover, retaliation is normally conducted from the air (usually drones) and, despite efforts to the contrary, inevitably includes civilian casualties (collateral damage) that inflame the host government and create anti-Americanism.

Becoming territory-possessors removes this advantage. If IS conquers and declares sovereign control over territory, that territory becomes a legitimate target for retaliation and attempts to dispossess the intruders.

When IS effectively occupied the northern Syrian Kurdish town of Kobani in late 2014 and the United States led air strikes that drove the conquerors out, no one complained about the U.S. actions.

The fourth distinguishing characteristic of IS has been its international appeal. Its core may be disaffected Sunnis in Iraq and Syria, but it has managed to broaden the net of its influence beyond those countries that are included in the current caliphate. This expansion into the international realm has included both physical recruitment efforts in Western Europe and the United States and financial appeals within other parts of the Sunni world. Both of these tentacles have heightened the international concern with the insidious expansion of IS appeal, and the threat it poses.

IS efforts to recruit have not been limited to but have been most prominently associated with those in North America and Europe. The appeal has been to potential *jihadis* and has apparently had its greatest impact on basically idle young men with both religious fervor and limited prospects otherwise. Both of these characteristics are associated with the recruitment of terrorists generally, and since the roots of IS are in AQI, it should not be entirely surprising. The original Al Qaeda, after all, was largely composed of foreigners who had joined the anti-Soviet effort in Afghanistan (the so-called *Afghanis*), of whom Zarqawi was an example. There is enough fundamentalist tradition within the Sunni sect of Islam to make this a fertile ground. Westerners, of course, become concerned by the prospects that such converts will be trained in terrorist methods and return to the West to wreak terrorist mayhem.

Funding has also been international. The heart of IS financing may be its *Mafiosi* activities, but it has also received a not inconsiderable amount of contributions from wealthy fundamentalist Sunnis in other countries. This source has been particularly notable from the oil-rich Gulf States, many of whose wealth comes from sales of petroleum to the West. Under pressure from the United States and other countries, regimes like that in Saudi Arabia have attempted to dry up this source, but with less than perfect success, at least partly due to the fact that these donors are also prominent, powerful supporters of the regimes themselves.

What Can Be Done About the Threat?

Although the threat that IS poses is primarily to the immediate area into which the caliphate is extending, its peril has been adopted by the West, and particularly the United States. The basis for this adoption is the stated goal of IS to pose a direct threat to the West (a legacy of its AQI roots) and the fear that it could expand more widely into the region, destabilizing the area and thereby imperiling international stability. The ambitions of the caliphate do, after all, extend beyond Iraq and Syria to Lebanon, Jordan, and even Israeli-occupied Palestine, and the actual physical attempt to extend its sway to any or all of these places would greatly complicate the situation. This definition of the threat clearly differentiates IS from the Syrian civil war. There is no direct—and thus arguably vital—threat to the United States from Syria. The threat from IS may be abstract and somewhere in the future, but it at least can be argued to pose a direct threat to the United States and Americans.

The situation becomes more complicated because the IS and Syrian problems are interwoven. Part of this overlap is obviously that parts of Syria are occupied by IS, but it is made much more vexing by the fact that support for opposition to one problem can actually assist the opposition in the other. Toppling the Assad regime, for instance, could materially aid the spread of the caliphate by removing the major barrier to its drive westward into the more populous and wealthy parts of Syria. "Destroying" IS (the current stated goal) could assist Assad by taking from the board the most serious, potent source of Sunni resistance to Assad's continuing rule.

This dynamic extends to and infects the efforts of others in the region. Other than the fundamentalists, no one really approves of IS, probably finding its tactics (e.g. beheadings) offensive or counterproductive, and most would just as soon that it went away. But eradicating IS would also help Assad, whom many Sunnis detest as much as or more than IS. As long as IS limits its campaigns to attacking Shiites and Kurds (both of whom many other Sunnis in the area also oppose), then a wholehearted campaign to eradicate IS has ambivalent appeal, and support for American efforts to form an effective anti-IS coalition are tepid and half-hearted.

Turkey's lack of enthusiasm—especially over countering IS attacks on Syrian Kurds—exemplifies this dilemma. The Turks dislike IS and its fundamentalist ideology: the specific underpinning of the Ataturk revolution in the 1920s was, after all, largely based on secularization to make the country competitive in the world. The Turks hate the Shiite regime of Assad on their southern border, and the Kurds in Syria and Iraq pose a potential threat if they unite with Turkish Kurds to push for a Kurdish state carved partially from Turkey. Many of the defenders of Syrian Kurds have come across the border from Turkey, but they have been given neither solace nor assistance by the Turkish government. This basic set of attitudes—a lack of enthusiasm for IS but a fear that eliminating IS would strengthen their traditional enemy in Baghdad affects most of the Sunni regimes in the area to one extent or another, and it largely explains why participation in the American-led coalition by most Sunni states has not been more wholehearted.

The same logic applies in reverse to the effort against Syria. Eliminating Assad remains an American policy objective, but it is a goal that gets a mixed response. Syria's friends and supporters are limited to the Shiite states, mainly Iran but also many in Iraq. One difficulty is who is going to overthrow the Assad regime. The only one member of the array of opposition groups that has any chance of doing that appears to be the Islamic

State. The current status quo leaves Assad in control of much of the population and wealth of Syria, which the Sunni states oppose, but turning those resources over to the larcenous caliphate is not an outcome any of them view with great favor.

What can the United States do in these circumstances? The consensus about Syria has always been that there are no good alternatives or answers, and this dynamic applies in spades to the decimation of IS, which is the current rhetorical objective. There are three basic approaches, each fraught with different problems. They are a massive intervention wherein the United States takes on the primary role of destroying IS in detail, a limited involvement wherein the United States provides assistance, including some armed force, but leaves the "heavy lifting" to forces in the region, or doing nothing and letting nature take its course.

The extreme solutions are sufficiently unattractive that they can be and have been effectively discarded. The American public would not stand for a massive deployment of American ground forces to Iraq and Syria, nor to the grisly mission of destroying the enemy "in detail." Whether such an incursion would work or turn into another endless morass is uncertain, as IS would probably simply try to melt away, assimilate into the population, and return to their terrorist roots. Moreover, such an approach would be very unpopular in the region. Iraqi Sunnis, who blame much of their negative fate since 2003 on the American military, would certainly not rejoice at their return to decimate other Sunnis, and the result could easily be something like another Anbar Uprising. The campaign would inevitably have to extend into Syria, which the Syrian government would oppose (they already complain about U.S. air operations in their sovereign air space). If the campaign were successful, moreover, a major beneficiary would be the Assad regime, the resistance to which would be weakened. This would hardly bring plaudits from those surrounding Sunni regimes who want Assad to fall.

Doing nothing is the other extreme. Its basic justification is that there is very little the United States can do to affect the outcome that does not have other negative effects, making any actions self-defeating. Moreover, the IS threat is quintessentially an internal matter in one Sunni state ruled by a Shiite minority (Syria) and another where a Sunni minority used to rule a Shiite majority but whose fortunes have been reversed (Iraq). These circumstances form the appeal of IS, but it is not clear how the United States or other outsiders could change that dynamic. The United States tried to affect fundamental change in Iraq, and it clearly did not produce salutary results. Containing and effectively reducing IS must be internally conceived and carried out, either through the reconciliation of Sunni and Shi'a in Iraq or through IS so alienating the Sunnis by their excesses that they deal with them—as they did in 2007. The United States, after all, did not create the schisms within Islam that are at the heart of this problem, and therefore it is impossible to see how the United States—and especially

American armed forces—can solve them. Ultimately, this is an internal regional problem. No politically non-suicidal American official would propose this solution, because it would be assailed from all sides on grounds discussed earlier (mainly the abrogation of American leadership in the world).

That leaves the middle ground of trying to assist but not to take the physical lead in halting and reversing the expansion of IS. American air-power has been the primary vehicle for this compromise, and its applica-tion had some effect in slowing IS advances around Baghdad and in the Kurdish regions in late 2014. Its major debility is that no one really believes such an approach can be decisive: if the goal is to "destroy" IS, aerial bombardment alone is not enough. As IS progressively becomes a territory holder, it necessarily becomes more static and thus vulnerable to attacks from the sky. Until either internal elements (other Sunnis) or regional actors decide to enter the fray in a large way, however, there is little prospect that the IS surge can be more than contained. That solution is not especially satisfying and does not meet the lofty rhetorical goals of destruction, but it may be the most that can practically be accomplished.

A Perfect Microcosmic Storm

The combined events in Syria and surrounding IS represent a microcosm of the very worst that the international environment offers in the immedi-ate future, but they also represent a fair definition of the "worst case" of the future with which policymakers must deal. The situation is uniquely stressful. It involves trying to reconcile and deal with two contradictory, complex, and very difficult situations tied together by IS in Syria. The Syrian civil war is quintessentially a DWIC—an internal conflict—whereas the IS threat is more international with strong internal importance in Syria and Iraq. The two events share a maze of complex and sometimes irre-concilable issues—how do you defeat IS without helping Assad, for instance? Neither has any easy solutions, and it is not particularly clear that outside military intervention beyond what is currently being done from the air can have much effect. Solving this complex may simply be beyond American capabilities. Fortunately, it is also occurring somewhere that American vital interests are not compellingly engaged. Is the most, or all, the United States can do in this situation essentially nothing?

Geopolitics does not conclusively support outside interference, espe-cially when the criterion of attainability of desired outcomes is part of the geopolitical calculation. In this circumstance, the alternative basis on which to justify policy is humanitarian, and there is no shortage of human suf-fering in both aspects of this tragedy. Historically that has not been enough, and humanitarian-motivated actions likely would ameliorate, not completely relieve, human suffering. Is the humanitarian justification an adequate basis for American activism?

The combination of Syria and IS may be the perfect storm of things that can go wrong in the contemporary world, and that storm may not be replicated any time soon. There will, however, be other internal conflicts akin to the Syrian conflict, and religiously or otherwise based movements will probably arise to challenge established governments in the future. If the whole of the crisis is unique, in other words, its parts are not. What will the United States do in the future when either kind of crisis, or in the worst case, their confluence, pops up?

One of the very clear lessons of the current experience is that the current national security paradigm does not provide adequate guidance about how to think about these kinds of situations. They are very different problems and challenges than those that confronted the Cold Warriors. They faced a very deadly, static foe on which they could concentrate. Contemporary thinkers face a more dangerous (but less deadly) threat that is constantly changing. One paradigm does not fit both circumstances.

Bibliography

Ajami, Fouad. *The Syrian Rebellion*. Palo Alto, CA: Hoover Institution Press, 2013.

Anderson, Scott. *Lawrence in Arabia: War, Deceit, Imperial Folly and the Making of the Modern Middle East*. New York: Anchor Books, 2013.

Arwan, Abdul Beri. *The Secret History of Al Qaeda*. Berkeley, CA: University of California Press, 2006.

Brisard, Jean-Charles. *Zarqawi: The New Face of Al-Qaeda*. New York: The Other Press, 2005.

Chandrasekaran, Rajiv. *Imperial Life in the Emerald City: Inside Iraq's Green Zone*. New York: Alfred A. Knopf, 2007.

Diamond, Larry. *Squandered Victory: The American Occupation and the Bungled Attempt to Bring Democracy to Iraq*. New York: Henry Holt and Company, 2005.

Feaver, Peter. "The Just War Tradition and the Paradox of Policy Failure in Syria." *Foreign Policy* (online), August 22, 2013.

Hall, M. Clement, and Charles Rivers (eds). *The History of Syria: 1900–2012*. New York: Create Space Independent Publishing Platform, 2013.

Hashemi, Nader, and Danny Postel (eds). *The Syrian Dilemma*. Cambridge, MA: MIT Press (Boston Review Books), 2013.

Hokayem, Emile. *Syria's Uprising and the Fracturing of the Levant*. London: Routledge (Adelphi Series), 2013.

Homans, Charles. "Just What Is a Just War? Anthropology of an Idea: Responsibility to Protect." *Foreign Policy*, November 2011, 34–35.

Lesch, David W. *Syria: The Rise and Fall of the House of Assad*. New Haven, CT: Yale University Press, 2013.

Packer, George. *The Assassin's Gate: America in Iraq*. New York: Farrar, Straus, Giroux, 2005.

Parker, Ned. "The Iraq We Left Behind: Welcome to the World's Next Failed State." *Foreign Affairs* 91, 2 (March/April 2012), 94–110.

Ricks, Thomas E. *Fiasco: The American Military Adventure in Iraq.* New York: Penguin Press, 2006.

Serwer, Daniel. "Iraq Struggles to Govern Itself." *Current History* 109, 731 (December 2010), 390–394.

Simon, Steven N. *After the Surge: The Case for U.S. Military Disengagement from Iraq.* New York: CRS 23, Council on Foreign Relations, 2007.

Sky, Emma. "Iraq, from Surge to Sovereignty." *Foreign Affairs* 90, 2 (March/April 2011), 117–127.

Snow, Donald M. *Distant Thunder: Patterns of Conflict in the Developing World.* 2nd edn. Armonk, NY: M. E. Sharpe, 1997.

Snow, Donald M. *When America Fights: The Uses of U.S. Military Power.* Washington, DC: CQ Press, 2000.

Snow, Donald M. *What After Iraq?* New York: Pearson Longman, 2009.

Snow, Donald M. *Cases in International Relations.* 6th edn. New York: Pearson, 2014.

Stern, Jessica, and M. Berger. *ISIS: The State of Terror.* New York: ECCO Books, 2015.

Tabler, Andrew J. "Syria's Collapse and How Washington Can Stop It." *Foreign Affairs* 92, 4 (July/August 2013), 90–100.

Van Dam, Nikolaos. *The Struggle for Power in Syria: Politics and Society under Assad and the Ba'ath Party.* London: I. B. Taurus, 2011.

Vincent, R. J. *Nonintervention and International Order.* Princeton, NJ: Princeton University Press, 1974.

Zakaria, Fareed. "Obama Needs to Dial Back His Syrian Strategy." *Washington Post* (online), October 17, 2014.

7 Paradigm for a New Era

The IS/Syria crisis is the latest and most complex developing world situation that has recently faced the United States, but it will not be the last developing world challenge and temptation that will confront this country. The quest for an appropriate response has revealed once again the absence of a clear set of American policy guidelines—a paradigm—within which to frame a response. Whether one will be crafted or emerge from this situation is uncertain; that such a framework would have been helpful in thinking about and dealing with the latest crisis in the Levant is not. One lesson clearly is that trying to forge a new paradigm is very hard but would have been very helpful.

By now, it should be obvious that the national security strategy that guided the United States through the world wars and the Cold War of the twentieth century has largely lost its relevance and appeal as a guidepost to organize policy and strategy for the new and very different international environment of the early twenty-first century. The Cold War paradigm responded to the array of national security challenges that dominated the international politics of the last century. Those conditions have changed significantly, and most of the policies have lost their direct relevance. It is by no means clear that the contemporary world environment resembles the Cold War environment enough for the old paradigm to remain a faithful guide to the present and future. If the old paradigm is indeed deficient, is there not a need to re-examine and refashion it for a new era?

This is not the first time the question has been raised. It represents a familiar, recurring theme that arises periodically in the American policy dialog, generally in response to some international shifts or to a change in the priorities and preferences of the American body politic, and it has been a recurring theme in these pages. Chapter 4 in particular examined both how the conditions and the constructs that undergirded the Cold War paradigm arose, and how those conditions and assumptions were progressively battered by the unsettling American experience in Vietnam, the rise of a developing world for which the Cold War paradigm's dictates seemed at least partially irrelevant, and finally by the physical demise of the Cold War opposition. Chapter 5 further examined the assault the old paradigm has undergone due to the traumas of the twenty-first century, for which its guidelines have proven of increasingly dubious value. The rationale for and salience of the old paradigm for confronting and organizing responses in the mid-2010s and beyond has largely evaporated.

The torch behind which to rally movement toward a new paradigm has been lit. In his January 28, 2014 State of the Union address, President Obama laid down the central need to reform the belief that underpins the Cold War paradigm—the use of American military force to dominate our conduct of the "holy war" against a communism long gone and not clearly replaced by an equivalent evil (the terrorist threat notwithstanding). "Our leadership and our security cannot depend on our military alone," he said. It is a good launching point for discussing policy toward the future.

But it is a perspective that continues to be resisted. The old paradigm, at least implicitly, continues to drive American national security policy. A statement by U.S. Secretary of Defense Ashton B. Carter in the January 2014 *Foreign Affairs* inadvertently makes the point. He argues, "At the outset of the wars in Afghanistan and Iraq, the Pentagon made two fatal miscalculations. First, it believed these wars would be over in a matter of months ... Second, the Pentagon was prepared for traditional military-versus-military conflicts." These are stunning admissions made with no sense of self-awareness of the assumption from which those judgments sprang—the Cold War paradigm.

The conditions for a serious discussion of paradigmatic alternatives are also propitious on various levels. In the past, adverse reactions to controversial national security actions and their consequences have precipitated discussions of appropriate action. In the 1970s, the embarrassing outcome of the Vietnam War fueled a strong, if temporary, aversion to military commitments. Ironically, the military's response was to turn away from these kinds of conflicts and to redouble its emphasis on the traditional forms of symmetrical conflict that would evaporate in 1991. The collapse of operational communism in Europe ended the physical Cold War confrontation. It also undercut the relevance of the Cold War paradigm, a dynamic many are still discovering. The trauma of 9/11 arrested introspection and allowed resuscitating the old paradigm in places it clearly did not fit like Iraq and Afghanistan. Those experiences have left the paradigmatic slate largely clear. The question is what new formulation will be drawn on that slate.

The world environment is changing in ways that make the traditional calculation of military efficacy less applicable to all situations, and this military effect has an impact on how the paradigm evolves in the face of changing world threats. Some of these implications clearly contradict traditional wisdom. The most notable of these, of course, is the pervasiveness of conflict in the developing world as the major *leitmotif* of international instability and violence. The West has no real answers to how to moderate or quell these problems, especially with force. If it could, the world would be an even more tranquil place than it already has become. As Russett and others have pointed out, the level and extent of violence in the world has been in steady decline for decades, and were tranquility somehow to break out in the developing world (admittedly a rather remote likelihood), the world would be a much more congenial place in which to live. Within the developed world, fighting among states has essentially disappeared: the last real warfare in Europe, for instance, was in the Balkans in the 1990s. What remains are the DWICs. The problem, of course, is that the United States and virtually everyone else has no accepted plan for bringing an end to this form of warfare. As Russett (2014) concludes, "Since the middle of the twentieth century, the number and severity of violent conflicts between and within states have declined markedly ... The average citizen is markedly safer than ever before." Many developing countries are exceptions.

That greater safety is, of course, selective. It does not apply to places like Syria or Iraq, where people are markedly less safe than they have been at other times, and the major international security question with obvious implications for American security is what to do to change that situation. Within the United States, the centerpiece of that debate will be over the proper intellectual organizing device, or paradigm, to understand the problem and to organize thinking about solutions. It is a fundamental problem.

The obvious need for and resistance to change will thus do battle in the upcoming debate. It would be utter, pretentious folly for the author to try to predict or prescribe the detailed outcomes of the debate over American security in the world or the most efficacious paradigm to organize that effort. Rather, the intent here is more restrained and modest, suggesting some important ways the world has changed to render the old paradigm inappropriate for dealing with new realities and some directions that policy and strategy might be redirected in ways more congruent with new realities.

The Changing National Security Environment

Think for a moment of the world situation on New Year's Day 2014 as a kind of snapshot of the contemporary national security environment. Most of the world was remarkably tranquil. There were no traditional, symmetrical wars between sovereign states raging anywhere in the world, all of the developed, OECD countries were at a stable peace with one another, and even the most pessimistic, self-interested scion of Eisenhower's military-industrial complex would have had a very difficult time making a believable argument that such a conflict was more than the most remote possibility. The only semblance of traditional international instability was in the Middle East, principally the ongoing conflict in the Levant.

Other than the increasingly unpopular American involvement in Afghanistan (a December 30, 2013 poll suggested that that war was now more unpopular in the United States than Vietnam), two sources of instability and violence were obvious. One of these, of course, was the ongoing civil conflict in Syria; the other was the pernicious expansionism of IS. Both were classic DWICs; the international system was essentially clueless about what to do about either.

Contrast this snapshot with one that could have been taken a century earlier. On January 1, 1914, the world at large was in a general state of peace, but the slippery slope toward the first horrible bloodletting of the twentieth century would accelerate when the Austrian Archduke Frederic Ferdinand was assassinated by Bosnian separatists in Sarajevo on June 28. Within weeks, the "guns of August" shattered the peace and would result in the horrendous slaughter that is euphemistically referred to as the Great War. Even that proved a mere prelude to the even more massive slaughter in World War II. Humankind's "better angels" took a clear beating during the first half of the century. When one is tempted to despair over the human condition today, a peek back in time is not a bad reminder that at least some things do get better.

Things have not, however, improved for everyone, and violence remains a continuing, nagging source of international instability. Because most of the violent conflicts in the world are internal within mostly artificial independent states where loyalties to more parochial bases often trump national unity, the violence that does occur tends, as has been argued here, to be particularly bloody and horrific, and modern informational technology makes the slaughter impossible to ignore—and often very hard to resist.

These observations inform the parameters around which the remaining discussion will revolve. It will begin by identifying and highlighting three ways, all of which have been mentioned before, in which the environment has changed. It will emphasize the ways in which the new environment contrasts with the environment it succeeds, thus necessitating a change in orientation. That discussion will form the backdrop against which to suggest some of the elements of a realist defense paradigm rooted in the centrality of the DWIC problem.

There is general agreement that the world environment has changed greatly since the demise of operational communism (the end of the Cold War), but that agreement does not extend to the conceptual and operational consequences of those changes. There is, for instance, general agreement that there is no longer a threat of the severity of a potential nuclear confrontation: the world is indeed a less deadly place. There is less agreement about whether the contemporary threat environment is less threatening generally. The world may be less deadly, but is it less dangerous? And if it is not less dangerous, can the United States afford to be less vigilant and self-sacrificing either in its level and quality of military preparedness or its ready willingness to employ force to protect threatened interests?

If change in the environment is what an Army War College student of mine called a BFO (blinding flash of the obvious) in 1991, its implications are not so apparent to all concerned. One way to look at this contrast is to examine that nature and extent of change through the lens of three different but sequential manifestations of change: the changing nature of world power distribution; the evolving locus and changing nature of violence and instability in the world; and change in the character and nature of threats and opportunities in the national security arena. Each helps set the parameters for a new security paradigm.

The Changing Power Balance

Cold War-era analysts and scholars devised a way to describe the distribution of world power that is still useful in understanding the dynamics of world politics, and especially the geopolitics of national security. This mode of analysis, most closely associated with the realist school of international relations, describes world politics in terms of the number of dominant political actors and how the relationships associated with that number define international interactions. Three forms of power distribution have been widely identified and described: unipolarity, bipolarity, and multipolarity.

The meanings of the terms are intuitive. A unipolar system is one in which there is only one dominant state. In such a situation, the major power generally has strong interests essentially everywhere and is a major factor in virtually all situations. Generally, a condition of dominance by a single power will result in opposition and the attempt by other states to counterbalance the dominant state. In a condition of bipolarity, two dominant powers oppose one another, and those dominant powers seek to associate and influence other states to support them in their competition with the rival power. Multipolarity implies several independent sources of power that may be relevant worldwide or at least in specific situations and locales. Multipolarity represents the greatest form of dispersion of global power.

The Cold War was a classic bipolar system. The two "poles" were the United States and the Soviet Union, and both developed an array of subsidiary states over which they could exercise great power. This system was centered in Europe, and the two powers used different means to maintain their sway: the Soviets used coercive military force in the form of a huge standing military, and the American economy was so strong and its resources so needed for postwar recovery that the economic instrument was its means to insure compliance. The result, of course, was the Cold War military conventional and nuclear military confrontation that was the principal national security manifestation of the system. The Cold War paradigm was the American operational response to this environment, and it became the dominant and enduring framework for national security.

The end of bipolarity was intellectually traumatizing. As noted earlier, the very real possibility of the nuclear vaporization of world society made the bipolar Cold War a very deadly place, but dealing with that deadliness also became a comfortable exercise. The comfort in large measure came from the predictability and highly structured nature of the competition.

This was especially true in the national security area, where the confrontation between two European-styled, conventional forces with nuclear weapons flowed directly from the Cold War paradigm, in which national security concerns, given the possible consequences of system failure, were clearly supreme. The situation was unambiguous: everyone knew who the enemy was, how to keep the enemy at bay, and the catastrophic consequences of failure. Cold War "marching orders" were orderly and clear and flowed from the paradigm. This clarity has largely been replaced by unsettling ambiguity in the contemporary environment. The world is still a "very dangerous place" where the United States cannot let its guard down. There is no Soviet threat to oppose, but the DWICs and terrorism have become the substitute source of danger and peril. The "brave new world" is arguably more dangerous if it is less deadly.

The demise of the Soviet Union ended the bipolar system and ushered in the current evolving transition. The world was effectively unipolar in the 1990s, and the United States was, in the words of Secretary of State Madeleine Albright, "the indispensable nation." Conservative newspaper columnist Charles Krauthammer declared a "unipolar moment" of American dominance, and analyst and former State Department officer Francis Fukuyama declared the "end of history" in the sense of the bipolar competition.

They, and others like them, were both right and wrong, as tends to be the case in new and uncharted waters. Not surprisingly, the assessments of what had disappeared were more prescient than the predictions of the future, since they were based in a past that had happened rather than a future that had not. They were thus less prescient about the direction and meaning of change. As a result, many of the dictates and ways of thinking of the Cold War remained in place virtually by default, as a hedge against a return of the "bad old days."

Things were, however, changing. The unipolar moment was not replaced by a rising opposing pole to balance the United States, but new forces were arising or being accentuated by the end of bipolarity. Individually and collectively, these insured that the United States would not sit comfortably astride the new system as its benevolent hegemon. These factors have become prominent in defining the condition surrounding a new paradigm.

The first and most traumatic source of that change, of course, was the dramatic introduction of international terrorism onto the scene on September 11, 2001. The characteristic that distinguishes contemporary terrorism is its international, sectarian base and its direction against Western governments, and especially the United States and Americans. Modern terrorism, of course, has been associated with radical interpretations of Islam that maintain their beliefs are threatened by Western values, including those associated with the "great Satan," the United States. They have mostly been located in and associated with more extreme elements in some Islamic states and in countries too weak to resist their activities. Some of the activities of these groups—and especially those associated with various permutations of Al Qaeda—are directed against those Western countries most active in the Islamic Middle East, which means principally the United States.

International terrorism directed against the United States defines it as an American national security problem. Organized actions by international groups, most dramatically demonstrated by the September 11 attacks, were something new in the American experience. The initial response was to extend the Cold War paradigm to terrorism, virtually substituting the Soviet threat with international terrorism and declaring "war on terror." It has not been an altogether comfortable fit.

The other source of change was the greater emergence of the developing world as a factor in world politics. Stripping away the veneer of the Cold War from the canvas of international politics allowed one to see the subtext that was already there: the developing world as a new and independent source of influence on system dynamics. The major effect was to reveal that the developing world had been the major source of turbulence in the international arena ever since independence came to the former colonial areas, principally in Asia and Africa. The Cold War obscured this dynamic both because the spotlight of Cold War machinations outshone developing world problems and because the major powers tended to place developing world dynamics in the framework of the Cold War competition. DWICs, for instance, were portrayed as Cold War battles, where the sides served as surrogates for the Cold War competitors.

The post-Cold War setting allowed the developing world to be assessed on its own merits, rather than as a Cold War playground. The major national security impact for the United States has been to realize that developing world dynamics have emerged as the major source of violence and instability in the world. Once again, this is really nothing new either, since most of the actual systemic violence of the Cold War period was in developing states. What is principally different is that these conflicts, of which the DWICs are the overwhelming examples, can no longer be explained or dealt with in the Cold War framework. An alternative way to think about them has yet to achieve consensus.

The global system is thus in a state of change in two principal ways with which a new paradigm must deal. First, it is becoming multipolar. There are several sources of independent power in the world today. That number is growing and likely will continue to grow, and it features a group of states that cannot be hierarchically controlled by the United States. The nature of the power on which this independence rests is different than the primarily military basis on which traditional realist calculations rested. Economics obviously plays a large role in multipolarity, and the result is a more subtle basis for power calculation than before. The U.S. may remain something like the unipolar military power, but it is not clear what that pre-eminence "buys" in terms of American influence in the world. In this confusion, an often shrill debate about whether the United States is fading from its pre-eminence in the world is occurring where the debaters lack both common reference points and solutions.

Another systemic effect is in the utility and forms of military power as an effective instrument of national power. It is no longer clear how being the most powerful military power translates into usable influence in a fragmented world system. It is even less clear if measures of military force have particular meaning in a world of DWICs where traditional force may not bring about favorable outcomes. Moreover, the DWICs are in places where marginal interests are involved anyway, meaning it may be questionable whether it is worth expending expensive force for marginal outcomes. These concerns about force are, of course, particularly salient in a national security sense.

The Locus and Nature of Violence

When mostly American critics bemoan the decline of the United States as the global (i.e. unipolar) power, they are implicitly referring to the reduced effectiveness of American arms for forcing compliance with American wishes and desires. Their reference is to a geopolitically based calculation of national power defined almost exclusively in traditional national security terms: the traditional Euro-centered way of looking at problems and their resolution through armed force. That system was the model for the three centuries after the 30 Years War, which ended in 1648. Consequential change accompanied by the threat or recourse to traditional, conventional military force was its norm. The Cold War, led by two European fringe players, the United States and the Soviet Union, was the last hurrah for that system.

This model remains the implicit standard by which power and influence is measured. When critics decry American decline, they sometimes refer to relative economic dynamics (e.g. the size of the Chinese economy approaching the American economy), but ultimately they are talking about military power. In some ways, the United States remains the unipolar power by this measure—size and capabilities of different categories of armed forces and the relative size of American monetary commitment to defense, for instance.

The problem is that it is unclear whether traditional means and measures of relative power are entirely relevant to the world today. In non-military ways, the world has become indeed multipolar, with different sources of competing power in non-military areas. In this competition, traditional military power has lost its salience as a way to gain or retain influence. Moreover, the kind of warfare on which traditional military calculations were based has largely disappeared from the pattern of world conflict. What used to pass for robustness and strength may have simply become muscle-bound clumsiness.

The purpose of national security policy is to influence the international environment to maximize the ability of the country to realize its interests. In the broadest terms, this recognition leads to two imperatives. From a national security vantage point, the most obvious and traditional concern is the negation of threats to interests. National security policy is primarily directed at this source of concern, and this was the Cold War emphasis. The most basic source of threat was military, symbolized by the superpower thermonuclear balance. The threat was Euro-centered and involved two symmetrically oriented and armed opponents. It was a direct extension of the European system's dynamics of the previous 300 years or more.

The other imperative was to produce an atmosphere removing or controlling barriers to national opportunities, and once again, these centered on Europe and East Asia, where the other developed states resided. The Soviet economy posed little threat to American access to developed world markets (no one wanted to buy anything the Soviets made, other possibly than some categories of weapons), and the political appeal of the communist system quickly faded. In this situation, the solution was primarily military: if the Russian bear's claws could be kept out of Europe—a military task—then American interests were protected.

The locus of violence now resides essentially exclusively in the developing world. That is in fact the way things have been since the developing countries began to escape the bonds of colonialism as independent units in which many people discovered they had little in common with their fellow citizens of the new states beyond their shared dislike for the departed European colonists. In terms of "opportunities" to become involved in international violence, the developing world became the only game in town in the contemporary world.

This situation should not surprise Americans. Despite the concentration on the European center of the Cold War, the United States has not employed armed force in anger in Europe since 1945. The exception, of course, was in the Balkans in the conflicts in Bosnia and Kosovo, but the Balkans was arguably more part of the developing than the developed world in the 1990s, and the structure of the conflicts was more akin to those associated with DWICs than anything envisioned in the Cold War paradigm. As Russett (2014) and others have pointed out, the United States has been involved in more violent conflicts than any other country in the period since 1945, but those involvements have been *exclusively* in the developing world. Some of these were justified as extensions of the "central battle" between the Cold War antagonists, but they were conducted in developing countries.

This locus of violence creates two conceptual problems for applying the Cold War paradigm: the matter of interests and the propriety of various solutions. Historically, the United States has not been as heavily invested in most of the developing world (the Middle East being an exception) as it has in the developed world. Put succinctly, most of America's most important interests have been in Europe, the Western Hemisphere, and East Asia, whereas the only really important American interests in the rest of the developing world over the past half century have involved access to petroleum energy. The developing world has simply not been as important to the United States as has the developed world.

Traditionally, important American interests have not been engaged in those places where instability is now occurring, and until the rise of international terrorism, threats to American interests were not especially prevalent in those areas either. The notable exception is oil-rich parts of the Middle East, where energy access has represented a vital interest. That area is also the source of terrorist threats. As a result, it is not at all surprising that American national security attention has largely shifted to this region. The growth of American shale oil and gas production may attenuate this situation, but much of its impact is still in the future.

The other basic dimension of change introduced by a developing world-centered system of violence is in the nature and character of the violence itself, and it is clearly related to the implications of the movement of violence into parts of the world where the United States has less vital interests. During the Cold War, there was a fundamental synergy between threats to the United States and Cold War paradigm solutions. America's most vital interests were clearly threatened by the Soviet-led menace, and conventional, traditional American military responses were equally clearly appropriate to the task of realizing American interests (or frustrating communist interests). There was a fundamental match between interests, threats, and responses.

That symmetry has not survived the end of the Cold War. Instead, it has been replaced by two fundamental mismatches which a new paradigm must reconcile. The first is the *interest-threat* mismatch—the situation where interests and threats to those interests are misaligned. In the simplest terms, the most important American interests (vital interests) are hardly threatened in the contemporary environment, and virtually all the threats that do exist are to LTV interests. The implication of this distinction is that nearly all the places where American force might be an appropriate response do not need that force (e.g. the defense of Western Europe), and all the places where that force might be applied do not warrant it.

The second dilemma is the *threat-force mismatch.* The places where American force might be applied in the contemporary environment are also places and situations for which that force is not designed and in which it has not proven especially effective. The DWICs, where most opportunities arise, are internal wars, desperately fought over issues pertinent to and only resolvable by the parties themselves. They are overwhelmingly asymmetrical, especially when faced with an outside intervener like the United States. The American military tradition does not find this a congenial way to fight and has struggled to adapt to asymmetrical conditions. The wars of American preference are like boxing matches fought in confined arenas with well accepted rules and boundaries. They are not ongoing street brawls. DWICs are much closer to no-holds-barred street fighting than they are carefully regulated competitions.

The Nature and Character of Threats and Opportunities

The gist of the message is that the traditional Cold War paradigm is no longer unquestionably relevant in the early twenty-first century. Since 1945, the United States has fought numerous conflicts within the framework of the Cold War paradigm, including major military efforts in Korea, Vietnam, and in the Kuwaiti desert. Two of these led to acceptable outcomes. The territorial integrity of South Korea was restored, and Kuwaiti sovereignty was re-established, although it took another engagement beginning in 2003 to punish fully the Iraqi regime that precipitated the war. American vital interests were arguably engaged in both conflicts: a hostile united Korean peninsula would have posed a basic threat to Japan, and Kuwaiti oil not controlled by the Saddam Hussein government in Baghdad was deemed vital to American energy well-being. Also, both were fought basically symmetrically, with American opponents standing toe-to-toe with conventional American military might. For both opponents, it was a mistake.

The first Persian Gulf War has produced the most important legacy for the present and future. In case any future opponent watching the almost casual efficiency with which the Iraqi armed forces were dispatched in 1991 had any prior illusions of fighting the United States symmetrically (on American terms), they were disabused of that notion. In that sense, Saddam Hussein did future potential American opponents a tremendous favor by demonstrating the futility of symmetrical war with the United States. In the future, no one else would make that same mistake again. Rather, the Vietnam War provided the blueprint on which to base resistance to the Americans.

The United States did not quickly understand this dynamic, and one can argue that the overwhelming success of American arms in the Kuwaiti desert was virtually the worst thing that could have happened to it. American Cold War planning and preparation seemed vindicated by the easy victory, and that very success was interpreted to mean the old model was still relevant and there was no need for fundamental military adaptation for the post-Cold War environment. It was the wrong lesson.

The other two major American involvements since the Cold War ended demonstrated the folly of this assessment. Certainly American forces brushed aside the token conventional resistance Iraq put up to the American invasion in 2003, but the Iraqis quickly converted to asymmetrical resistance which the United States never defeated (the 2007 Anwar Awakening notwithstanding). The same model was applied in Afghanistan, and after

13 years of combat, it did not end successfully. The success in Kuwait obscured the point that American interventions, certainly in the manner they were conceptualized and conducted, were doomed from the beginning: they failed because that is all they could do. Going down the same path in the future will only likely yield similar results.

Moreover, it is not entirely clear that the United States has any real business imposing itself militarily in these situations. It is one thing to undertake difficult, even quixotic, tasks when one has no choice because unquestionably vital interests are engaged and must be defended at all costs. But such American interests are almost *never* involved in the kinds of places where DWICs occur. There is indeed an interest-threat mismatch, but the American national security establishment has a difficult time dealing with that reality. All the conflicts in which the United States may feel the temptation to act have two daunting characteristics that must be recognized and accounted for in terms of the dilemmas they pose. The first is that they are wars of choice and not necessity: necessity requires the engagement of vital interests that are clearly not present. Second, they are forms of warfare at which the United States has not succeeded in the past, and unless things change, they are situations that will yield future frustration too.

Back to the Future: A Realist-Based Paradigm

Returning to a national security paradigm based in the philosophy of realism does not sound like a very radical proposition. Americans have, over the years, believed that realism is and should be the basis of policy, and indeed the Cold War paradigm had a strong realist base. It can be argued that the current paradigmatic problem facing the United States is that the country has, especially in the early years after 9/11, implicitly rejected realism.

It is also an approach deeply rooted in Cold War-era strategy. In the wake of the Vietnam War, President Nixon articulated what became known as the Nixon Doctrine. The essence was that in other than situations of vital importance, the United States would offer a range of forms of military and non-military assistance, but not American troops. In the early Reagan administration, the Weinberger Doctrine (articulated by Secretary of Defense Caspar Weinberger) offered similar restraint. During the first Bush administration, Chairman of the Joint Chiefs of Staff Colin Powell stated criteria for intervention that became known as the Powell Doctrine. Richard Betts reiterated these in a recent *Foreign Affairs* article (Betts 2014). They are using force only as a last resort that enjoys widespread public support, only employing force when vital interests are invoked, and using enough force to guarantee success. They were good criteria in the last century; they still are.

Realism was appealing in the Cold War because its philosophy is heavily grounded in the possession and use of power, including military power, both to describe how international politics works and as a way to succeed in the international environment. The hard edge of power—military force—defined the heart of the Cold War competition, and military prowess had described the basis of international politics for the centuries preceding 1945. That reality led to the Cold War conceptual framework for competing in the world that emphasized military power as the prime solution to problems. That idea was attractive to those within society that viewed themselves as the most hard-headed and realistic element in the national security arena.

Returning to a paradigm based in realism does not imply remilitarizing the American approach to policy. The most salient characteristic of traditional realism is its message regarding criteria for the *use*, as opposed to *possession*, of military force. The heart of that American realist tradition can be stated succinctly: *Military force should only be used when the vital national interests of the United States are engaged. Force is a last resort only to be considered when all other means fail. When less than vital interests are engaged, the direct application of American force should be avoided.* This is the sense of realism that should form the basis for a new national security paradigm for this country. It is the way Americans have traditionally thought about the use of force. Most Americans should have little trouble readopting a value many have always held. This proposal really reflects a return to the past: back to the future!

During the Cold War, American military actions had to be framed in terms of vital interests to be acceptable. Adherence began to erode, however, as the conduct of what was in the vital interest of the United States was expanded and arguably stretched beyond its reasonable limits. The Korean War was justified by the intolerability of a Japan menaced by a united, communist Korea, and the vital importance that assertion implied was generally accepted. The justification that arguably broke the camel's back was in Vietnam. Justifications for the massive American involvement changed across time, as policymakers struggled for a cause that would excite a wary population. At the core, however, all these explanations emphasized the realist criterion of vitality, attempting to convince the American public that an unfavorable outcome would be intolerable for the United States. In the end, of course, neither victory nor intolerable consequences occurred. Victory eluded the Americans, because the structure of that conflict—a classic DWIC unrecognized by those in power for what it was—made it essentially impossible for the United States to prevail. Not winning did not affect the country's security interests in any vital manner.

This same kind of argumentation was made in the wake of 9/11 to justify the excursions into Iraq and Afghanistan. It was a two-step argument. The first step was to maintain that American direct military intervention was vital to American interests: in Iraq due to what proved to be the phantom Iraqi possession of weapons of mass destruction and ties to terrorism, in Afghanistan in order to hunt down and snuff out Al Qaeda. Both of these assertions were debatable, and they were gradually rejected by increasing numbers of Americans. To those who supported the actions, however, the handwriting was on the wall: if the American public insists on vital importance as the enabling condition for employing American force, the advocacy of an expansive American hegemony was in trouble.

This realization created the need for the second argument. Its core was that the realist criterion was too restrictive and, if applied rigidly, kept the United States from becoming involved in places where American military presence might be useful. The neo-conservatives who became central national security players in the George W. Bush administration after 9/11 were the leading proponents of this position. These neo-cons (as they were known) had a decidedly radical agenda that centered on strengthening and expanding American hegemony. At the heart of their rationale was an assertion of benevolent intent, arguing the United States would become essentially the sword of democratic advocacy, the end result of which would be a happier, more peaceful world. Achieving that end, however, would require the fairly liberal application of American force in a variety of situations, including some where the traditional criterion of vital importance could not be convincingly reached.

The neo-conservative construction prevailed in the early 2000s, and it made an expansion of the realist criterion absolutely necessary, since there was no likelihood its proposals could carry the day with the American public otherwise. The idea that the possible expansion of democracy in the region was vital to American interests was the quintessence of this idea and it was simply a conceptual "bridge too far." Only an expanded view of using American force would allow pursuing the neo-con dream.

The Contemporary National Security Context

The basic question that drives an American assessment of the international security environment is, "where will the U.S. have enough and sufficiently important interests to justify force?" It is a realist perspective because it frames the matter using vital interests as the basic benchmark for a potential positive answer. It rejects the neo-con assertion that vitalness is too confining a standard for contemplating American recourse to arms. The application of the realist standard should, in the contemporary environment, provide a considerable decrease in the active deployment of American force, a benefit both to an overextended and largely exhausted American military and to a country wherein the large outlays of scarce resources for dubious military adventures have become an unwanted, deleterious burden. It also represents a return to the United States acting like its own self-image as the beacon of peace and stability in the world.

There is little question that the relaxation of the standard of vitalness has resulted in the excess and unnecessary usage of American force abroad. The actual reasons for invading and conquering Iraq certainly could not have survived a strict application of the realist criterion, and neither could a large-scale involvement in Afghanistan after al Qaeda left that country in 2001 for exile in Pakistan, from which it still operates. Indeed, the negative reactions of retired flag rank officers to both interventions were phrased mostly in realist terms and became beacons in the evaluation and rejection of direct military incursions in places like Libya and Syria. None of these places were worth "going to war over" by the United States under strict realist requirements. The degree to which a realist paradigm allows American involvement short of direct force, however, is a remaining question.

The places where US force might realistically be called for are obviously in the developing world. The most obvious examples are the DWICs in Africa and Asia (including the Middle East). Using realist criteria, most of these conflicts fall on the less-than-vital side of the demarking line for employing force: they are places and situations not worth the expenditure of American blood and treasure. This does not mean they are unworthy of American concern and even American action; it does mean that they do not warrant a serious consideration of deploying American force in them. If one takes these kinds of conflicts "off the board" for using American force, the prospects for employment are reduced very considerably.

The problem is that the distinction between vital and LTV interests is not precise. The distinction is not so much a discrete line of demarcation as it is a confidence interval, and within the interval are situations about which different observers can and do disagree. Put another way, the idea of vitality is not inter-subjective: it does not mean exactly the same thing to all observers. What is vital to one individual or group may not be to another individual or group.

The subversive erosion of earlier notions of vitalness in the Cold War paradigm came from this difficulty. The most prominent example was Vietnam. American intervention in that war was justified as vital to American national security through such constructs as the "domino theory" (the idea that if Vietnam fell to communism, it would start a domino effect whereby neighbors would fall, and that momentum would continue until the United States itself might be at risk). In retrospect and devoid of the emotions of the moment, such rationalizations may seem ludicrous, but they did not at the time.

These examples suggest a danger that lurks within the realist criterion and against which efforts must be undertaken. That is the attempt basically to highjack the argument of vitalness and to apply it where it does not truly apply. The reason for attempting the appropriation of vitalness is obvious: if one can convince the body politic that something is indeed vital to their interests, then whatever action one might propose gains much greater credibility than it might otherwise have. The motives behind doing so are not necessarily devious: what is honestly vital to one observer may not in fact be vital to another. A core of honest difference may surround any debate.

One can try to specify in as much detail as possible what standards are involved in achieving vitalness, but the process will never be perfect or foolproof. No matter how precise the standards and criteria, there will always be new, apparently unique situations to which the current standards do not apply. The best one can probably reasonably hope for is a generally accepted common standard and the promise of a vigorous debate when exceptions are claimed. The resolve to avoid a rush to positive military judgment is always strongest after a regretted military involvement: the periods after Vietnam and presumably today. The trick is keeping up the vigilance when unpleasant memories have faded (which they do).

Another objection to restricting the use of American force is the familiar charge that doing so will be interpreted as evidence of American weakness, even retreat as a world power by American adversaries. In this view, an assertive United States is necessary to maintain American supremacy in the world—essentially the American status as the unipolar power. If American interests exist everywhere, and the United States is unwilling to defend those interests, with force if necessary, America's place in the world will decline.

Such a formulation suggests that force remains the virtually sole lingua franca of international power politics. While this may be true in dire situations, one way to counter the assertion of this position is to suggest that American power and prestige is not served by wading instinctively into military situations where its interests are questionable, where its ability to achieve its ends is not at all certain and where, in the end, the United States may fail to achieve its goals. In those cases, is American prestige really reinforced by an ultimately feckless effort? Does the current turmoil over IS in Iraq following a long U.S. regional involvement demonstrate American resolve or lack of judgment? Would doubling down and getting back into the sectarian violence there show American resolution? Or would it demonstrate American stupidity?

The returned imposition of the realist criterion of vitalness as the centerpiece will clearly limit the number and extent of overseas employments of American force in harm's way in the near future. Some of that reduction has already been evident in the decisions not to place American forces on the ground in Libya and Syria or to reintroduce them into the degenerating situation surrounding IS. Those restraints have avoided what would have been fractious, divisive impacts on the American public environment.

The Broader Context and Implications of Paradigm Change

Ultimately, the test of national security policy is how well it protects national interests in a world environment not always amenable to those interests. This is also the primary objective of overall foreign policy, and the unique province of national security policy is that it deals specifically with those interests that have or may have a military content. Most importantly, national security policy must be concerned primarily with the protection of those interests that are important enough that military force may be a necessary part of their realization.

This mission definition gives the national security enterprise a unique gravity that derives from the potential consequences of its failure to protect vital interests. Many areas of foreign and domestic policy can fail with consequences that are inconveniencing and serious. National security policy potentially deals with matters that ultimately include national survival and the physical safety and well-being of the state.

This sense of gravity makes national security analysis uniquely conservative among policy areas in the true sense: it deals with conserving and promoting the most basic values of the state. If someone botches some aspect of agricultural subsidies, the result may be higher consumer costs for some food product. If those charged with national security underestimate a threat or prepare improperly or inadequately for a threat, the result can be literally cataclysmic. Such dramatic instances may be exceedingly few, but there may only need to be one critical mistake.

These influences affect national security policy formulation in two distinct ways germane to paradigm change. One is resistance to change. A major part of the challenge is an understanding of the range of threats and reducing uncertainty about the likelihood that they will be challenged by identifying and negating all sources of potential peril. Once that is done and seems to work, there is a very real resistance to change, because change may introduce new sources of uncertainty into calculations.

This leads to the second distinct effect, which is over-preparation. One can reduce greatly the uncertainty in any relationship, including national security confrontations, but one can never remove that uncertainty altogether. As a result, there is always a tendency to err on the side of caution. Having too much preparation may be far less dangerous than having too little in situations where there is neither the time nor the capacity to correct deficiencies in the event of crises. Moreover, the longer a given level and quality of preparation seems to work (its presence and the lack of threat actualization coincide), the more faith one gains in the actions taken and the more resistance there is likely to be to modifying, and especially reducing, the results of that preparation.

Reforming the Cold War paradigm thus takes place in an atmosphere in which there is built-in, institutional resistance to the effort. The existing paradigm was forged in the extremely adversarial, stressful ideological clash between communism and Western democracy at the end of World War II, and this context gave it a moral, even evangelical quality that went beyond the more normal power politics of the period before it. It also nurtured a peculiar breed of "Cold Warriors" with a virtual missionary zeal to conform the world to the virtues of Western society and in opposition to what they viewed as the abject evil of the communist challenge.

This evangelical strain reinforces the Cold War paradigm and adds fervor both to its extension into places like the competition with terrorism and the debate over its extensive modification. What all this means is that the task of reforming the Cold War paradigm is likely to be a formidable one. It is also something that must be done for the United States to respond to the contemporary world environment in which it must operate to protect and optimize the national interest.

Responding to a Changed World Environment

The characteristics that distinguished the Cold War and helped shape the Cold War paradigm are gone. The world with which national security policy must deal is very different than before. The center of the world's problems is no longer in central Europe and its major military challenge is no longer conventional, symmetrical interstate war. A framework appropriate to the Cold War is now inappropriate, even irrelevant, to dealing with the world as it now exists.

The bipolar world has given way to a contemporary system that features what one can call *complex multipolarity*. The condition of multipolarity is not, of course, unique to the present; much of the period of the eighteenth and nineteenth centuries in the European balance of power was essentially multipolar. The classic nineteenth century balance of power system, for instance, was premised on a balance among five major states (Britain, France, Russia, Prussia/Germany, and the Austro–Hungarian Empire). Its basic dynamic was the absence of exclusive alliances among any members, the ability of any member to unite with any other(s), and a shared commitment to the idea that this equality of power was desirable and served to maintain a peace from which they all benefited. This system dominated from the end of the Napoleonic Wars in 1815 until the Franco–Prussian War of 1870.

The evolving international system shares the essential characteristic of a multipolar system in that there are multiple independent sources of power and influence in the system. American unipolarity, to the extent it ever existed as more than an abstract construct, has given way to a multipolar order, the composition of which is both physically different from the nineteenth century system and holds different values and priorities. This evolving system is not Euro-centered, as were its predecessors: the United States is still a member, and arguably a few European countries like Germany, Russia, France, and Britain have a role, but the center of power has moved to the former periphery of the system, notably to economic and population powerhouses like India and China, to economic powers like Japan and Korea, and beyond Asia to places like South Africa and Brazil.

The second sense of change comes from the kinds of countries that are now joining the power system. They create an emphasis both on different instruments of power and on different uses of existing instruments. The new members are not traditional powers in the sense of possessing large, traditional, European style armed forces that are configured for traditional projections of armed force. The new countries, with the exception of China, spend modestly on traditional military preparations (especially when compared to the United States), and none possess nor seem particularly interested in developing armed forces useful in projecting military power far from their own shores. A few have large forces for essentially local purposes (the stand-off between India and Pakistan, for instance), but only China can even remotely be thought of as a military rival of the traditional, European-based states. The traditional military instrument of power, which has been the basis of most power calculation for centuries, has little meaning in the actions of these countries toward one another. Calculating American military power as a determinant of the power relationship between the United States and South Africa and Brazil, for instance, is an exercise in irrelevance. In this sense, the United States remains the unipolar military power in a traditional, conventional and nuclear sense, even though it is increasingly a distinction without practical import.

In this new order, the economic instrument of power has become increasingly important in defining international status. The economic factor is probably more important today because of a globalizing economy and the effective shrinking of the globe, one result of which is to enhance the economic lever. The possession and ability to manipulate commodities like international energy supplies or the amount and terms of capital movement have always played a part in international discourse, but not so centrally as today. As independent sources of decisions over these kinds of concerns diversify through the addition of new states with agendas that are different than those of the traditional international "players," the calculation of power and its application must change as well.

From a national security vantage point, the question is how new forces alter the threat environment and how to respond to it. The new actors are not generally more stable or less violence prone than the traditional major actors. As products of the developing world, the "neighborhoods" in which the new powers reside contain many of the kinds of artificial countries in which DWICs break out and which are subject to centrifugal internal forces. India and Pakistan, for instance, may not pose any direct personal vital threats to American security, but that does not mean they do not concern American peace and prosperity. They do remain locked in a heavily armed, including nuclear, competition that, should it deteriorate, would face the United States with serious dilemmas, each has serious internal difficulties arising from multinational forces, and each has countries on its border with deep problems. Some of these, such as Afghanistan, have already drawn the United States into the web, and there may be other temptations from places like Kashmir or even conceivably Tibet. The Middle East is particularly rife with dangerous possibilities that involve serious American interests, and virtually every place in the world has difficulties that affect the United States in some way.

None of these problems is entirely new: the Indian subcontinent has been turbulent since the partition in 1947 and thus has been a matter of some level of American concern ever since. The major source of change in the world is that these problems are now much more prominent than they formerly were. Almost all these places fell beneath the consensual status of vitalness in the traditional Cold War sense, and they may still reside below that threshold. It is the job of a national security paradigm for a new environment to sift through the priorities, the appropriate ways to address them, and thus the direction and content of a new American national security paradigm based in realism.

The Road Ahead

In the end, it comes back to the basics. The heart of the national security equation remains conceptually compact. It is about interests, threats, and risks, and how the calculation of those factors guides strategy, policy, and the issues associated with them. If one has a firm grasp on those basics at any point in time, one will have a pretty good idea of the state of the national security predicament that the country faces.

The dynamics that drive national security concerns also drive the national foreign policy enterprise. What are the underlying American interests at any point in time and in particular situations? How important are those interests, and what threatens them? How important is it to thwart, negate, or reduce those impacts? What are the consequences of different responses and outcomes? The answers translate into the level of risk that attaches to different courses of action. Taking risks is inevitable when resources are finite, as they inevitably always are. Which risks are tolerable? Which are not?

Reasonable and reasoning people disagree on all these matters when it comes to their application, and it is the role of policymakers and the policy process to sort through the challenges and to reach decisions that hopefully maximize national security. In other than rare situations of great clarity and consensus, there will always be disagreement and dissent about particular solutions. Some of that dissent will prove to be accurate, and some of it will not. The process attempts to reconcile the differences.

All policies arise from and operate in a framework of presumptions about the most appropriate general ways to reconcile responses. They represent doctrine. At the pinnacle of this framework is the basic paradigm or orientation the country has toward the structure of national security challenges. That paradigm ideally allows the development of strategies—plans of action—to meet those challenges and help guide the formulation and implementation of policies that support the strategy and its paradigmatic vision in the face of issues that arise. The central argument here has been that the top of the pyramid, the paradigm, needs restructuring and that doing so would simplify responding to the contemporary environment.

A reorientation of the American national security paradigm to a central grounding in realism is really a recalibration of practice to return to more historical American values. The most prominent of these values include when and under what circumstances the United States will employ armed force in pursuit of its national goals. Sending in American force to solve the world's problems has become virtually normal behavior, justified as evidence of the American role in the world and the American determination to act as the world's pre-eminent country; by contrast, the reluctance, even refusal, to flex American military muscle is viewed as a pusillanimous retreat from power in the world. This tendency has been growing since the United States waded "waist deep in the big muddy" of Vietnam (the title of a Richard Rovere book on the war), a war in which the United States had no real vital interests and which it could not and did not win. For a time after Vietnam, the lesson of "no more Vietnams" said the country should not repeat that disaster. The lesson was forgotten. A return to realism, the cardinal violation of which was begun in Vietnam, can return American policy to that wise standard. There may be other ways to get to that same end, but an explicit reinstatement of the realist principle of vitalness is the most direct way and is based on fundamental American values.

What would a return to an American paradigm based in realism do? Most importantly, it would state the realist criterion of only using force in the pursuit of vital American interests as the first pillar of American security policy. Before any use of American force could be contemplated, the first question would become, "what vital interests of the United States require the use of American arms to insure those vital interests are not compromised unacceptably?" Although advocacies of American force employment are routinely justified as being "vital," that assertion has become hollow and is rarely defended or articulated in a convincing way. Advocacies of prominent American military involvement in Libya and Syria are examples. Rather, vital interests are simply asserted. The bland assertion is largely the heritage of the neo-con lament that vitalness is too restrictive. They were wrong when they made the assertion. They still are.

A return to a grounding of the American paradigm in the realist criterion will hopefully enliven the debate about the boundary between vital and LTV interests and establish more easily identifiable conditions to justify force than has been true in the past. At a minimum, it may require proponents of using force more explicitly to justify *why* American force is necessary to defend *American* vital interests than has been the case. Such a development would find considerable favor within those portions of the American military establishment who are physically required to make the sacrifices associated with force deployment in harm's way. It would mean limiting the use of force to where it is truly needed and hopefully to where it has a real chance of achieving its goals.

It would also respond to the evolving multipolar international environment. Most of the violence and instability in the world now occurs in the developing world where, by and large, American vital interests are not clearly engaged, or are only engaged in subtle and indirect ways for which the application of conventional American force is inappropriate and often unwanted. This particularly applies to potential involvements in the DWICs, which are the major sources of U.S. temptation. Would, for instance, the proposal to invade Iraq have survived a detailed, in-depth examination on national security grounds that might have required those asserting vital interests to *prove*, rather than simply to *assert*, the existence of Iraqi WMD and ties to terrorism? Would a detailed oversight of American force employment in Afghanistan after the end of 2001, when Al Qaeda had been removed from the country and the Taliban were failing, have justified what became America's longest war? The realist criterion was applied, albeit indirectly, to Libya, and the United States did not put boots on the ground. The same has been true in Syria. Has the United States been irreversibly harmed by the events in either of these places?

The counter-case that is often made is that if the United States rules out using American force in many situations because the bar is set too high, the prestige of the United States will recede, as will American relevance in the world. This assertion is most often made about the Middle East, where America's most spectacular employments have occurred in recent decades. This criticism is most often associated with supporters of Israel, who believe an American professed reluctance to put forces in harm's way will leave the state of Israel more clearly on its own in a hostile environment.

This case entails two basic fallacies. The first is that the willingness to employ American force somehow automatically enhances the American reputation as a "tough guy" on whom one can rely. Is it not possible, however, that the contrary image of the United States blundering into situations in which it has no real business and in which it cannot succeed projects a more accurate perspective? Is this not particularly true when the United States intervenes, fails to achieve its proposed goals, and then retreats with those goals (which generally turn out to have been not so important) unachieved?

The second fallacy is that the realist criterion creates a "yes-no" kind of dictate for any American involvement in situations, when in fact it only really applies to the direct insertion of American force. There are a wide range of responses the United States can contemplate in different situations short of "sending in the Marines." In a multipolar world where traditional force is not so clearly the answer to all challenges to national interest, a reassertion of the realist principle could instead reinvigorate the articulation and use of other measures that fall between the extremes. Avoiding the logical fallacy of the excluded middle might actually improve the sophistication of the American arsenal of instruments of power rather than disabling them.

A return to the realist principle would have several potential impacts, three of which are worth mentioning. Cumulatively, these influences could help enliven a new national debate surrounding the post Cold War paradigm. These arguments are a positive impact on the pattern of U.S. force employment; an increased search for and reliance on other instruments of power, including more limited forms of force; and an impact on the kinds of areas where the United States should contemplate using force. This latter concern has a special impact on so-called humanitarian interventions.

Probably the most salutary short-term effect of the return to vitalness would be the reduction of American military commitments to conflicts in the developing world where vital interests are scarce, and especially the use of overstretched ground forces. Now that the military commitment to Afghanistan is completed (and it is a process that might have been sped up by imposing the vitalness criterion on its continuation), American overseas deployment of combat ground forces will be reduced to those who are deployed but not employed in places like Western Europe and Korea, and the great bulk could be brought back to the United States for refurbishment and reinvigoration. Over a dozen years of continuous deployments—including multiple tours in the Middle East—has taken its toll on the force. Because the criterion of vitalness would raise the bar for future deployments, one could expect a reduced "op tempo" (operational tempo or rate of use) for the force.

Such a reduction would reduce some of the growing anomaly of the all-volunteer force. As already noted, that force is not infinitely expandable. It has arguably reached or surpassed its quantitative limits, for which the need repeatedly to deploy the same troops is testimony. The size and considerable costs associated with the AVF are more appropriate for a time of essential peace, when large demands, such as those of the period since 2001, are not made on this finite resource. At the same time, these deployments have cost the American treasury large amounts of money that could have been used for other priorities or that could have provided savings applicable to the national debt, to which Iraq and Afghanistan have been major contributors. The United States is both war-weary and in a penurious state of mind; the reduced use of force that would make it through the screen of the realist principle could contribute to the domestic American political climate.

A second benefit would be the reorientation of American foreign policy away from the rapid recourse to force to the use of instruments of policy more consonant with the values of the international environment. The utility of the economic, political, and other elements of power relies somewhat on the existence of military force as a last resort, but making it clear that the involvement of Americans in harm's way is indeed a last resort could energize the creativity of American policy in two ways. On one hand, it could create ancillary policies that rely on non-military measures, such as more creative uses of multilateral diplomacy or the subtleties of the economic instrument. At the same time, the more complete development of and reliance upon non-traditional military power in its various guises would seem to be more responsive to the environment, as well as limiting the recourse to American force. The United States might, in the process, burnish its tarnished image as Ronald Reagan's "shining house on the hill," rather than as the world's bully. U.S. low-key but highly effective sanctions against Russian adventures in the Crimea and Ukraine suggest some of the creative alternatives to American force.

Third, the knowledge that force is once again truly the means of last resort could also reinvigorate the debate over how the country should approach the world's instabilities, and especially their most glaring deficiencies. One of the ironies of the current debate has been that political liberals, in general averse to waving the American cudgel, have found themselves caught in the dilemma of having to endorse, or at least not to condemn, the use of force in humanitarian disasters like the ongoing tragedy in Syria. Humanitarian intervention in Syria would never meet the criterion of vitalness unless the definition of vitalness is expanded greatly to include the well-being of mankind. A national debate on vitalness might open the way for a more thorough definition of what the United States does and does not consider important enough to expend American blood and treasure to protect.

A realist reorientation does not solve all the world's problems. In the case of DWICs, it may make some worse in the short run, because the parties themselves would have to work out their own problems without American "help." Since that assistance has had dubious results in the past, taking the United States out of the situation in an active military way is not necessarily a bad thing. As Andrew Bacevich recently pointed out in a *Washington Post* op-ed, the country has taken active military action in *fourteen* Middle Eastern countries since 1980. Have all of those produced results that advanced American interests or helped the situations for those who live there? In a specific instance, did eight years of American military presence in Iraq make the IS threat in Anbar Province any easier for the Iraqis or Americans to deal with? It is hard to see how.

What a realist-based paradigm does is to force the United States to find more creative ways to influence situations where its level of interests do not unambiguously justify the insertion of American force to influence outcomes. If, as argued here, only the internal parties can ultimately solve their internal problems, the approach is ultimately realistic.

A realist-based national security paradigm also argues physical restraint is a better approach in a moral sense. With vitalness as its enabler, it will reduce sharply the situations in which the United States interposes itself with armed force: the result is a morally restrained version of the Cold

War counterpart. Whether restraint will produce a better world environment—one more amenable to American values—can and should be debated at length. It will, however, likely avoid some actions that actually make things worse, not better. Is that a bad thing?

Bibliography

Bacevich, Andrew. "Even If We Defeat the Islamic State, We'll Still Lose the Bigger War." *Washington Post* (online), October 3, 2014.

Betts, Richard K. "Pick Your Battles: Ending America's Permanent State of War." *Foreign Affairs* 93, 6 (November/December 2014), 15–24.

Byman, Daniel. "Why Drones Work: The Case for Washington's Weapon of Choice." *Foreign Affairs* 92, 4 (July/August 2013), 32–43.

Builder, Carl. *The Masks of War: American Military Styles in Strategy and Analysis.* A RAND Corporation Research Study. Santa Monica, CA: RAND Corporation, 1989.

Carter, Ashton B. "Running the Pentagon Right: How to Get the Troops What They Need." *Foreign Affairs* 93, 1 (January/February 2014), 101–112.

Cronin, Audrey Kurth. "Why Drones Fail: When Tactics Drive Strategy." *Foreign Affairs* 92, 4 (July/August 2013), 44–54.

Fukuyama, Francis. *The End of History and the Last Man.* New York: Free Press, 1992.

Gates, Robert. *Duty: Memoirs of a Secretary at War.* New York: Knopf, 2014.

Goldstein, Joshua. *Winning the War on War: The Decline of Armed Conflict Worldwide.* New York: Plume, 2012.

Haass, Richard N. *Wars of Necessity, Wars of Choice: A Memoir of Two Iraq Wars.* New York: Simon and Schuster, 2010.

Haass, Richard N. "The Unraveling: How to Respond to a Disordered World." *Foreign Affairs* 93, 6 (November/December 2014), 70–79.

Hoffman, Bruce. *Inside Terrorism.* 2nd edn. New York: Columbia University Press, 2006.

Jervis, Robert. *The Illogical of American Nuclear Strrategy.* Ithaca, NY: Cornell University Press, 1984.

Kinzer, Stephen. *Overthrow: America's Century of Regime Change from Hawaii to Iraq.* New York: Times Books (Macmillan), 2007.

Kinzer, Stephen. *The Brothers: John Foster Dulles, Allen Dulles, and Their Secret World War.* New York: Times Books (Henry Holt and Company, LLC), 2013.

Krauthammer, Charles. "The Unipolar Moment." *Foreign Affairs* 10, 1 (Winter 1990/1), 23–33.

Mearsheimer, John J. "Why We Shall Soon Miss the Cold War." *Atlantic Monthly* 262, 2 (August 1990), 35–50.

Nacos, Brigette I.. *Terrorism and Counterterrorism: Understanding Threats and Responses in the Post-9/11 World.* New York: Penguin Academics, 2006.

Obama, Barack. "State of the Union." Text reprinted in *Washington Post* (online), January 29, 2014.

Oneal, John, and Bruce Russett. *Triangulating Peace: Democracy, Interdependence, and International Organizations.* New York: W.W. Norton, 2000.

Pinker, Steven. *The Better Angels of Our Nature: Why Violence Has Declined*. New York: Penguin Books, 2012.

Rovere, Richard H. *Waist Deep in the Big Muddy: Personal Reflections on 1968*. Boston, MA: Little Brown, 1968.

Russett, Bruce. "The Waning of Warfare." *Contemporary History* 113, 759 (January 2014), 30–32.

Snow, Donald M. *The Necessary Peace: Nuclear Weapons and Superpower Relations*. Lexington, MA: Lexington Press, 1987.

Snow, Donald M.. *National Security for a New Era*. 1st edn (2002), 5th edn (2014). New York: Longman and Pearson.

Snow, Donald M. *September 11, 2001: The New Face of War?* New York: Longman, 2002.

Snow, Donald M., and Patrick Haney. *American Foreign Policy for a New Era*. New York: Pearson, 2013.

Stern, Jessica. *Terrorism in the Name of God: Why Religious Militants Kill*. New York: ECCO, 2003.

Index

geopolitics 27–8, 158, 165; terrorism 28; use of force 58, 59–60; war 38
Germany 1, 24
Gert, Bernard 63
Gorbachev, Mikhail 86, 87
governmental gridlock 21–2, 23, 24–5, 144; federal budget 21
Gulf States 76, 146, 150, 152, 155

Haney, Patrick J. 22, 93
Hezbollah 76, 138
Hoffman, Abbie 127
the Holocaust 59, 63–4, 138
humanitarian intervention 43, 58–80, 139; 1990s clash of competing imperatives 64–5; authorized agent 66, 68; common morality/moral imperative 59, 60–9 *passim*, 77, 79 (controversy 61; religion, tradition, and rational human nature 63); 'do-something syndrome' 68–9, 70–3 (selectivity of 73); DWIC 58, 74, 75, 76–7; failure 66, 68, 74, 75; human atrocities, increased frequency of 59, 60; human rights 64–5; just war theory 64, 66, 67; justification 58–61; legitimacy and mandate for 67; natural disaster relief 77; natural law 62, 63, 64, 67, 68; principle of non-interference 63, 64; principle of non-intervention 62–3, 67; reactions to 77–9; realism 183; restraint 68, 69; sovereignty 60, 62–3, 64–5, 67; Syria 61, 76, 79, 99, 139, 158, 184; uncertainty 74, 76; unintended consequences 68, 69, 73–7 (greater-than-expected harm to the outsider 75, 76–7); yin-yang principle 68–77; *see also* R2P
Hussein, Saddam 16, 45, 71–2, 75, 136, 153, 171; *see also* Iraq

ICISS (International Commission on Intervention and State Sovereignty) 66–7, 68, 74; *see also* R2P
India 179
interest: conceptual basis of national security 11–13, 180; conflict of interest 12, 13; interest/threat match 81, 82, 89, 170; interest/threat mismatch 17, 82, 170, 172; interest/threat relationship 13–14, 82; interest/threat/risk contemporary relationship 108–109; national interest 11–13;

national security, disagreement over 13, 14, 20; physical safety 11, 12; sense of security 12; *see also* interests, importance of; national security interests, importance of 13, 14, 81, 169–70; national security, disagreement over 13, 14, 20, 109; LTVs 13, 16–17, 20, 82, 109, 170; LTVs/VIs distinction 175–6, 181; VIs 13, 14, 81, 109, 170, 172; VIs and the use of force 13, 173, 174–6, 181–2, 183, 184; *see also* interest
International Criminal Court 141; United States 65
international environment 18–20, 23; interest/threat/risk contemporary relationship 108–109; intermestic intersection 22–5; *see also* international environment, major changes
international environment, major changes 107–108, 162, 163–72, 178–80; changing power balance: multipolarity and economic power 165–8, 178–9; cyberwar 108, 131; locus and nature of violence 165, 168–71; nature and character of threats and opportunities 165, 171–2; non-state actors 107–108, 109; unconventional, asymmetrical war 108; *see also* international environment
Iran 16, 71, 146, 156
Iraq 4; American invasion of 16, 29, 55, 71, 72, 98, 127, 153, 162, 171, 173; artificial state 136, 137, 146; DWIC 58; ethnic/tribal and religious roots of conflict 136, 137; invasion of Kuwait 16, 71, 171; Iran-Iraq War 16, 71; the Iraqi Conundrum: interests, threats, risks 15–17; Iraqi Shiites 75; ISIS(L) 17, 136, 153, 158; Kurds 70–2, 73; Persian Gulf War 70, 108, 114, 171; realism 174; terrorism 17, 20; WMD 16, 173, 182; *see also* Hussein, Saddam; ISIS(L)
ISIS(L) (Islamic State of Iraq and Syria/of the Levant) 60, 126, 130, 148–58, 164; AQI 136, 148, 149, 151, 155; al-Baghdadi, Abu Bakr 149, 150; a criminal enterprise 151–2 (criminal sources of funds 76, 151–2, 155); definition 149–50; a different challenge 150–5; drone/UAV 121; DWIC 136; fundamentalism 150,

mismatch 17, 82, 170, 172; interest/
threat relationship 13–14, 82; interest/
threat/risk contemporary relationship
108–109; lack of current clear threat
unifying strategy and policy 2, 18, 81
(current threats are in the psychological realm 109); risk 'formula' 3–4;
subjectivity 3, 4, 14, 109; terrorism
(nature of the terrorist threat 126–9; a
threat that provides focus for strategy
and policy 2, 19, 81, 125–6); threat/
force mismatch 170; variability of 3, 4,
14; *see also* national security
Tibet 179
Turkey 150, 152, 156

UAV *see* drone/UAV (unmanned aerial
vehicle)
Ukraine 2, 102, 184
UN (United Nations): Syria 140; UN
Charter 82; UN General Assembly,
R2P 66, 67; UN Security Council 67
use of force 1, 172, 181; American
military culture 31; disagreement on 1,
13; expense of 13; geopolitics 58,
59–60; as last resort 172, 173, 183–4;
moral dimension 59; neo-conservatism
174; paradigm for a new era 167–8;
realism 13, 59, 99, 172 (VIs and the
use of force 13, 173, 174 6, 181–2,
183, 184); restricting the use of force as
sign of American weakness/decline
168, 176, 181, 182; threat/force mismatch 170; *see also* the military

Vietnam War 29, 31–2, 34, 36, 53, 90,
171, 172, 175; asymmetrical warfare
96; casualties 69; conscription 94,
110; failure 97, 162, 181; ingratitude
78–9; unpopularity 94
violence and instability: DWIC as
source of 85, 98, 101, 162–3, 164,
166, 167, 169, 179–80; human atrocities, increased frequency of 59, 60;
locus and nature of contemporary
violence 165, 168–71

Walzer, Michael 60, 61, 66
war 34–57; abolition of 37; air warfare
41; American way of war 34, 96–7,
171; combatants/non-combatants
distinction 40–1; cyberwar 108, 131;

definition 35, 37 (war as a political
act 46–7, 54–5); geopolitics 38;
interstate war 47–8, 108, 163; intrastate war 47, 48, 54, 101 (intervention
in civil conflict 48); laws/rules of war
40, 41–3, 108, 138–9; legal declara
tion of war 36 (power of the Congress to declare war 36; President
36); limited war 44–5, 47–8, 53;
political support 44; potential
nuclear war 48; public support 45,
51, 52, 56, 94, 101; recourse to war,
management of 38–9; restraint in 44,
184–5; ROEs 41, 42, 47; success and
victory 46–7; total war 43–6, 47, 53;
war/armed conflict legal distinction
35–6; war crime 40, 64, 141, 147;
warrior 39; *see also* asymmetrical
warfare; collateral damage; DWIC;
just war; nuclear weapon; symmetrical warfare; war, reasons for;
World War I; World War II
war, reasons for 37, 38–9, 43–8; instrumentality of war 46; political objective 46, 51–2 (attainability 51, 52;
clarity and simplicity 51, 52; importance 51, 52; moral loftiness 51–2)
War of 1812: 10, 26, 36, 47, 52
Washington, George 29
Weigley, Russell 31, 96
Weinberger, Caspar: Weinberger Doctrine 172
Weiss, Thomas 60–1, 64–5
Westphalian state 62; Westphalian
peace 35, 62
Williams, T. Harry 31
World War I 29, 164; poison gas 41–2
World War II 49–53, 164; casualties 49;
combatants/non-combatants distinction 40; general agreement on
national security policy 2, 15; political objective 47; ROEs 41; strategy
2; symmetrical warfare 31, 35, 94;
World War II military model 49–51
(in the contemporary world 51–3;
unsuitable for DWIC 54–6)
Wright, Quincy 37

Yemen 123, 131

Zakaria, Fareed 153

9 7 8 1 1 3 8 9 0 2 9 2 3

An environmentally friendly book printed and bound in England by www.printondemand-worldwide.com

PEFC Certified

This product is
from sustainably
managed forests
and controlled
sources

PEFC™
PEFC/16-33-415

www.pefc.org

#0187 - 030316 - C0 - 229/152/17 - PB - 9781138902923